D1572589

EPICTETUS

EPICTETUS

DISCOURSES AND ENCHIRIDION

Based on the Translation of
Thomas Wentworth Higginson

WITH AN INTRODUCTION BY IRWIN EDMAN

PUBLISHED FOR THE CLASSICS CLUB BY

WALTER J. BLACK · NEW YORK

Contents

THE DISCOURSES

BOOK I

v

BOOK II

CONTENTS   vii

BOOK III

BOOK IV

THERE are certain books on philosophy more favored by the lay reader than by the professional philosopher. They are the writings of men who took philosophy both more and less seriously than the technical experts. Among the Stoics, and particularly among the Roman Stoics, philosophy was the most serious of human concerns. It was the basic counsel and resource in the perplexities of life, the major refuge and the only durable consolation. Philosophy, among the Roman Stoics, was a form of wisdom literature, written by "wise men" and by those aspiring to wisdom. The writings of the Roman Stoics were addressed to an educated public seeking personal security and equilibrium. It was not detached analysis of the ultimate structure of being. It was not thinking for its own sake. It was contemplation offered as therapeutic, reflection as a way of becoming detached from the cares and contingencies of the world.

Among the Roman Stoics, two stand out, one an emperor and one a slave, and there is a literary irony in the fact that the works of both, the meditations of the ruler-general and the collected sayings of the slave, should have become for generations upon generations the solace and sanctuary of educated men all over the Western world. It may indeed be said that to the literate public the very word philosophy has come to be associated with those counsels of resignation, evenness, obedience, conformity to nature and acceptance of one's status which we have come to know from the writings of Marcus Aurelius and the pupil-remembered utterances of Epictetus.

It is one of the curiosities of intellectual history that the "discourses" of Epictetus should have become so famous. In

ix

the first place, they are only in a limited sense his own. They were his lectures as recalled by his devoted pupil Arrian. In the second place, they are by no means, as presented in the essays we know as the *Discourses* of Epictetus (apparently roughly remembered lecture notes) very original or very creative as philosophy. Musonius, with whom Epictetus studied, seems to have been a much more inventive philosopher. Certainly the earlier Stoics who worked out whole systems of logic, physics, and metaphysics were, from the point of view of the student of philosophy, more important intellectual figures. Even as literature the Stoics had abler representatives. Cleanthes' "Hymn to Zeus" is a great paean to the divine spirit of the world. In the way of meditation Marcus Aurelius is richer and subtler. But Epictetus had the historical good fortune to strike a certain note, half essay and half sermon, something between that of a preacher and a sober man of the world. This note attracted the imagination of the educated Roman public and of the early Christian fathers. It appealed at once to Skeptics and representative men of affairs. Epictetus' sayings became the private meditation of monks and ministers of state. He was full of nuggets, if not of gold yet of durable moral metal. He was a reminder to the reader in both success and in adversity of how to live without distraction or distortion, how to rule oneself by obeying reason.

Epictetus of Hierapolis was born about 50 B. C. and died about 30 A. D. He was brought up as a slave in the home of a freedman of Nero. But it is important to remember that the social status of a slave in a Roman household was something different than the word connotes to a modern ear. A slave was a slave often only by the accidents of war. He was a cultivated foreigner, usually a cultivated Greek. He was a respected member of the household, often a revered tutor. He was given much responsibility and much freedom. He was often eventually given, as was Epictetus, his freedom. Even before his manumission Epictetus was given a liberal education by his master. When he did become free, he became a popular teacher of philosophy. And a popular teacher of philosophy in Roman society filled something of the functions of both an expositor and a psychiatrist. The patrician young were his pupils and eminent men of state sought his counsel. Among those whom Epictetus influenced was the young Marcus Aurelius.

Philosophers have not always been popular with reigning powers, especially when they seemed to have ideas on the conduct of life as well as on the nature of the universe. The Emperor Domitian was uneasy about the influence of philosophers. They might discredit the state religion which made the emperor a deity. He banished all philosophers from Rome and Italy. Epictetus came under the ban. He lived abroad until his death, lecturing on philosophy.

What *was* the philosophy of this slave whose words were remembered by a relatively obscure pupil, of this philosophical writer who was no original genius in the sense that older members of the Stoic school might have claimed to be original? He had no system; he had no novel ideas. At his worst, to those not amenable to his spell, he sounds like Polonius. The earlier Stoics had a theory of the universe as a system of absolute reason. They had a theory of physics or of nature and matter, they had a system of ethics, a code of virtues, mostly ascetic ones, a conception of good as consistency and ultimately of consistency with nature defined in terms of universal reason. Epictetus seemed to have heard of these theories and indeed to have been well schooled in them. But there is no system to be made of his recalled sayings, and though there are allusions here and there in his discourses to the logical principles of the judgment of the absolute "wise man," to the unswervable rectitude of the good, Epictetus is really not interested in logic or metaphysics. He is interested in morals and in morals chiefly as instruction and in instruction chiefly as an ascetic discipline. His "discourses" have the sententiousness

suggested by the word. They are counsels to men who knew
the world, who have seen it and seen around it and through
it. They are advices from a wise man not expecting too much
of whatever he may do in life and society but dedicated
almost with resignation to do his best. The earlier Stoic school
had admonished complete independence of politics and affairs.
The Stoics, including Seneca, borrowed their detachment.
They wished to be faithful, like Socrates, to "an inner light."
They wished to set over against the shoddy politics and pro-
vincial tyrannies of any one mean city, the standards of universal justice; they wished as a class to be an "organ of imperial
reason." There had been among cultivated men progressive
disillusion with the goods afforded by the external world or
the securities afforded by external politics. Chrysippus had
renounced political activity with the comment: "If I counsel
honorably I shall offend the citizens, if basely the gods." He
asked instead, "What can I be to *Zeus?*"

The Cynics, from whom the Stoics took much of their
moral philosophy, had been accused, justly, of carrying detachment to absurd extremes. The earlier Stoics had made an
almost equally haughty and astringent thesis of detachment.
Epictetus moderates the tone of ascetic renunciation. He
still pleads for detachment in the sense of not committing
oneself to external supports of one's happiness, not to be
swayed easily by fortunes or misfortunes over which one had
no control.

"For as Zeus dwells within himself, and is tranquil by himself, and thinks of his own administration and its nature, and
is employed in thoughts suitable to himself, so ought we be
able to talk to ourselves, not to feel the want of others also,
not be unprovided with the means of passing our time, to
observe the divine administration, and the relation of ourselves to everything else. . . . When a man has this peace,
not proclaimed by Caesar (for how should he be able to
proclaim it?) but by God through Reason, is he not content

when he is alone? when he sees and reflects: Now no evil can happen to me, for me there is no robber, no earthquake, everything is full of peace, of tranquillity." (III, 13.)

Epictetus, then like all the Stoics, insisted—in his mild way —that inner serenity was the only serenity, that only what was in the control of man's "unconquerable mind" mattered to his well being or could nourish it. But because he, like all Stoics, thought that the universe was well ordered and made sense, he gives constant counsels of the decorous conservative. Children should obey their parents, husbands and wives should be faithful to each other, the slave should bow to the will of the master. One should know one's station and its duties and do one's duties with decent conformity, if not with enthusiasm. Know that you are a son, says Epictetus, know that you are a brother. Make "concessions" and "sacrifices" to what is due, to what is obligatory in these relations.

Much of Epictetus reads like copybook maxims. Remaining unmoved by external good and ill, each one should do the decorous, the expected, the traditionally right, the decently conventional in the normal situation and relations of life. The maxims of Epictetus seem more copybook than they are, often because they have been copied into so many copybooks since his day and have been the staple of traditional allusions of two millennia of men of letters, of statesmen in their journals and diaries, of monks and preachers in their meditations and sermons.

The maxims of Epictetus are at once admonitions to be free of distractions of secondary and illusory pleasures and urgings to duty. In fact the voice of Epictetus is the voice of a teacher to a pupil, a pupil in the moral life. Not pleasure is the end of life, nor is concern for the avoidance of pain its second chief concern as the Epicureans had taught in an uncertain and frightening world. Duty is the end of life, not Duty in some grandiose and vast blank categorical imperative, but duty in the smaller relations of life, to one's friends, to one's

tasks, to one's neighbor, to oneself. Part of the somber charm
of Epictetus is the seriousness with which he takes the trivial
incidents of daily life and uses them as clues to the larger moral
issues of duty, the way in which small obligations illuminate
the over-arching obligation to be unwavering in one's devotion to the inner compulsion to do the appropriate outer
deed. The advice is often homely enough. Our author advises
the philosophy student to come to him "with his hair carefully trimmed rather than dirty and rough." The body is less
important than the soul, but keeping the body clean is a
good way to begin to know what order in the soul is. In the
same way, athletics, not important in themselves, are important as an initiation into hardship and discipline. Temperate
use of wine is allowed and Epictetus is not too exigent on the
theme of chastity. What he is concerned with is decency,
personal dignity, modesty, proportion. His moral advices are
those of a respectable citizen, one who accepts without too
much criticism the status quo. Hence his warning against
gossip, slander, idle talk, his advice to the young not to talk
too much or too brashly. Each man should do some useful
work, and unlike most philosophers in the ancient world,
Epictetus did not scorn manual work. You should be independent, too, in another sense, free of dependence on the admiration or honor given by others. You need to be respected
by your mind and acceptable to the divine order of the universe.

In religion, too, Epictetus is conventional. The usual duties
of ritual and prayer are those of a member of a reputable
community of all men who are all "children of Zeus." The
duties of religion are the decorum of the moral life, its rites
are the symbols of that reasonable order and justice which
made resignation and obedience intelligible.

Epictetus is one of those philosophers who has caught the
imagination for centuries because he expresses with quietude
and sincerity the sense of the duties of life, of the importance

of the good will whatever the consequences, and of the values of inner serenity over outer goods dependent on chance and time. There is no rapture in him, nor depths of analysis, but there is the expression of that decorum of life and its duties which it is possible to pursue even in the face of adversity or good fortune. In a sense all is vain, as in Ecclesiastes, except that one sees beyond vanity, and one can at least do what is demanded of the circumstances of existence, which added up make a divine good sense in the world.

IRWIN EDMAN

Editor's note: For greater clarity in the Discourses, *the speeches of students and questioners, whether real or imaginary, have been enclosed in quotation marks.*

Arrian to Lucius Gellius

I NEITHER composed the Discourses of Epictetus in the sense in which books of this kind can properly be said to have been composed, nor did I myself bring them to public notice, any more than I composed them. But whatever I heard from his own mouth, that I tried to set down in the very same words, so far as possible, and to preserve as memorials for my own use, of his manner of thinking, and his frank utterance.

These Discourses are such as a person would naturally deliver from his own thoughts, *extempore*, to another; not such as he would prepare to be read by others afterwards. Being such, I cannot tell how, without either my consent or knowledge, they have fallen into the hands of the public. But it matters little to me if I do not appear an able writer, and not at all to Epictetus if anyone treats his Discourses with contempt; since it was very evident, even when he uttered them, that he aimed at nothing more than to move the minds of his hearers toward virtue. If they produce that one effect, they have in them what, I think, philosophical discourses ought to have. And if they fail of it, let the readers be assured, that when Epictetus himself spoke them, the hearer could not help being affected in the very manner he intended he should be. If by themselves the Discourses have less efficacy, perhaps it is my fault, or perhaps it is unavoidable.

Farewell.

I

Of the Things Which Are and the Things Which Are Not in Our Own Power

Of human faculties in general, you will find that each is unable to contemplate itself, and therefore to approve or disapprove itself. How far does the proper sphere of grammar extend? As far as the judging of language. Of music? As far as the judging of melody. Does either of them contemplate itself, then? By no means.

Thus, for instance, when you are to write to your friend, grammar will tell you what to write; but whether you are to write to your friend at all, or no, grammar will not tell you. Thus music, with regard to tunes; but whether it be proper or improper, at any particular time, to sing or play, music will not tell you.

What will tell, then?

That faculty which contemplates both itself and all other things.

And what is that?

The reasoning faculty; for that alone we find is able to place an estimate on itself—what it is, what its powers, what its value, and likewise on all the rest. For what else is it that says gold is beautiful, since the gold itself does not speak? Evidently, that faculty which judges of the appearances of things.[1] What else passes judgment on music, grammar, the other faculties, proves their uses, and shows their proper occasions?

Nothing but this.

As it was fit, then, this most excellent and superior faculty alone, the power to make right use of the appearances of things, the gods have placed under our control; but no other matters have they placed under our control. Was it because they would not? I rather think that, if they could, they would have granted us these too; but they certainly could not. For, placed upon earth as we are, and confined to an earthly body and to earthly companions, how was it possible that, in these respects, we should not be hindered by external things?

But what says Zeus? "O Epictetus, if it had been possible, I would have made this little body and property of thine free, and not liable to hindrance. But now do not mistake; it is not thy own, but only a fine mixture of clay. Since, then, I could not give thee this, I have given thee a certain portion of myself; this faculty of choosing and refusing, of desire and aversion, or, in a word, of making use of the appearances of things. Taking care of this, and making thine own to consist of this, thou wilt never be baffled, never hindered; thou wilt not groan, wilt not blame, wilt not flatter anyone. How, then? Do these advantages seem small to thee?" Heaven forbid! "Let them suffice thee, then, and thank the gods."

---

[1] The word here translated "the appearances of things," will sometimes be found rendered, in other passages, "the phenomena of existence," and sometimes "things as they appear." It was a favorite word with the Stoics, and can be adequately translated by no single English word, or even phrase, implying as it does not merely the uncertainty of all impressions, but the unimportance of the emotions they involved.

But now, although it is in our power to care for one thing, and apply ourselves to one, we choose rather to care for many, and to encumber ourselves with many—body, property, brother, friend, child, and slave—and, by this multiplicity of encumbrances we are burdened and weighed down. Thus, when the weather does not happen to be fair for sailing, we sit in distress and gaze out perpetually. Which way is the wind? North. What good will that do us? When will the west wind blow? When it pleases, friend, or when Aeolus pleases; for Zeus has not made you dispenser of the winds, but Aeolus.[1]

"What, then, is to be done?"

To make the best of what is in our power, and take the rest as it occurs.

"And how does it occur?"

As God wills.

"What, then, must I be the only one to lose my head?"

Why, would you have all the world, then, lose their heads for your consolation? Are not you willing to stretch out your neck, like Lateranus,[2] when Nero commanded him to be beheaded? For, though he shrank a little after receiving a weak blow, he stretched it out again. And before this, when Epaphroditus,[3] the freedman of Nero, interrogated him about the conspiracy, "If I have a mind to say anything," replied he, "I will tell it to your master."

---

[1] Homer, *Odyssey*. Classics Club edition, p. 117.

[2] Plautius Lateranus, a consul elect, was put to death by command of Nero, for being involved in the conspiracy of Piso. His execution was so sudden that he was not permitted to take leave of his wife and children, but was hurried off and killed by the hand of the tribune Statius. He suffered in obstinate silence, and without making any reproach to Statius, who was concerned in the same plot. Tacitus, *Annals*, xv. c. 60.

[3] Epaphroditus was the master of requests and freedman of Nero, and the master of Epictetus. He assisted Nero in killing himself, for which he was condemned to death by Domitian. Suetonius, *Life of Nero*, c. 49; *Domitian*, c. 13.

"What resource have we, then, upon such occasions?" Why, what else but to distinguish between what is mine, and what not mine—what I can and what I cannot do? I must die; must I die groaning too? I must be exiled; does anyone keep me from going smiling, and cheerful, and serene? "Betray a secret?" I will not betray it, for this is in my own power. "Then I will fetter you." What do you say, man? Fetter me? You will fetter my leg, but not even Zeus himself can get the better of my free will. "I will throw you into prison; I will behead that paltry body of yours." Did I ever tell you that I alone had a head that could not be cut off? These are the things that philosophers ought to study; these they ought daily to write, and in these exercise themselves.

Thraseas [1] used to say, "I would rather be killed today than banished tomorrow." But how did Rufus [2] answer him? "If you prefer death as the heavier misfortune, how foolish a preference! If as the lighter, who has given you your choice? Why not study to be content with what is allotted you?"

Well, and what said Agrippinus? [3] "I will not be a hindrance to myself." Word was brought him, "Your case is pending in the Senate." "Good luck attend it. But it is eleven o'clock" (the hour when he used to exercise before bathing)—"let us go to our exercise." This being over, a messenger tells him, "You are condemned." "To banishment," says he, "or to death?" "To banishment." "What of my estate?" "It is not

---

[1] Thraseas Paetus was a Stoic philosopher put to death by Nero.

[2] Rufus was a Tuscan, of the equestrian order, and also a Stoic philosopher. When Vespasian banished the other philosophers, Rufus was alone excepted.

[3] Agrippinus was banished by Nero, for no other crime than the unfortunate death of his father, who had been causelessly killed by the command of Tiberius; and this furnished a pretense for accusing him of hereditary disloyalty. Tacitus, *Annals,* xvi. c. 28, 29.

taken away." "Well, then, let us go as far as Aricia,[1] and dine there."

This it is to have studied what ought to be studied; to have placed our desires and aversions out of reach of tyranny and chance. I must die—if instantly, I will die instantly; if in a short time, I will dine first, and when the hour comes, then will I die. How? As becomes a man who is giving back what is not his own.

How, Upon Every Occasion, to Preserve Our Character

To a reasonable creature, that alone is unbearable which is unreasonable, but everything reasonable may be borne. Beatings are not in themselves unbearable. "How so?" See how the Spartans [2] bear whipping, after they have learned that it is a reasonable thing. Hanging is not unbearable; for, as soon as a man has taken it into his head that it is reasonable, he goes and hangs himself. In short, we shall find by observation that no creature is oppressed so much by anything as by what is unreasonable; nor on the other hand, attracted to anything so strongly, as to what is reasonable.

But it so happens that different things are reasonable and unreasonable to different persons, just as good and bad, ad-

[1] Aricia, a town about sixteen miles from Rome, the first stage in his road to banishment.

[2] The Spartans, to make a trial of the fortitude of their children, used to have them publicly whipped at the altar of Artemis, and often with so much severity that they died.

vantageous and disadvantageous are. On this account, chiefly, we stand in need of a liberal education, to teach us to adapt our ideas of reasonable and unreasonable to particular cases, conformably to nature. But to judge of the reasonable and the unreasonable, we use not only our estimates of things about us, but of what fits each person's particular character. Thus, it is reasonable for one man to perform a menial service, who considers only that if he does not perform it he will be whipped and lose his dinner, but that if he does, he has nothing hard or disagreeable to suffer; whereas to another it appears unbearable, not only to perform such a service himself, but to respect anyone who does. If you ask me, then, whether you shall do this menial service or not, I will tell you it is a pleasanter thing to get a dinner than not, and a greater disgrace to be whipped than not to be whipped; so if you measure yourself by these things, go and do the service.

"Ay, but it does not fit my character."

It is you who are to consider that, not I; for it is you who know yourself, what value you set upon yourself, and at what rate you sell yourself; for different people sell themselves at different prices.

Hence Agrippinus,[1] when Florus was deliberating whether he should go to Nero's shows, and take some part in them himself, bid him go. "But why do not you go, then?" says Florus. "Because," replied Agrippinus, "I do not deliberate about it." For he who once starts to ask the question and to calculate the value of external things, comes very near to those who forget their own character. Why, then, do you ask me whether to choose death or life? I answer, life. Pain or pleasure? I answer, pleasure. "But if I do not act a part, I shall lose my head." Go and act it, then, but I will not. "Why?" Because you think of yourself as only one thread of the many

---

[1] Nero was remarkably fond of theatrical entertainments, and used to introduce upon the stage the descendants of noble families, whom want had rendered venal. TACITUS, *Annals*, xiv. c. 14.

that make up the tunic. "What then?" You have only to care how to be like the rest of mankind, as the one thread wants not to be distinguishable from the others. But I would be the purple,[1] that small and brilliant part, which gives a luster and beauty to the rest. Why, then, do you tell me to resemble the multitude? At that rate, how shall I be the purple?

This Helvidius Priscus,[2] too, saw, and acted accordingly; for when Vespasian sent to forbid his going to the Senate, he answered, "It is in your power to prevent my continuing a senator; but as long as I am one I must go."—"Well, then, at least be silent when you are there."—"Do not ask my opinion and I will be silent."—"But I must ask it."—"And I must speak what seems to me to be right."—"But if you do, I will put you to death." "When did I ever tell you I was immortal? You will do your part, and I mine; it is yours to kill, and mine to die intrepid; yours to banish, mine to depart untroubled."

What good, then, did Priscus do, who was but a single person? Why, what good does the purple do to the garment? What, but to be beautiful in itself, and to set a good example to the rest? Another man, perhaps, if in such circumstances Caesar had forbidden his going to the Senate, would have answered, "I thank you for excusing me." But such a man he would not have forbidden to go—well knowing that he would either sit like a statue, or, if he spoke, would say what he knew to be agreeable to Caesar, and even overdo it by adding still more.

Thus acted also a wrestler, who was in danger of death, unless his private parts were amputated. His brother, who was

---

[1] An allusion to the purple border which distinguished the dress of the Roman nobility.

[2] Helvidius Priscus was remarkable for his learning and philosophy and his love of country. He behaved, however, with haughtiness, on several occasions, to Vespasian, who sentenced him to death with great reluctance, and even forbade the execution when it was too late. SUETONIUS, *Vespasian*.

a philosopher, came to him, and said, "Well, brother, what do you propose to do? Shall we cut off this part, and return again to the field?" He refused, and courageously died.

When someone asked whether he acted thus as a wrestler, or as a philosopher, I answer, as a man, but as a man who had been proclaimed champion at the Olympic games; who had been used to such places, and not merely rubbed down in the school of Bato.[1] Another would have had his very head cut off, if he could have lived without it. This is that regard for character, so powerful with those who are accustomed of their own accord to consider it in their deliberations.

"Come then, Epictetus, shave off your beard."[2] If I am a philosopher, I answer, "I will not shave it off." "Then I will take off your head." If that will do you any good, take it.

Someone asked, "How shall each of us perceive what fits his character?" How, replied Epictetus, does a bull, when a lion approaches, alone recognize his own fitness, and fling himself into the defense of the whole herd? It is evident that with the fitness comes, at the same time, the consciousness of it. In the same manner, whoever of us has such qualifications will not be ignorant of it. But neither is a bull nor a gallant-spirited man formed all at once. We are to exercise, and prepare ourselves, and not plunge rashly into what does not concern us.

Only consider at what price you sell your free will, O man! At least, do not sell it for a trifle. The highest greatness and excellence perhaps belong to others, to such as Socrates. But why, then, if we are born with a nature like his, do not all, or the greater number, become such as he? What, are all horses swift? Are all dogs sagacious? What, because my gifts are humble shall I neglect all effort for myself? Heaven for-

---

[1] Bato was a well-known athletic trainer at Rome.

[2] Domitian ordered the banishment of all philosophers. To avoid this inconvenience, those who wished to disguise their profession shaved off their beards.

bid! Epictetus will not surpass Socrates—granted; but if I do not lag behind him that is enough for me. I shall never be a Milo, and yet I do not neglect my body; nor a Croesus, and yet I do not neglect my property; nor should we stop any effort in despair of reaching the highest.

CHAPTER THREE

From the Doctrine That God Is the Father of Mankind, How We May Proceed to Its Consequences

IF a man could be thoroughly persuaded, as he ought to be, of this principle, that we are all originally sprung from God, and that God is the father of men and gods, I believe he never would think of himself meanly or ignobly. Suppose Caesar were to adopt you, there would be no bearing your haughty looks; and will you not feel ennobled on knowing yourself to be the son of God? Yet, in fact, we do not feel ennobled. But having two things united in our composition, a body in common with the brutes, and reason in common with the gods, many of us incline toward our unhappy and mortal kindred, and only a few toward that which is happy and divine. And, as everyone necessarily treats each particular thing according to the notion he forms about it, so those few who believe that they are made for faith and honor and a wise use of things will never think meanly or ignobly of themselves. But the multitude do the opposite. "For what am I? A poor contemptible man, with this miserable flesh of mine."

Miserable indeed, but you have also something better than your poor flesh. Why, then, do you overlook that and pine away in attention to this?

Because of our animal kinship, some of us incline toward it and become like wolves—faithless and crafty and mischievous; others, like lions—wild and savage and untamed; but most of us like foxes, which, even in the animal kingdom, are low and degraded. For what is a slanderous and ill-natured man but a fox, or something even more wretched and mean? Watch and take heed, then, that you do not sink so low.

CHAPTER FOUR

Of Progress

HE who is making progress, having learned from the philosophers that good should be sought and evil shunned, and having learned, too, that prosperity and peace are obtainable by man only when he does not miss what he seeks and does not incur what he would avoid—such a man totally excludes and banishes all wayward desire, and shuns merely those things over which he can have control: if he should attempt to shun things over which he has no control, he knows that he will sometime meet what he shuns, and be unhappy. Now if virtue promises happiness, prosperity, and peace, then progress in virtue is certainly progress in each of these. For whatever the goal to which perfection in anything absolutely brings us, progress is always an approach towards it.

How comes it, then, that while we confess the greatness of virtue, we yet seek and make an ostentatious show of progress in other things? What is the work of virtue? Well being.

Who is in a state of progress then? He who has best studied
Chrysippus? [1] Why, does virtue consist in having read
Chrysippus through? If so, progress is nothing else than
understanding a great deal of Chrysippus; but now, while
declaring that virtue produces one thing we declare that the
approach to virtue, which is progress, produces something
else.

This person, they say, is already able to understand Chrysippus, by himself. "Certainly, sir, you have made vast
progress!" What progress? Why do you delude him? Why
do you blind him to a sense of his real needs? Why do you
not show him the real work of virtue, that he may know
where to look for progress? Look for it there, poor fellow,
where your work lies. And where does your work lie? In
learning what to desire and what to shun, that you may neither
be disappointed of the one nor meet with the other; in practicing what to choose and what refuse, that you may be not
prone to fail; in practicing judicial assent and doubt, that you
may be not liable to be deceived. These are the first and most
necessary things. But if you merely seek, in trembling and
lamentation, to keep away all possible ills, what real progress
have you made?

Show me then your progress on this point. Suppose I should
say to a wrestler, Show me your muscle. And he should
answer me, See my dumb-bells. Your dumb-bells are your
own affair; I want to see the effect of them.

"Take the treatise 'On Choice' [2] and see how thoroughly
I have perused it."

I am not asking about this, O slave, but how you act in
choosing and refusing, how you manage your desires and
aversions, your intentions and purposes, how you meet events
—whether you are in harmony with nature's laws or opposed

---

[1] Chrysippus was regarded as the highest authority among the later
Stoics; but not one of his many books has come down to us.

[2] Probably the title of one of Chrysippus' works.

to them. If in harmony, give me evidence of that, and I will say you are progressing; if the contrary, you may go your way, and not only comment on your books, but write some like them yourself; and what good will it do you? Do you not know that the whole volume is sold for five denarii?[1] Does he who comments on it, then, value himself at more than that sum? Never make your life to lie in one thing and yet seek progress in another.

Where is progress then?

If any of you, withdrawing from externals, turns to his own will, to train and perfect and make it harmonious with nature—noble, free, unrestrained, unhindered, faithful, honorable; if he has learned, too, that whoever longs for or dreads things outside his own control can neither be faithful nor free, but must necessarily take his chance with them, and must necessarily be subject to the persons who can procure or prevent what he wants or shuns; if, rising in the morning, he observes and keeps to this rule; bathes regularly, eats frugally, and to every matter that arises applies the same fixed principle—as a racer does to racing, and an orator to his oratory—this is he who truly makes progress; this is he who has not labored in vain. But if he is wholly intent on reading books, and labors only over them, and makes them the goal of his travels, I bid him go home immediately and do his daily duties there, since the end of his travels is nothing.

The only real thing is to study how to rid life of lamentation, and complaint, and of *Alas!*, and *I am ruined*, and misfortune, and failure; and to learn what death, what exile, what prison, what poison is; that one may be able to say in a prison, like Socrates, "My dear Crito, if it so pleases the gods, so let it be";[2] and not, "Poor me, an old man, have I kept my gray hairs for this!" Do you inquire who it is who says this? Do

---

[1] The denarius (the penny of the New Testament) was a Roman coin of small value.

[2] Plato, *Crito;* see Classics Club edition, p. 66.

you think I am quoting some mean and despicable person? Does not Priam say it? Does not Oedipus? Indeed, how many kings say it? For what is tragedy but the dramatized sufferings of men, bewildered by their admiration for things external? If we have to be taught by fictions that things beyond our will are nothing to us, I should rejoice in such a fiction that would teach me to live tranquil and serene. But what your own aims are, it is your business to consider.

Of what good, then, is Chrysippus to us?

To teach you that those things are not false on which tranquillity and peace depend. "Take my books, and you will see how true and conformable to nature those things are which give me peace." How great a happiness! And how great the benefactor who shows the way! To Triptolemus all men have raised temples and altars, because he gave us a cultivated kind of food;[1] but to him who has discovered and brought to light and communicated to all the truth, which is the means, not merely of living, but of living well—who among you has ever raised an altar, or a temple, or dedicated a statue; or worships God in his name? We offer sacrifices in memory of those who gave us corn and the vine; and shall we not give thanks to God for those who have nurtured such fruit in the human breast—the truth which makes us blessed?

---

[1] Triptolemus was said to have introduced agriculture and vegetable food among men, under the guidance of Demeter.

CHAPTER FIVE

Against the Academics[1]

THERE are men, said Epictetus, who will oppose very evident truths, and yet it is not easy to find an argument which may persuade them to alter their opinions. The cause of this is neither the man's own strength nor the weakness of his teacher; but when a man becomes obstinate in error, reason cannot always reach him.

Now there are two sorts of obstinacy: one, of the intellect; the other, of the will. A man may obstinately set himself not to assent to evident truths, nor to quit the defense of contradictions. We all dread a bodily paralysis, and would make use of every contrivance to avoid it; but one of us is troubled about a paralysis of the soul. Indeed, by Zeus, even in the case of the soul, when a person is in a state where he cannot apprehend or understand anything, we think him in a sad condition; but when his sense of shame and dignity are under an absolute paralysis, we go so far as to call this strength of character!

Are you certain that you are awake? "I am not," replies such a person, "for neither am I certain when in a dream I seem to myself to be awake." Is there no difference, then, between these two appearances? "None." Shall I argue with this man any longer? What steel or what caustic can I apply to make him aware of his paralysis? If he is aware of it, and pretends not to be so, he is even worse than dead. He sees not his inconsistency, or, seeing it, holds to the wrong. He moves not, makes no progress; he rather grows worse. His sense of

---

[1] The New Academy taught a type of skepticism based on the belief that it was impossible to establish universal truths.

shame is gone; his reasoning faculty is not gone, but brutalized. Shall I call *this* strength of character? By no means—unless we call the same that which in the vilest debauchees makes them publicly speak and act out their worst impulses.

CHAPTER SIX

Of Providence

FOR everything that happens in the world it is easy to give thanks to Providence, if a person has but these two qualities in himself: a habit of viewing broadly what happens to each individual, and a grateful temper. Without the first he will not perceive the usefulness of things which happen; and without the second, he will not be thankful for them. If God had made colors, and had not made the faculty of seeing them, what would have been their use? None. On the other hand, if he had made the faculty of observation, without objects to observe, what would have been the use of that? None. Again, if he had formed both the faculty and the objects, but had not made the light of day? Neither in that case would they have been of any use.

Who is it, then, who has fitted this to that and that to this? Who is it that has fitted the sword to the scabbard, and the scabbard to the sword? Is there no such Being? From the very structure of a complete work, we are accustomed to declare positively that it must be the product of some artificer, and not the result of mere chance. Does every such work, then, prove an artificer, and yet visible objects, the sense of seeing, and light, not prove one? And male and female, and their inclination to each other, and the use of their several organs—do not these things prove an artificer? Most certainly they do.

But further; this constitution of understanding, by which we are not simply impressed by sense objects, but take and subtract and add and combine, and pass from point to point by inference—is not all this sufficient to prevail on some men, and compel them not to leave an artificer out of their scheme? If not, let them explain to us what the power is that brings about each of these things, and how it is possible that chance should produce things so wonderful and so skillfully designed.

What then, do these things belong to us alone?

Many, indeed—things that are peculiarly necessary for a rational animal; but you will find many which are common to us and to irrational animals.

Then, do they too understand what happens?

Not at all; for to use is one thing, and to understand, another. But God had need of animals to make use of things as they appear, and of us to understand that use. It is sufficient, therefore, for them to eat, and drink, and sleep, and continue their species, and perform other such offices as belong to each of them; but to us, to whom he has given likewise a faculty of understanding, these offices are not sufficient. For if we do not proceed in a wise and systematic manner, and suitably each to his own nature and constitution, we shall never attain our end. For where the constitution of beings is different, their work and their ends are different likewise. So where the constitution is adapted only to use, there use alone is sufficient; but where there is also an ability to understand the use, unless that too be duly exercised the end of such a being will never be attained.

Well, then, every animal is constituted either for food, or for labor in husbandry, or to produce cheese, or for some other like use; and for these purposes what need is there of understanding things, and being able to discriminate between them? But God has introduced man, as a spectator of himself and of his works; and not only as a spectator, but as an interpreter of them. It is therefore shameful for a man to begin and end where irrational creatures do. He is indeed to begin there, but to end where nature itself has fixed our end; and that is, in contemplation and understanding, and in a scheme of life harmonious with nature.

Take care, then, not to die without ever contemplating these things. You take a journey to Olympia to behold the work of Phidias,[1] and each of you thinks it a misfortune to die without an acquaintance with such things. Will you not have a care to see and understand those works for which there is no need to take a journey, but which are ready and at hand? Will you never perceive what you are, or for what you were born, or for what purpose you are admitted to behold this spectacle?

"But in life there are some things unpleasant and difficult."

And are there none at Olympia? Are you not hot? Are you not crowded? Are you not without conveniences for bathing? Are you not soaked when it rains? Do you not have uproar, and noise, and other unpleasant things? But, by comparing all these with the remarkable quality of the spectacle, I suppose you bear and endure them. Well, and have you not received faculties by which you may endure every event in life? Have you not been given fortitude? Have you not been given patience? What signifies to me anything that happens, while my soul is above it? What shall disconcert or trouble or appear grievous to me? Shall I fail to use my powers for the purpose for which I received them; and shall I lament and groan at every casualty?

"Yes, but my nose is running!" Why then have you hands, slave? Is it not to wipe your nose? Do you say it is unreasonable that there should be running noses in the world? How much better for you to wipe your nose than complain! Pray,

---

[1] The great gold and ivory statue of Zeus.

what figure do you think Hercules would have made if there had not been a lion, and a hydra, and a stag, and a boar, and wicked and brutal men, whom he expelled and cleared away? And what would he have done if none of these had existed? Is it not plain that he must have wrapped himself up and slept? In the first place, then, he would never have become a Hercules by slumbering away his whole life in such luxury and ease; or if he had, what good would he have been? What would have been the use of his arm and his strength, of his patience and greatness of mind, if such circumstances and occasions of action had not roused and exercised him?

What then, should he have provided these things for himself; and introduced a boar and a lion and a hydra into his country?

This would have been madness and folly. But as they were in being, and to be met with, they were proper subjects to call out and exercise Hercules. Do you therefore likewise, recognize this and consider the faculties you have, and after taking a view of them say, "Bring on me now, O Zeus, what difficulty thou wilt, for I have faculties granted me by thee, and powers by which I may win honor from every event"? No; but you sit trembling, for fear this or that should happen, and lamenting and mourning and groaning at what does happen; and then you accuse the gods! In what does such baseness end but in impiety? And yet God has not only granted us these faculties by which we may bear every event without being depressed or broken by it, but, like a good king and a true father, has placed their exercise above restraint, compulsion, or hindrance, and wholly within our own control; nor has he reserved a power, even to himself, of hindering or restraining them. With these things free, and your own, will you not use them, nor consider what you have received, nor from whom? But you sit groaning and lamenting, some of you, blind to him who gave them, and not acknowledging your benefactor; while others basely turn themselves to complaints and accusations against God! I undertake to show you that you have means and faculties to exhibit greatness of soul, and a manly spirit. What occasion you have to find fault and complain, pray show me if you can.

Of the Use of the Forms
of Right Reasoning

It is not understood by most persons that the proper use of arguments by inference and hypothesis and interrogations, and logical forms generally, has any relation to the duties of life. In every matter the question is, how a wise and good man may go honestly and consistently through with it. We may say, therefore, either that the wise man will not involve himself in difficult problems or that, if he does, he will not think it worth his while to deal with them thoroughly; or if we allow neither of these alternatives, we must confess that some study should be made of those subjects on which the solution of problems chiefly depends. For what is the object of reasoning? To lay down true positions, to reject false ones, and to suspend judgment in doubtful ones. Is it enough, then, to learn merely this? It is enough, say you. Is it enough, then, for one who wants to commit no mistake in the use of money, merely to be told why we accept the good coins and reject the bad? It is not enough. What must he have besides? The skill to test and distinguish between the good coins and the bad. Therefore, in reasoning too, to read the rule is not enough; but we must be able to prove and distinguish between the true and the false and the doubtful. This is clear.

And what further is the aim of reasoning? To admit the logical consequence of whatever you have properly granted. Well, and is it enough merely to know this? It is not; but we must learn how it happens that one thing is the consequence of another, and when a thing follows from one premise, and when from many premises. Is it not further necessary that he who would acquit himself skillfully in argument should both himself prove whatever he asserts and be able to follow the proofs of others, and not be deceived by those who use sophistry as if they were reasoning fairly? Hence arises the science and practice of logical forms; and it appears to be indispensable.

But it may sometimes happen that from the premises which we have honestly granted there follows some consequence which, though false in itself, is nevertheless a fair inference. What then ought I to do? Accept a falsehood? Impossible. Take back my concessions? But this will not be allowed. Or assert that the consequence does not fairly follow from the premises? Nor is even this permitted. What, then, is to be done in the case? Is it not this? As having once borrowed money is not enough to make a person a debtor, unless he still continues to owe money and has not paid it, so having granted the premises is not enough to make it necessary to accept the inference; but we must stand by our premises. If the premises remain to the end what they were when we granted them, it is absolutely necessary to revoke the grant, and refuse to accept the inference. For this inference is no consequence of ours, nor belongs to us, when we have revoked our grant of the premises. We ought then thoroughly to consider our premises and their different aspects, on which anyone, by laying hold—either on the question itself or on the answer, or on the inference, or something else—may embarrass the unthinking man who did not foresee the result. So that in this way we may not be led into any unbecoming or confused position.

The same rule holds for hypotheses and hypothetical arguments. For it is sometimes necessary to assume an hypothesis, as a kind of step to the rest of the argument. Is every proposed hypothesis, then, to be granted, or not every one? And if not every one, which? And is he who has granted an hypothesis forever to abide by it? Or is he sometimes to revoke it, and accept only the consequences, but not accept the contradictions? Yes, but a person may say on your accepting a possible hypothesis, "I will force you into an impossibility." With such a man as this, shall the wise man never debate, but avoid all argument and conversation with him? And yet who besides the wise man is capable of managing an argument, and sagacious in reasoning, and proof against being deceived and imposed on by sophistry? Or will he indeed debate, but without regarding whether he behaves rashly and heedlessly in the argument? How, then, can he be wise, as we are supposing him? And without some training and education in reasoning, how can he hold his own? If they show he can, then all our theories are superfluous and absurd, and unconnected with our idea of a good man.

Why, then, are we still indolent, and slothful, and sluggish, seeking pretenses to avoid labor and late hours of work to render our reason accurate? "But suppose, after all, I should make a mistake in this field—it is not as if I had murdered my father." Slave, in this case, you had no father to murder; but the only fault you could commit in the case, you have committed. I myself said this very thing to Rufus when he reproved me for not finding the weak point in some syllogism. "Why," said I, "it isn't as if I had burnt down the capitol!" "Slave," answered he, "did the thing here involve the capitol? Or are there no other faults but burning the capitol, or murdering a father?" And is it no fault to treat rashly, and vainly, and heedlessly, the things which pass before our eyes—not to comprehend an argument or a demonstration, or a sophism; nor, in short, to see what is strong in reasoning and what is weak? Is there nothing wrong in this?

CHAPTER EIGHT

That Logical Subtleties Are Not Safe to the Uninstructed

IN as many ways as equivalent terms may be varied, in so many may the technical and rhetorical forms of reasoning be varied likewise. Take, for instance, the syllogism: "If you have borrowed and not paid, you owe me money; but you have not borrowed and not paid; therefore you do not owe me money." To perform these processes skillfully is the peculiar mark of a philosopher. For if a rhetorical argument is an imperfect syllogism, he who is versed in the perfect syllogism would be equally ready to detect an imperfect one.

"Why, then, do we not exercise ourselves and others after this manner?"

Because, even now, when we are not exercising ourselves in these things, and are not diverted, by me at least, from the study of morality, yet we made no eminent progress toward the beautiful and good. What is to be expected, then, if we take on this enterprise too? Especially as it would not only withdraw us from more necessary studies, but likewise afford a capital occasion for conceit and insolence. For the power of arguing and of persuasive reasoning is great; particularly if it is constantly practiced, and receives an additional ornament from rhetoric. In general, any such power is dangerous to weak and uninstructed persons, as being apt to render them arrogant and elated. For by what means can one persuade a young man who excels in these pursuits that he ought not to be an appendage to his accomplishments, but they to him? Does he not trample all such advice, and walk about elated and puffed up, not bearing that anyone should touch him, and remind him where he is defective, and in what he is wrong?

"What, then, was not Plato a philosopher?"

Yes, and was not Hippocrates a physician? Yet you see how he expresses himself. But what has his style to do with his being a physician? Why do you confound things accidentally united in the same men?

If Plato was handsome and stalwart, must I set myself to becoming handsome and stalwart—as if this was necessary to philosophy, because a certain person happened to be at once handsome and a philosopher? Will you not perceive and distinguish what are the things that make men philosophers, and what belong to them on other accounts? Pray, if I were a philosopher, would it be necessary that you should be lame too like me?

What then? Do I reject these special faculties? By no means; neither do I reject the faculty of sight. But if you ask me what is the good of man, I can only tell you that it is a kind of power of choice.

How from the Doctrine of Our Relationship to God We Are to Deduce Its Consequences

IF what philosophers say of the kinship between God and men be true, what should anyone do but, like Socrates, when he was asked from what country he came, never to say that he was an Athenian, or a Corinthian, but a citizen of the universe? For why, if you limit yourself to Athens, do you not farther limit yourself to that mere corner of Athens where your body was brought forth? Is it not evident that you take some more authoritative place which includes, not only that corner and your whole house, but the whole country of your fathers, and thence call yourself an Athenian or a Corinthian? He, then, who understands the administration of the universe, and has learned that the principal and greatest and most comprehensive of all things is this vast system, extending from men to God; and that from him have descended the seeds of being not only to one's father or grandfather, but to all things that are produced and born on earth; and especially to rational natures, since they alone are qualified to partake of communion with the Deity, being linked with him by reason—why should not such a man call himself a citizen of the universe? Why not a son of God? And why shall he fear anything that happens among men? Shall kinship to Caesar, or any other of the great at Rome, enable a man to live secure, above contempt, and void of all fear whatever; and shall not having God for our maker, and father, and guardian, free us from griefs and fears?

26

"But wherewithal shall I be fed? For I have nothing."

To what do slaves trust, or fugitives, when they run away from their masters? To their estates, their servants, their plate? To nothing but themselves. Yet they do not fail to find food. And must a philosopher, think you, leave his own abode to rest and depend on others, and not take care of himself? Must he be more helpless and fearful than the brute beasts?—each of which is self-sufficient, and lacks neither proper food nor any suitable or natural provision. I think that your old teacher ought not to have to be working to keep you from thinking or speaking too meanly or ignobly of yourselves, but should rather be working to keep young men of spirit who, knowing their affinity to the gods and how we are, as it were, fettered by the body and its possessions, and by the many other things that thus are needful for the daily pursuits of life, from resolving to throw them all off, as troublesome and vexatious and useless, and depart to their divine kindred.

This is the work that ought to employ your master and teacher, if you had one. You would come to him and say: "Epictetus, we can no longer bear being tied down to this poor body—feeding, and resting, and cleaning it, and vexed with so many low cares on its account. Are not these things indifferent and nothing to us, and death no evil? Are we not kindred to God; and did we not come from him? Suffer us to go back whence we came. Suffer us to be released at last from these fetters that bind and weigh us down. Here thieves and robbers, courts and tyrants, claim power over us, through the body and its possessions. Suffer us to show them that they have no power."

In which case it would be my part to answer: "Friends, wait for God, till he give the signal and dismiss you from this service; then depart to him. For the present, endure to remain at this post where he has placed you. The time of your abode here is short and easy for men like you; for what tyrant, what thief, or what court can be formidable to those who count as nothing the body and its possessions? Wait, do not foolishly depart."

Thus ought it to be between a teacher and noble youth. But how stands it now? The teacher is a dead man, and you are dead. When you have eaten enough today, you sit weeping about tomorrow, and how you shall get food. Why, if you have it, slave, you will have it; if not, you will depart. The door is open; why lament? What room is there for tears, what occasion for flattery? Why should any one person envy another? Why be impressed with awe by those who have great possessions, or are set in high rank, especially if they are powerful and irascible? For what can they do to us? The things they can do, we care nothing about; the things for which we care, they cannot reach. Who, then, after all, shall be master over one thus disposed? How did Socrates behave in regard to these things? As it became one conscious of kinship with the gods. He said to his judges:

"If you should tell me, 'We will acquit you on condition that you will no longer talk in the way you have hitherto done, or make any disturbance among either our young or our old people,' I would answer: 'It is absurd of you to think that if your general had stationed me in any post I ought to maintain and defend it, and choose to die a thousand times rather than desert it, but that if God has assigned me any station or mode of life, I ought to desert that for you.' " [1]

This it is for a man to recognize truly his relationship with God. But we habitually think of ourselves as mere stomach and intestines and genital parts, because we fear, because we desire. And we flatter those who can help us in these matters; we dread them too.

A man asked me once to write for him to Rome. He was one vulgarly esteemed unfortunate, for he had formerly been

---

[1] Epictetus is giving in his own words his recollection of a passage in Plato's *Apology*. See Classics Club edition, p. 46.

illustrious and rich, and was afterwards stripped of all his possessions, and reduced to living here. I wrote for him in a humble style; but after reading my letter he returned it to me and said: "I wanted your assistance, not your pity; for no evil has befallen me."

Thus Rufus, to test me, used to say: "Your master[1] is going to do this or that to you." When I answered him, "It is what happens to a man," he said, "Why, then, should I petition him, when I can get the same result from you?[2] For what one has of his own, it is superfluous and vain to receive from another. Shall I, then, who can receive nobleness and a manly spirit from myself, receive an estate, or a sum of money, or a place, from you? Heaven forbid! I will not be so insensible of my own possessions. But if a person is fearful and abject, what else is necessary but to apply for permission to bury him as if he were dead? "Please forward to us the corpse of such a one."[3] For, in fact, such a one is that and nothing more. If he were anything more, he would be aware that man is not to be made miserable at the will of his fellow man.

---

[1] Epictetus, it will be remembered, had been a slave.

[2] The meaning seems to be, "It is not worth while for me to petition your master so long as you are able to bear your fate so manfully."

[3] As a friend might ask for the body of a criminal who had been executed.

CHAPTER TEN

To Those Who Seek Preferment at Rome

IF we philosophers applied ourselves as heartily to our own work as the old politicians at Rome to their schemes, perhaps we too might be accomplishing something. I know a man older than I am, who is now in charge of the grain supply at Rome. When he passed through this place, on his return from exile, I recall how he inveighed against his former life, and how he promised that for the future, when he had returned to Rome, he would devote himself solely to spending the remainder of his days in peace and tranquillity. "For how few are now left to me!" he said. "You will not do it," said I. "When you are once within reach of Rome you will forget all this; and if you can but once gain admittance to court, you will rejoice and thank God." "If you ever find me, Epictetus," said he, "putting so much as one foot inside the court, think whatever you please of me." Well, now, what did he do? Before he entered the city he was met by a letter from Caesar. On receiving it he forgot all those resolutions; and has ever since been accumulating one property after another. I should be glad now to have an opportunity of reminding him of the words he uttered on the road, and of pointing out how much better a prophet I was than he.

What then? Do I say that man is made for an inactive life? No, surely. But how can you say the life of a philosopher is not full of action? For my own part, I wake at dawn with my head full of my lessons for the coming day, and then say to myself, quickly, What is it to me how such a one recites? My present business is to sleep.

What comparison can be made between their kind of activity and ours? If you consider what it is they do, you will see; for about what are they employed the whole day but in calculating, contriving, consulting—about some grain or a piece of land, or other such interests? Is there any likeness, then, between reading a petition, "I entreat you to give me a permit to export corn," and this, "I entreat you to learn from Chrysippus what the administration of the universe is, and what place a reasonable creature holds in it; learn, too, what you yourself are, and wherein your good and evil consist"? Are these things at all alike? Do they require the same kind of study? And is it no more shameful to neglect the one than the other?

Well, then, are we philosophers the only ones who take things easily? No, but you young men do so far more. And as we old men, when we see young ones playing, are tempted to trifle with them; so, much more, if we saw them earnest and ardent, we should be eager to labor with them in serious pursuits.

CHAPTER ELEVEN

Of Family Affection

WHEN an important personage once came to visit him, Epictetus, having inquired into the particulars of his affairs, asked him whether he had a wife and children. The other replying that he had, Epictetus likewise inquired, In what manner do you live with them? "Very miserably," he said. How so? For men do not marry, and have children, in order to be miserable, but rather to make themselves happy. "But I am so very miserable about my children that the other day, when my daughter was sick and appeared to be in danger, I could not bear even to be with her, but ran away, till it was told me that she was recovered." And pray do you think this was acting right? "It was acting naturally," said he. Well, do but convince me that it was acting naturally, and I can as well convince you that everything natural is right. "All, or most of us fathers, are affected in the same way." I do not deny the fact; but the question between us is, whether it is right. For by this way of reasoning it must be said that diseases occur for the good of the body, because they do happen; and even that vices are natural, because all, or most of us, are guilty of them. Show me, then, how such a behavior as yours appears to be natural.

"I cannot undertake that; but rather you show me that it is neither natural nor right."

If we were disputing about black and white, what criterion must we call in, to distinguish them?

"The sight."

If about hot and cold, or hard and soft, what?

"The touch."

Well, then, when we are debating about natural and unnatural and right and wrong what criterion are we to take?

"I do not know."

And yet to be ignorant of a criterion of colors, or of smells, or tastes, might perhaps be no very great loss; but do you think that he suffers only a small loss who is ignorant of what is good and evil, and natural and unnatural to man?

"No, the very greatest."

Well, tell me; are all things which are judged good and proper by some rightly judged to be so? Thus is it possible that the several opinions of Jews, and Syrians, and Egyptians, and Romans, concerning food, should all be right?

"How can it be possible?"

I suppose, then, it is absolutely necessary that, if the opinions of the Egyptians be right, the others must be wrong; if those of the Jews be good, all the rest must be bad.

"How can it be otherwise?"

And where there is ignorance, there is also want of wisdom and knowledge in the most necessary points.

"It is granted."

Then, as you are sensible of this, you will for the future apply yourself to nothing, and think of nothing else, but how to learn the criterion of what is agreeable to nature; and to use that in judging of each particular case. At present the assistance I have to give you towards what you desire is this: Does affection seem to you to be a right and a natural thing?

"How should it be otherwise?"

Well, and is affection natural and right, and reason not so? "By no means."

Is there any opposition, then, between reason and affection? "I think not."

Suppose there were; if one of two opposites be natural, the other must necessarily be unnatural, must it not?

"It must."

What we find, then, to accord at once with love and reason, that we may safely pronounce to be right and good.

"Agreed."

Well, then; you will not dispute that to run away and leave a sick child is contrary to reason. It remains for us to consider whether it be consistent with affection.

"Yes, let us consider that."

Did you, then, from an affection to your child, do right in running away and leaving her? Has her mother no affection for the child?

"Yes, surely she has."

Would it have been right, then, that her mother too should leave her, or would it not?

"It would not."

And does not her nurse love her?

"She does."

Then ought she likewise to leave her?

"By no means."

And does not her school attendant love her?

"He does."

Then ought he also to have run away and left her—the child being thus left alone and unassisted, because of the great affection of her parents and her friends, or perhaps left to die among people who neither loved her nor took care of her?

"Heaven forbid!"

But is it not unreasonable and unjust that what you think right in yourself, on account of your affection, should not be allowed to others, who have the very same affection with you?

"That is absurd."

Pray, if you were ill yourself should you be willing to have your relatives, including your wife and children, so very affectionate as to leave you helpless and alone?

"By no means."

Or would you wish to be so loved by your friends that in their excessive affection they would leave you alone when you were ill? Or would you not prefer, if it were possible, to be loved in this way by your enemies, so as to be left alone by them? If so, it is clear that your behavior was by no means an act of affection. But now, was there no other motive that induced you to desert your child?

"How is that possible?"

I mean some such motive as induced a person at Rome to hide his face while a horse was running to which he earnestly wished success; and when, beyond his expectation, it won the race he was obliged himself to be sponged, to recover from his faintness.

"And what was this motive?"

At present, perhaps, it cannot be made clear to you. It is sufficient to be convinced, if what philosophers say be true, that we are not to seek any motive merely from without; but that there is the same [unseen] motive in all cases, which moves us to do or forbear any action; to speak or not to speak; to be elated or depressed; to avoid or pursue—that very impulse which has now moved us two; you, to come and sit and hear me; and me, to speak as I do.

"And what is that?"

Is it anything else than that we wanted to do so?

"Nothing else."

And if we had wanted to do otherwise, what else should we have done than what we wanted to do? This, and not the death of Patroclus, was the real source of the lamentation of Achilles —for every man is not thus affected by the death of a friend— that he wanted to grieve. This too was the cause of your running away from your child, that you wanted to run away; and if hereafter you should stay with her, it will be because you want to stay. You are now returning to Rome because you want to do so; but if you should alter your opinion you will not return. In a word, neither death, nor exile, nor pain, nor anything of this kind, is the real cause of our doing or not doing any action, but our opinions and the decisions of our will. Do I convince you of this, or not?

"You do."

Well, then, such as the cause is, such will be the effect. From this day forward, then, whenever we do anything wrong, we will ascribe it to the decision of our will which led us to the act; and we will endeavor to remove and extirpate that, with greater care than we would remove wens and tumors from the body. In like manner, we will ascribe what we do right to the same cause; and we will accuse neither servant, nor neighbor, nor wife, nor children, as the cause of any evil to us— persuaded that if we had not made certain decisions, we should not carry them to such consequences. The control of these decisions lies in us, and not in any outward things. Of the decisions of our will we ourselves, and not things outward, are the masters.

"Agreed."

From this day, then, we will not so closely inquire as to any external conditions—estate or slaves, or horses, or dogs—but only make sure of our own principles.

"Such is my desire," said the visitor.

You see, then, that it is necessary for you to become a student, that creature whom everyone laughs at, if you really desire to make an examination of decisions of your will; but this, as you should know, is not the work of an hour or a day.

CHAPTER TWELVE

Of Contentment

CONCERNING the gods, some affirm that there is no deity; others, that he indeed exists, but is slothful, negligent, and without providential care; a third class admits both his being and his providence, but only in respect to great and heavenly objects, not earthly; a fourth recognizes him both in heaven and earth, but only in general, not individual matters; a fifth, like Odysseus and Socrates, says, "I cannot be hid from thee in any of my motions." [1]

We must first examine each of these opinions, and see which is, and which is not rightly spoken. Now, if there are no gods, wherefore serve them? If there are, but they take no care of anything, how is the case bettered? Or, if they both are, and take care; yet, if there is nothing communicated from them to men, and therefore certainly nothing to me, how much better is it? A wise and good man, after examining these things, submits his mind to him who administers the universe, as good citizens do to the laws of the state.

---

[1] Homer, *Iliad*. See Classics Club edition, p. 150.

He, then, who comes to be instructed, ought to come with this aim: "How may I in everything follow the gods? How may I acquiesce in the divine administration? And how may I be free?" For he is free to whom all happens agreeably to his desire, and whom no one can unduly restrain.

"What, then, is freedom mere license?"

By no means; for madness and freedom are incompatible.

"But I would have that happen which appears to me desirable, however it comes to appear so."

You are mad; you have lost your senses. Do not you know that freedom is a very noble and valuable thing? But for me to choose at random, and for things to happen agreeably to such a choice, may be so far from a noble thing, as to be of all things the most undesirable. For how do we proceed in writing? Do I choose to write the name of Dion (for instance) as I will? No, but I am taught to desire to write it as it ought to be written. And what is the case in music? The same. And what in every other art or science? Otherwise, it would be of no purpose to learn anything if it were to be adapted to each one's particular humor. Is it, then, only in the greatest and principal matter, that of freedom, permitted me to desire at random? By no means; but true instruction is this—learning to desire that things should happen as they do. And how do they happen? As the appointer of them has appointed. He has ordained that there should be summer and winter, plenty and dearth, virtue and vice, and all such contrarieties, for the harmony of the whole. To each of us he has given a body and its parts, and our possessions and companions. Mindful of this, we should enter upon a course of education and instruction, not in order to change the constitution of things—for this is neither practicable nor desirable—but that, things being as they are with regard to us, we may have our minds accommodated to the facts. Can we, for instance, flee from mankind? How is that possible? Can we, by conversing with them, transform them? Who has given us such a power? What, then, remains, or what method is there to be found, for such a commerce with them that, while they act according to the appearances in their own minds, we may nevertheless be affected conformably to nature?

But you are wretched and discontented. If you are alone, you call it a desert; and if with men, you call them cheats and robbers. You find fault too with your parents, and children, and brothers, and neighbors. Whereas you ought, if you live alone, to call that repose and freedom, and to esteem yourself as resembling the gods; and when you are in company, not to call it a crowd, and a tumult, and a trouble, but an assembly, and a festival—and thus to accept all things contentedly. What, then, is the punishment of those who do not so accept them? To be—as they are. Is anyone discontented with being alone? Let him remain in his desert. Discontented with his parents? Let him be a bad son; and let him mourn. Discontented with his children? Let him be a bad father. Shall we throw him into prison? What prison? Where he already is; for he is in a situation against his will, and wherever anyone is against his will, that is to him a prison—just as Socrates was not truly in prison, for he was there willingly.

"What, then, must my leg be lame?"

And is it for one paltry leg, wretch, that you accuse the universe? Can you not forego that, in consideration of the whole? Can you not give up something? Can you not gladly yield it to him who gave it? And will you be angry and discontented with the decrees of Zeus—which he, with the Fates, who spun in his presence the thread of your birth, ordained and appointed? Do not you know how very small a part you are of the whole?—that is, as to body; for, as to reason, you are neither worse nor less than divine. For reason is not measured by size or height, but by the decisions of its will. Will you not, therefore, place your good there wherein you are equal with the gods?

"But how wretched am I, in such a father and mother!"

What, then, was it granted you to come beforehand, and make your own terms, and say, "Let such and such persons, at this hour, be the authors of my birth"? It was not granted; for it was necessary that your parents should exist before you, and so you be born afterwards. Of whom? Of just such as they were. What, then, since they are such, is there no remedy afforded you? Surely, you would be wretched and miserable if you knew not the use of sight, and shut your eyes in presence of colors; and are not you more wretched and miserable in being ignorant that you have within you the needful nobility and manhood wherewith to meet these accidents? Events proportioned to your reason are brought before you; but you turn your mind away at the very time when you ought to have it the most open and discerning. Why do not you rather thank the gods that they have made you superior to those events which they have not placed within your own control, and have rendered you accountable for that only which is within your own control? They discharge you from all responsibility for your parents, for your brothers, for your body, possessions, death, life. For what, then, have they made you responsible? For that which is alone in your own power —a right use of things as they appear. Why, then, should you draw those cares upon yourself for which you are not responsible? This is giving oneself needless trouble.

CHAPTER THIRTEEN

How Everything May Be Performed to the Divine Acceptance

WHEN a person inquired how anyone might eat to the divine acceptance, If he eats with justice, said Epictetus, and with gratitude, and fairly, and temperately, and decently, must he not also eat to the divine acceptance? And if you call for hot water, and your servant does not hear you, or, if he does, brings it only warm, or perhaps is not to be found at home, then to abstain from anger or petulance, is not this to the divine acceptance?

"But how is it possible to bear such things?"

O slavish man! will you not bear with your own brother, who has God for his Father, as being a son from the same stock, and of the same high descent? But if you chance to be placed in some superior station, will you presently set yourself up for a tyrant? Will you not remember what you are, and over whom you bear rule—that they are by nature your relations, your brothers; that they are the offspring of God?

"But I have them by right of purchase, and not they me."

Do you see what it is you regard? You bend your gaze downward towards the earth, and what is lower than earth, and towards the unjust laws of men long dead; but up towards the divine laws you never turn your eyes.

CHAPTER FOURTEEN

That All Things Are Under the Divine Supervision

WHEN a person asked him, how anyone might be convinced that his every act is under the supervision of God, Do not you think, said Epictetus, that all things are mutually connected and united?

"I do."

Well; and do not you think that things on earth feel the influence of the heavenly powers?

"Yes."

Else how is it that in their season, as if by express command, God bids the plants to blossom and they blossom, to bud and they bud, to bear fruit and they bear it, to ripen it and they ripen; and when again he bids them drop their leaves, and withdrawing into themselves to rest and wait, they rest and wait? Whence again are there seen, on the waxing and waning of the moon, and the approach and departure of the sun, so great changes and transformations in earthly things? Have, then, the very leaves, and our own bodies, this connection and sympathy with the whole, and have not our souls much more? But our souls are thus connected and intimately joined to God, as being indeed members and distinct portions of his essence; and must he not be sensible of every movement of them, as belonging and connatural to himself? Even you can think of the divine administration, and every other divine subject, and together with these of human affairs also; you can at once receive impressions on your senses and your understanding from a thousand objects; at once assent to some things, deny or suspend your judgment concerning others, and preserve in your mind impressions from so many and various objects, by whose aid you can revert to ideas similar to those which first impressed you. You can retain a variety of arts and the memories of ten thousand things. All this you do, and is not God capable of surveying all things, and being present with all, and in communciation with all? Is the sun capable of illuminating so great a portion of the universe, and of leaving only that small part of it unilluminated, which is covered by the shadow of the earth, and cannot he who made and moves the sun, a small part of himself,[1] if compared with the whole—cannot he perceive all things?

"But I cannot," say you, "attend to all things at once." Who asserts that you have equal power with Zeus? Nevertheless, he has assigned to each man a director, his own good genius, and committed him to that guardianship—a director sleepless and not to be deceived. To what better and more careful guardian could he have committed each one of us? So that when you have shut your doors, and darkened your room, remember never to say that you are alone; for you are not alone, but God is within, and your genius is within; and what need have they of light to see what you are doing? To this God you likewise ought to swear allegiance as the soldiers do to Caesar. For they, in order to receive their pay, swear to prefer before all things the safety of Caesar; and will you not swear, who have received so many and so great favors; or, if you have sworn, will you not fulfill the oath? And what must you swear? Never to distrust, nor accuse, nor murmur at any of the things appointed by God; nor to shrink from doing or enduring that which is inevitable. Is this oath like the former? In the first oath persons swear never to dishonor Caesar; by the last, never to dishonor themselves.

---

[1] The Stoic doctrine identified the universe, of which the sun is but a part, with God.

CHAPTER FIFTEEN

What Philosophy Promises

WHEN someone consulted Epictetus, how he might persuade his brother to forbear treating him ill, Philosophy, he answered, does not promise to procure any outward good for man; otherwise it would include something beyond its proper theme. For as the material of a carpenter is wood; of a statuary, brass; so of the art of living, the material is each man's own life.

"What, then, is my brother's life?"

That, again, is matter for his own art, but is external to you; like property, health, or reputation. Philosophy undertakes none of these. In every circumstance I will keep my will in harmony with nature. To whom belongs that will? To him in whom I exist.

"But how, then, is my brother's unkindness to be cured?"

Bring him to me, and I will tell him; but I have nothing to say to *you* about *his* anger.

But the inquirer still further asking for a rule for self-government, if he should not be reconciled, Epictetus answered thus:

No great thing is created suddenly, any more than a bunch of grapes or a fig. If you tell me that you desire a fig, I answer you, that there must be time. Let it first blossom, then bear fruit, then let the fruit ripen. Since, then, the fruit of a fig tree is not brought to perfection suddenly, or in one hour, do you think to possess instantaneously and easily the fruit of the human mind? I warn you, expect it not.

CHAPTER SIXTEEN

Of Providence

BE not surprised if other animals have all things necessary to the body ready provided for them, not only meat and drink, but lodging; if they want neither shoes nor bedding nor clothes, while we stand in need of all these. For they not being made for themselves, but for service, it was not fit that they should be so formed as to be waited on by others. For consider what it would be for us to take care, not only for ourselves, but for sheep and asses too—how they should be clothed, how shod, and how they should eat and drink. But as soldiers are furnished ready for their commander, shod, clothed, and armed—for it would be a grievous thing for a colonel to be obliged to go through his regiment to put on their clothes—so nature has furnished these useful animals, ready provided, and standing in need of no further care; so that one little boy, with only a crook, drives a flock.

But we, instead of being thankful for this, complain of God that there is not the same kind of care taken of us likewise; and yet, good heaven! any one thing in the creation is sufficient to demonstrate a Providence, to a humble and grateful mind. Not to instance great things, the mere possibility of producing milk from grass, cheese from milk, and wool from skins—who formed and planned this? No one, say you. O surprising irreverence and dullness!

Come, let us omit the primary works of nature; let us contemplate her merely incidental traits. What is more useless than the hairs upon one's chin? And yet has she not made use even of these, in the most becoming manner possible? Has she not by these distinguished the sexes? Does not nature in each of us call out, even at a distance, I am a man; approach and address me as such; inquire no farther; see the characteristic? On the other hand, with regard to women, as she has mixed something softer in their voice, so she has deprived them of a beard. But no; [some think] this living being should have been left undistinguished, and each of us should be obliged to proclaim, "I am a man!" But why is not this characteristic beautiful and becoming and dignified? How much more beautiful than the comb of cocks; how much more noble than the mane of lions! Therefore we ought to preserve the characteristics made by the Creator; we ought not to reject them, nor confound, so far as in us lies, the distinction between the sexes.

Are these the only works of Providence with regard to us? And what speech can fitly celebrate their praise? For, if we had any understanding, ought we not, both in public and in private, incessantly to sing and praise the Deity, and rehearse his benefits? Ought we not, whether we dig or plow or eat, to sing this hymn to God: Great is God, who has supplied us with these instruments to till the ground; great is God, who has given us hands and organs of digestion; who has given us to grow insensibly, to breathe in sleep? These things we ought forever to celebrate; and to make it the theme of the greatest and divinest hymn, that he has given us the power to appreciate these gifts, and to use them well. But because the most of you are blind and insensible, there must be someone to fill this office, and lead, in behalf of all men, the hymn to God; for what else can I do, a lame old man, but sing hymns to God? Were I a nightingale, I would act the part of a nightingale; were I a swan, the part of a swan; but since I am a reasonable creature, it is my duty to praise God. This is my business; I do it; nor will I ever desert this post, so long as it is permitted me; and I call on you to join me in the same song.

That the Art of Reasoning Is Necessary

SINCE it is reason which shapes and regulates all other things, it ought not itself to be left in disorder; but by what shall it be regulated? Evidently, either by itself, or by something else. Well, either that too is reason, or something else superior to reason, which is impossible; and if it be reason, what again shall regulate that? For if this reason can regulate itself, so can the former; and if we still require any further agent, the series will be infinite and without end.

"But," say you, "the essential thing is to prescribe for qualities of character."

Would you hear about these, therefore? Well, hear. But if you say to me that you cannot tell whether my arguments are true or false, and if I happen to express myself ambiguously, and you bid me make it clearer, I will then at once show you that this is the first essential. Therefore, I suppose, the Stoics first put the art of reasoning—just as before the measuring of corn, we settle the measure; for, unless we first determine the measure and the weight, how shall we be able to measure or weigh? Thus, in the present case, unless we have first learned and fixed that which is the standard of judgment of other things, and by which other things are known and judged, how shall we be able accurately to know anything else? How is it possible? Well, a bushel measure is only wood, a thing of no value, but it measures corn; and logic is of no value in itself. That we will consider hereafter, but grant it now; it is enough that it distinguishes and examines, and, as one may say, measures and weighs all other things. Who says this? Is it only Chrysippus, and Zeno, and Cleanthes? Does not Antisthenes say it? And who is it, then, who has written that the beginning of a right education is the examination of terms? Does not Socrates say it? Of whom, then, does Xenophon write, that he began by the examination of terms, what each signified?

Is this, then, the great and admirable thing, to understand or interpret Chrysippus?

Who says that it is? But what, then, is the admirable thing?

To understand the will of nature.

Well, then; do you conform to it yourself? In that case, what need have you for anyone else? For if it be true that men err but unwillingly,[1] and if you have learned the truth, you must needs act rightly.

But, indeed, I do not conform to the will of nature.

Who, then, shall interpret that?

They say, Chrysippus. I go and inquire what this interpreter of nature says. Soon I cannot understand his meaning; I seek one to interpret that. I call on him to explain everything as clearly as if it were in Latin. Yet what right has this last interpreter to boast? Nor has Chrysippus himself, so long as he only interprets the will of nature, and does not follow it; and much less has his interpreter. For we have no need of Chrysippus on his own account; but that, by his means, we may apprehend the will of nature; just as no one values a diviner on his own account, but that, by his assistance, men hope to understand future events and heavenly indications; nor the auguries, on their own account, but on account of what is signified by them; neither is it the raven, nor the crow, that is admired, but the divine purposes displayed through their means.

Thus I come to the diviner and interpreter of these higher

---

[1] The saying of Socrates, "No man errs, voluntarily," appears in Plato's *Protagoras*, 345.

things, and say, "Inspect the auguries for me: what is signified for me?" Having taken, and inspected them, he thus interprets them: "You have a free will, O man, incapable of being restrained or compelled. This is written here in the auguries. I will show you this, first, in the faculty of assent. Can anyone restrain you from assenting to truth? No one. Can anyone compel you to admit a falsehood? No one. You see, then, that you have here a free will, incapable of being restrained, or compelled, or hindered. Well, is it otherwise with regard to pursuit and desire? What can displace one pursuit? Another pursuit. What [can displace] desire and aversion? Another desire and another aversion." "If you offer *death* as an alternative," say you, "you compel me." No, not the alternative does it, but your conviction that it is better to do such a thing than to die. Here, again, you see that it is your own conviction which compels you—that is, choice compels choice; for if God had constituted that portion which he has separated from his own essence, and given to us, capable of being restrained or compelled, either by himself, or by any other, he would not have been God, nor have fitly cared for us.

"These things," says the diviner, "I find in the auguries. These things are announced to you. If you will, you are free. If you will, you will have no one to complain of, no one to accuse. All will be equally according to your own will, and to the will of God."

For the sake of this oracle, I go to this diviner and philosopher; admiring not alone him for his interpretation, but also the things which he interprets.

CHAPTER EIGHTEEN

That We Ought Not to Be Angry
with the Erring

IF what the philosophers say be true,[1] that all men's actions proceed from one source, namely feeling; that as they assent from a feeling that a thing is so, and dissent from a feeling that it is not, and suspend their judgment from a feeling that it is uncertain; so, likewise, they seek a thing from a feeling that it is for their advantage—and it is impossible to esteem one thing advantageous, and yet desire another; to esteem one thing a duty, and yet pursue another—why, after all, should we be angry at the multitude?

"They are thieves and robbers," someone says.

What do you mean by thieves and robbers? They are in an error concerning good and evil. Ought you, then, to be angry, or rather to pity them? Do but show them their error, and you will see that they will amend their faults; but if they do not see the error, they will rise no higher than their convictions.

"What, then; ought not this thief and this adulterer to be put to death?"

Nay, call him rather one who errs and is deceived in things of the greatest importance; blinded, not in the vision which distinguishes white from black, but in the reason which discerns good from evil. By stating your question thus, you would see how inhuman it is—and just as if you were to say, "Ought not this blind or that deaf man to be destroyed?" For, if the greatest hurt be a deprivation of the most valuable

---

[1] This was a precept commonly accepted by the Stoics.

things, and the most valuable thing to everyone be rectitude of will; when anyone is deprived of this, why, after all, are you angry? You ought not to be affected, O man! contrary to nature, by the evil deeds of another. Pity him rather. Yield not to hatred and anger, nor say, as many do: "What! shall these execrable and odious wretches dare to act thus?" Whence have *you* so suddenly learned wisdom?

Why are we thus enraged? Because we make idols of those things which such people take from us. Make not an idol of your clothes, and you will not be enraged with the thief. Make not an idol of a woman's beauty, and you will not be enraged with an adulterer. Know that thief and adulterer cannot reach the things that are properly your own; but those only which belong to others, and are not within your power. If you can give up these things, and look upon them as not essential, with whom will you any longer be enraged? But while you idolize them, be angry with yourself, rather than with others. Consider this: you have a fine suit of clothes, your neighbor has not. You have a window; you want to air them. He knows not in what the good of man consists, but imagines it is in a fine suit of clothes, just as you imagine. Shall he not come and take them away? When you show a cake to greedy people, and are devouring it all yourself, would you not have them snatch it from you? Do not tempt them. Do not have a window, do not air your clothes.

I, too, the other day, had an iron lamp burning before my household deities. Hearing a noise at the window, I ran. I found my lamp was stolen. I considered that he who took it away did nothing unaccountable. What then? I said, tomorrow you shall find an earthen one. A man loses only what he has. "I have lost my coat." Yes, because you had a coat. "I have a pain in my head." You certainly can have none in your horns. Why, then, are you out of humor? For loss and pain can be only of such things as are possessed.

But the tyrant will chain—what? A leg. He will take away—

what? A head. What is there, then, that he can neither chain nor take away? The moral purpose. Hence the advice of the ancients, Know thyself.

"What, then, ought we to do?"

Practice yourself, for heaven's sake, in little things, and thence proceed to greater. "I have a pain in my head." Do not lament. "I have a pain in my ear." Do not lament. I do not say you may never groan, but do not groan in spirit; or if your servant be a long while in bringing you something to bind your head, do not croak and go into hysterics, and say, "Everybody hates me." For who would not hate such a one?

Relying for the future on these principles, walk erect and free, not trusting to bulk of body, like a wrestler; for one should not be invincible in the sense that an ass is.

Who, then, is invincible? He whom the inevitable cannot overcome. For such a person I imagine every trial, and watch him as an athlete in each. He has been victorious in the first encounter. What will he do in the second? What, if he should be exhausted by the heat? What, if the field be Olympia? And so in other trials. If you throw money in his way, he will despise it. Is he proof against the seductions of women? What if he be tested by fame, by calumny, by praise, by death? He is able to overcome them all. If he can bear sunshine and storm, discouragement and fatigue, I pronounce him an athlete unconquered indeed.

CHAPTER NINETEEN

Of the Right Treatment
of Tyrants

WHEN a person possesses some superiority, either real or imaginary, he will necessarily be puffed up with it, unless he has been well instructed. A tyrant openly says, "I am supreme over all." And what can you bestow on me? Can you exempt my desires from disappointment? How should you? For do you never incur what you shun? Are your own aims infallible? Whence came you by that privilege? Pray, on shipboard, do you trust yourself, or the pilot? In a chariot, whom but the driver? And whom in all other arts? Just the same. In what, then, does your power consist?

"All men pay regard to me."

So do I to my desk. I wash it and wipe it, and drive a peg for my oil flask.

"What, then; are these things to be valued beyond me?"

No, but they are of some use to me, and therefore I pay regard to them. Why, do I not pay regard to an ass? Do I not wash his feet? Do I not clean him? Do not you know that everyone pays such regard even to himself; and that he does it to you, just as he does to an ass? For who pays regard to you as a man? Show that. Who would wish to be like you? Who would desire to imitate you, as he would Socrates?

"But I can take off your head."

You say rightly. I had forgot that one is to pay regard to you as to a fever, or the cholera; and that there should be an altar erected to you, as there is to the goddess Fever at Rome.

What is it, then, that disturbs and terrifies the multitude—the tyrant and his guards? By no means. What is by nature free cannot be disturbed or restrained by anything but itself; but its own convictions disturb it. Thus, when the tyrant says to anyone, "I will chain your leg," he who chiefly values his leg cries out for pity; while he who chiefly values his own moral purpose says, "If you imagine it for your interest, chain it."

"What! do you not care?"

"No, I do not care."

"I will show you that I am master."

"You? How should you? Zeus has set me free. What! do you think he would suffer his own son to be enslaved? You are master of my carcass; take it."

"So that, when you come into my presence, you pay no attention to me?"

"No, I pay attention only to myself; or, if you will have me recognize you also, I will do it, but only as if you were a pot."

This is not selfish vanity; for every animal is so constituted as to do everything for itself. Even the sun does all for himself, and for that matter so does even Zeus himself; but when he would be styled the dispenser of rain and plenty, and the father of gods and men, you see that he cannot attain these offices and titles unless he contributes to the common good. And he has universally so constituted the nature of every reasonable creature, that no one can attain its own good without contributing something for the good of all. And thus it becomes not selfish to do everything for oneself; for do you expect that a man should desert himself and his own concerns, when all beings have one and the same original instinct, self-preservation? What follows then? That where we recognize those absurd convictions, which treat things outward as if they were the true good or evil of life, there must necessarily be a regard paid to tyrants; and I wish it were to tyrants only, and not to the very officers of their bedchamber too. For how can a man grow wise on a sudden, when Caesar has put him in charge of his chamberpot? Immediately we say, "Felicio talked very sensibly to me!" I wish he were turned out of office, that he might once more appear to you the fool he is.

Epaphroditus [1] owned a shoemaker, whom, because he was good for nothing, he sold. This very fellow being, by some strange luck, bought by a courtier, became shoemaker to Caesar. Then, you might have seen how Epaphroditus honored him. "How is good Felicio, pray?" And, if any one of us asked what the great man himself was about, it was answered, "He is consulting about affairs with Felicio." Did he not sell him previously as good for nothing? Who, then, has all on a sudden made a wise man of him? This it is to reverence externals.

Is anyone exalted to the office of tribune? All who meet him congratulate him. One kisses his eyes, another his neck, and the slaves his hands. He goes to his house; finds it illuminated. He ascends the capitol; offers a sacrifice. Now, who ever offered a sacrifice for having good desires; for conforming his aims to nature? Yet we thank the gods for that wherein we place our good.

A person was talking with me today about applying for the priesthood in the temple of Augustus. I said to him, Let the thing alone, friend; you will be at great expense for nothing. "But my name," said he, "will be written in the annals." Will you stand by, then, and tell those who read them, "I am the person whose name is written there"? And even if you could tell everyone so now, what will you do when you are dead? "My name will remain." Write it upon a stone, and it will remain just as well. And, pray, what remembrance will there be of you outside of Nicopolis? [2] "But I shall wear a crown of gold." If your heart is quite set upon a crown, make and put on one of roses; for it will make the prettier appearance.

---

[1] Epaphroditus once owned Epictetus.
[2] The city in which Epictetus taught during the latter part of his life.

CHAPTER TWENTY

In What Manner Reason Contemplates Itself

EVERY art, and every faculty, contemplates certain things as its principal objects. Whenever, therefore, it is of the same nature with the objects of its contemplation, it necessarily contemplates itself too: but where it is of a different nature, it cannot contemplate itself. The art of shoemaking, for instance, is exercised upon leather, but is itself entirely distinct from the materials it works upon; therefore it does not contemplate itself. Again, grammar is exercised on articulate speech. Is the art of grammar itself, then, articulate speech? By no means. Therefore, it cannot contemplate itself. To what purpose, then, is reason appointed by nature? To a proper use of the phenomena of existence. And what is reason? The art of systematizing these phenomena. Thus, by its nature, it becomes contemplative of itself too.

Again, what subjects of contemplation belong to prudence? Good and evil, and that which is indifferent. What, then, is wisdom itself? Good. What folly? Evil.

You see, then, that wisdom necessarily contemplates both itself and its contrary. Therefore, the first and greatest work of a philosopher is to try to distinguish the phenomena of existence, and to admit none untried. Even in money, where our interest seems to be concerned, you see what an art we have invented, and how many ways an assayer uses to try its value—by the sight, the touch, the smell, and, lastly, the hearing. He throws the piece down, and attends to the jingle; and is not contented with its jingling only once, but, by frequent attention to it, trains his ear for sound. So, when we think it of consequence whether we are deceived or not, we use the utmost attention to discern those things which may deceive us. But, yawning and slumbering over our poor neglected reason, we are imposed upon by every appearance, nor know the mischief done. Would you know, then, how very languidly you are affected by good and evil, and how vehemently by things indifferent, consider how you feel with regard to bodily blindness, and how with regard to being deceived, and you will find that you are far from being moved, as you ought, in relation to good and evil.

"But trained powers and much labor and learning are here needed."

What then? Do you expect the greatest of arts to be acquired by slight endeavors? And yet the principal doctrine of the philosophers is in itself short. If you have a mind to know it, read Zeno, and you will see. It is not a long story to say, "Our end is to serve the gods," and "The essence of good consists in the proper use of the phenomena of existence." If you say, what then is God? what are phenomena? what is particular, what universal nature?—here the long story comes in. And so, if Epicurus should come and say that good lies in the body, here, too, it will be a long story; and it will be necessary to hear what is the principal, and substantial, and essential part in us. It is unlikely that the good of a snail should be placed in the shell; and is it likely that the good of a man should? You yourself, Epicurus, have in you something superior to this. What is that in you which deliberates, which examines, which recognizes the body as the principal part? Why light your lamp, and labor for us, and write so many books? That we may not be ignorant of the truth? But what are we? What are we to you? Thus the argument becomes a long story.

CHAPTER TWENTY-ONE

Of the Desire of Admiration

WHEN a man maintains his proper attitude in life, he does not long after externals. What would you have, O man?

"I am contented, if my desires and aversions are conformable to nature; if I seek and shun that which I ought, and thus regulate my purposes, my efforts, and my opinions."

Why, then, do you walk as if you had swallowed a ramrod?

"Because I could wish moreover to have all who meet me admire me, and all who follow me cry out, What a great philosopher!"

Who are those by whom you would be admired? Are they not the very people who you used to say were mad? What, then, would you be admired by madmen?

CHAPTER TWENTY-TWO

Of General Principles

THE same general principles are common to all men, nor does one such principle contradict another; for which of us does not admit that good is advantageous and eligible, and in all cases to be pursued and followed? Who does not admit that justice is fair and becoming? Where, then, arises the dispute? In adapting these principles to particular cases; as when one cries, "Such a person has acted well—he is a gallant man"; and another, "No, he has acted like a fool." Hence arise disputes among men. This is the dispute between Jews and Syrians and Egyptians and Romans—not whether the right be preferable to all things, and in every instance to be sought; but whether the eating swine's flesh be consistent with right, or not. This, too, you will find to have been the dispute between Achilles and Agamemnon; for call them forth. What say you, Agamemnon—ought not that to be done which is fit and right? "Yes, surely." Achilles, what say you—is it not agreeable to you, that what is right should be done? "Yes; I desire it beyond everything." Apply your principles then. Here begins the dispute. One says, "It is not fit that I should restore Chryseis to her father." The other says, "Yes; but it is." One or the other of them, certainly, makes a wrong conception of the principle of fitness. Again, the one says, "If it be fit that I should give up Chryseis, it is fit, too, that I should take some of your prizes." The other answers, "What, that you should take my mistress?" "Ay; yours." "What, mine only? Must I only, then, lose my prize?"

What, then, is it to be properly educated? To learn how to apply the principles of natural right to particular cases, and, for the rest, to distinguish that some things are in our power, while others are not. In our own power are the will, and all voluntary actions; out of our power, the body and its parts, property, parents, brothers, children, country, and, in short, all our fellow beings. Where, then, shall we place the good? In what shall we define it to consist? In things within our own power. But are not health and strength and life good? And are not children, parents, country? Who will deny that?

Let us, then, try another point of view. Can he who suffers evil, and is disappointed of good, be happy? He cannot. And can he preserve a right behavior with regard to society? How is it possible that he should? I am naturally led to seek my own highest good. If, therefore, it is my highest good to have an estate, it is for my good likewise to take it away from my neighbor. If it is my highest good to have a suit of clothes, it is for my good likewise to steal it wherever I find it. Hence wars, seditions, tyranny, unjust invasions. How shall I, if this be the case, be able any longer to do my duty towards Zeus? If I suffer evil, and am disappointed, he takes no care of me. And what is he to me if he cannot help me; or again, what is he to me if he chooses I should be in the condition that I am? Then I begin to hate him. What, then, do we build temples, do we raise statues, to Zeus, as to evil demons, as to the goddess Fever? How, then, is he the preserver, and how the dispenser of rain and plenty? If we place the essence of good on any such ground, all this will follow. What, then, shall we do?

This is the inquiry which interests him who philosophizes in earnest, and to some result. Do I not now see what is good, and what is evil, or am I mad? Suppose I place good only in things dependent on my own will? Why, everyone will laugh at me. Some gray-headed old fellow will come, with his fingers covered with gold rings, and will shake his head, and say, "Hark ye, child, it is fit you should learn philosophy; but it is fit, too, you should have common sense. All this is nonsense. You learn syllogisms from philosophers; but how you are to act, you know better than they." Then what displeases you if I do know? What can I say to this unfortunate? If I make no answer, he will burst; so I must answer thus: "Bear with me, as with lovers. I am not myself; I have lost my senses."

CHAPTER TWENTY-THREE

Against Epicurus

EVEN Epicurus is sensible that we are by nature sociable beings; but having once placed our good in the mere outward
shell, he can say nothing afterwards inconsistent with that;
for again, he strenuously maintains that we ought not to
admire or accept anything separated from the nature of good,
and he is in the right to maintain it. But how, then, arise any
affectionate anxieties, unless there be such a thing as natural
affection towards our offspring? Then why do you, Epicurus,
dissuade a wise man from bringing up children? Why are you
afraid that upon their account he may fall into anxieties? Does
he fall into any for his slave Mouse,[1] that feeds within his
house? What is it to him, if his little Mouse begins to cry? But
Epicurus knew that, if once a child is born, it is no longer in
our power not to love and be solicitous for it. On the same
grounds he says that a wise man will not engage himself in
public business, knowing very well what must follow. If men
are only so many flies, why should he not engage in it?

And does he, who knows all this, dare to forbid us to bring
up children? Not even a sheep, or a wolf, deserts its offspring;
and shall man? What would you have—that we should be as
silly as sheep? Yet even these do not desert their offspring. Or
as savage as wolves? Neither do these desert them. Pray, who
would mind *you*, if he saw his child fallen upon the ground
and crying? For my part, I am of opinion that your father and
mother, even if they could have foreseen that you would have
been the author of such doctrines, would not have thrown
you away.

---

[1] The reference is thought to be to Mys (Mouse), a favorite house
slave of Epicurus.

CHAPTER TWENTY-FOUR

How We Ought to Struggle With Difficulties

IT is difficulties that show what men are. For the future, in case of any difficulty, remember that God, like a gymnastic trainer, has pitted you against a rough antagonist. For what end? That you may be an Olympic conqueror; and this cannot be without toil. No man, in my opinion, has a more profitable difficulty on his hands than you have, provided you will but use it, as an athletic champion uses his antagonist.

Suppose we were to send you as a scout to Rome.[1] But no one ever sends a timorous scout, who, when he only hears a noise, or sees a shadow, runs back frightened, and says, "The enemy is at hand." So now, if you should come and tell us, "Things are in a fearful way at Rome; death is terrible, banishment terrible, calumny terrible, poverty terrible; run, good people, the enemy is at hand"; we will answer, Get you gone, and prophesy for yourself; our only fault is that we have sent such a scout. Diogenes was sent as a scout before you, but he told us other tidings. He says that death is no evil, for it is nothing base; that calumny is only the noise of madmen. And what account did this spy give us of pain, of pleasure, of poverty? He says that to be naked is better than a purple robe; to sleep upon the bare ground, the softest bed; and gives a proof of all he says by his own courage, tranquillity, and freedom, and, moreover, by a healthy and robust body. "There is no enemy near," he says; "all is profound peace." How so, Diogenes? "Look upon me," he says. "Am I hurt?

---

[1] Since Domitian had banished philosophers from Rome a scout is sent to find out what is going on of interest to them.

Am I wounded? Have I run away from anyone?" This is a
scout worth having. But you come, and tell us one tale after
another. Go back and look more carefully, and without fear.

"What shall I do, then?"

What do you do when you land from a ship? Do you take
away with you the rudder, or the oars? What do you take,
then? Your own, your bundle and your flask. So, in the present
case, if you will but remember what is your own, you will not
covet what belongs to others. If some tyrant [1] bids you put
off your consular robe—"Well, I am in my equestrian robe."
Put off that too. "I have only my coat." Put off that too.
"Well, I am naked." I am not yet satisfied. "Then e'en take
my whole body. If I can throw off a paltry body, am I any
longer afraid of a tyrant?"

"But such a one will not leave me his heir." What, then,
have I forgotten that such possessions are never really mine?
How, then, do we call them ours? As we call a bed in an inn
ours. If the landlord, when he dies, leaves you the bed, well
and good; but if to another, it will be his, and you will seek
one elsewhere; and consequently, if you do not find one, you
will sleep upon the ground; only sleep fearlessly and pro-
foundly, and remember that tragedies find their theme among
the rich and kings and tyrants. No poor man fills any other
place in one than as part of the chorus; whereas, kings begin
indeed with prosperity: "Garland the palace"; but continue;
and about the third and fourth act comes: "Alas, Citheron!
why didst thou receive me!" [2] Where are thy crowns, wretch;
where is thy diadem? Cannot thy guards help thee?

Whenever you are brought into any such society, think
then that you meet a tragic actor, or, rather, not an actor, but
Oedipus himself. "But such a one is happy; he walks with a

---

[1] The reference is probably to the Emperor Diocletian.
[2] Sophocles, *Oedipus Tyrannus*, v. 1390. Citheron was the mountain
on which the infant Oedipus had been left to die.

numerous train." Well, I too fall in with the crowd and walk with a numerous train.

But remember the principal thing—that the door is open. Do not be more fearful than children; but as they, when the play does not please them, say, "I will play no longer," so do you, in the same case, say, "I will play no longer," and go; but, if you stay, do not complain.

CHAPTER   TWENTY-FIVE

On the Same Subject

IF these things are true; and if we are not stupid or insincere when we say that the good or ill of man lies within his own will, and that all beside is nothing to us, why are we still troubled? Why do we still fear? What truly concerns us is in no one's power; what is in the power of others concerns not us. What embarrassment have we left?

"But you must direct me."

Why should I direct you? Has not Zeus directed you? Has he not given you what is your own, incapable of restraint or hindrance; and what is not your own, liable to both? What directions, then, what orders, have you brought from him? "By all means guard what is your own; what belongs to others do not covet. Honesty is your own; a sense of virtuous shame is your own. Who, then, can deprive you of these? Who can restrain you from making use of them, but yourself? And how do you do it? When you make that your concern which is not truly your own, you lose that which is." Having such precepts and directions from Zeus, what sort do you still want from me? Am I better than he, or more worthy of credit? If you observe these precepts, what others do you need? Are not these his? Apply the recognized principles; apply the demonstrations of philosophers; apply what you have often heard, and what you have said yourself; what you have read, and what you have carefully studied.

How long is it right to devote oneself to these things and not break up the game?

As long as it goes on well. A king is chosen by lot at the Saturnalian festival, supposing it to be agreed to play at that game; he orders: "Do you drink; you mix the wine; you sing: you go; you come." I obey, that the game may not be broken up by my fault.

[Then he orders] "I bid you think yourself to be unhappy." I do not think so; and who shall compel me to think so?

Again, suppose we agree to play Agamemnon and Achilles. He who is appointed for Agamemnon says to me, "Go to Achilles, and force away Briseis." I go. "Come." I come. We should deal with life as with these imaginary orders.

"Suppose it to be night." Well, suppose it. "Is it day then?" No; for I admitted the hypothesis that it was night. "Suppose that you think it to be night." Well, suppose it. "But you must really think that it is night." That by no means follows from the hypothesis. Thus it is in the case illustrated. Suppose you have ill luck? Suppose it. "Are you then unlucky?" Yes. "Are you thoroughly unfortunate?" Yes. "Well; but you must really regard yourself as miserable." But this is no part of the assumption, and there is a power who forbids me [to admit that].

How far, then, are we to carry such analogies? As far as is useful; that is, till we go farther than is reasonable and fit.

Moreover, some are peevish and fastidious, and say, I cannot dine with such a fellow, to be obliged to hear him all day recounting how he fought in Mysia. "I told you, my friend, how I gained the eminence." There I begin to suffer another siege. But another says, "I had rather get a dinner, and hear him prate as much as he pleases."

Do you decide between these opinions; but do not let it be with depression and anxiety, and the assumption that you are miserable, for no one compels you to that. Is there smoke in my house? If it be moderate, I will stay; if very great, I will go out. For you must always remember, and hold to this, that the door is open. "You are forbidden to live at Nicopolis." Then I will not live there. "Nor at Athens." Well, nor at Athens. "Nor at Rome." Nor at Rome. "But you shall live at Gyaros."[1] I will live there. But suppose that living at Gyaros seems to me like living in a house full of smoke. I can then retire where no one can forbid me to live, for it is an abode open to all, and put off my last garment, this poor body of mine; beyond this, no one has any power over me.

Thus Demetrius said to Nero: "You sentence me to death; and Nature sentences you." If I prize my body first, I have surrendered myself as a slave; if my estate, the same; for I at once betray where I am vulnerable. Just as when a reptile pulls in his head, I bid you strike that part of him which he guards; and be you assured, that wherever you show a desire to guard yourself, there your master will attack you. Remember but this, and whom will you any longer flatter or fear?

"But I want to sit where the senators do."

Do not you see, that by this you incommode and torment yourself?

"Why, how else shall I see the show in the amphitheater advantageously?"

Do not insist on seeing it, O man! and you will not be incommoded. Why do you vex yourself? Or wait a little while; and when the show is over, go sit in the senators' places and sun yourself. For remember, that this holds universally—we

---

[1] An island in the Aegean Sea, to which the Romans used to banish criminals.

incommode and torment ourselves; that is, the decisions of our will do it for us. What is it to be reviled, for instance? Stand by a stone and revile it, and what will you get by it? If you, therefore, would listen only as a stone, what would your reviler gain? But if the reviler has the weakness of the reviled for a vantage ground, then he carries his point.

"Strip him" [bids the tyrant]. What mean you by *him?* Take my clothes, strip them, at your pleasure. "I meant only to insult you." Much good may it do you.

These things were the study of Socrates; and by these means he always preserved the same countenance. Yet we had rather exercise and study anything, than how to become unrestrained and free. "But the philosophers talk paradoxes." And are there not paradoxes in other arts? What is more paradoxical than to prick anyone's eye, that he may see? Should one tell this to one ignorant of surgery, would not he laugh at him? What wonder then, if in philosophy also many truths appear paradoxical to the ignorant?

CHAPTER   TWENTY-SIX

What the Rule of Life Is

As someone was reading hypothetical propositions, Epictetus remarked that it was a rule in these to admit whatever was in accordance with the hypothesis, but much more a rule in life to do what was in accordance with nature. For, if we desire in every matter and on every occasion to conform to nature, we must on every occasion evidently make it our aim, neither to omit anything thus conformable, nor to admit anything inconsistent. Philosophers, therefore, first exercise us in theory, which is the more easy task, and then lead us to the more difficult; for in theory there is nothing to hinder our following what we are taught, but in life there are many things to draw us aside. It is ridiculous, then, to say we must begin with these applications, for it is not easy to begin with the most difficult; and this excuse children should make to those parents who dislike that they should study philosophy. "Am I to blame then, sir, and ignorant of my duty, and of what is incumbent on me? If this is neither to be learned, nor taught, why do you find fault with me? If it is to be taught, pray teach me yourself; or, if you cannot, let me learn it from those who profess to understand it. For what think you; that I voluntarily fall into evil, and miss good? Heaven forbid! What, then, is the cause of my faults? Ignorance. Are you not willing, then, that I should get rid of my ignorance? Who was ever taught the art of music, or navigation, by anger? Do you expect, then, that your anger should teach me the art of living?"

This, however, can properly be said only by one who is really in earnest. But he who reads these things, and applies to the philosophers, merely for the sake of showing, at some entertainment, that he understands hypothetical reasonings, what aim has he but to be admired by some senator, who happens to sit near him? [1] Great possessions may be won by such aims as that, but what we hold as wealth passes there for folly. It is hard, therefore, to overcome by appearances, where vain things thus pass for great.

I once saw a person weeping and embracing the knees of Epaphroditus, and deploring his hard fortune, that he had not more than 150,000 drachmae left. What did Epaphroditus say then? Did he laugh at him, as we should do? No; but cried

---

[1] This passage is omitted as inexplicable by a previous translator. A passage just below Higginson has also omitted, as the text is admitted to be in a hopeless state.

out with astonishment: "Poor man! How could you be silent under it? How could you bear it?"

The first step, therefore, towards becoming a philosopher is to be sensible of one's own governing principles; for on knowing it to be weak, no person will immediately employ it in great attempts. But, for want of this, some who can scarce digest a crumb will yet buy and swallow whole treatises; and so they throw them up again, or cannot digest them; and then come colics, fluxes, and fevers. Such persons ought to consider what their capacity is. However, it is easy to convince an ignorant person, so far as concerns theory; but in matters relating to life, no one will submit himself to confutation, and we hate those who have confuted us. Socrates used to say that we ought not to live a life unexamined.[1]

Of the Varied Appearances of Things to the Mind, and What Means Are at Hand by Which to Regulate Them

APPEARANCES to the mind are of four kinds. Things either are what they appear to be; or they neither are, nor appear to be; or they are, and do not appear to be; or they are not, and yet appear to be. To hit the mark in all these cases, is the wise man's task. Whatever unduly constrains us, to that a remedy must be applied. If the sophistries of Pyrrhonism, or

---

[1] Plato, *Apology*. See Classics Club edition, p. 56.

the Academy, constrain us, the remedy must be applied there; if specious appearances, by which things seem to be good which are not so, let us seek for a remedy there. If it be custom which constrains us, we must endeavor to find a remedy against that.

"What remedy is to be found against custom?"

Establish a contrary habit. You hear the vulgar say, "Such a one, poor soul! is dead." Well, his father died; his mother died. "Yes, but he was cut off in the flower of his age, and in a foreign land." Observe the contrary ways of speaking, and abandon such expressions. Oppose to one habit a contrary habit; to meet sophistry we must have the art of reasoning, and the frequent use and exercise of it. Against specious appearances we must set clear convictions, bright and ready for use. When death appears as an evil, we ought immediately to remember that evils are things to be avoided, but death is inevitable. For what can I do, or where can I fly from it? Let me suppose myself to be Sarpedon, the son of Zeus, that I may speak as nobly. "I go either to excel, or to give another the occasion to excel."[1] If I can achieve nothing myself, I will not grudge another his achievement.

But suppose this to be a strain too high for us; do not these following thoughts befit us? Whither shall I fly from death? Show me the place, show me the people, to whom I may have recourse, whom death doth not overtake. Show me the charm to avoid it. If there be none, what would you have me do? I cannot escape death; but cannot I escape the dread of it? Must I die trembling and lamenting? For the very origin of the disease lies in wishing for something that is not obtained. Under the influence of this, if I can make outward things conform to my own inclination, I do it; if not, I feel inclined to tear out the eyes of whoever hinders me. For it is the nature of man not to endure the being deprived of good; not to en-

[1] Imitated from the *Iliad*. See Classics Club edition, p. 187.

dure the falling into evil. And so, at last, when I can neither control events, nor tear out the eyes of him who hinders me, I sit down, and groan, and revile him whom I can—Zeus, and the rest of the gods; for what are they to me, if they take no care of me?

"Oh! but then you will be impious."

What then? Can I be in a worse condition than I am now? In general, remember this, that unless we make our religion and our treasure to consist in the same thing, religion will always be sacrificed.

Have these things no weight? Let a Pyrrhonist, or an Academic, come and oppose them. For my part, I have neither leisure nor ability to stand up as an advocate for common sense. Even if the business were concerning an estate, I should call in another advocate. To what advocate, then, shall I now appeal? I will leave it to anyone who may be upon the spot. Thus, I may not be able to explain how sensation takes place, whether it be diffused universally, or reside in a particular part; for I find perplexities in either case; but that you and I are not the same person, I very exactly know.

"How so?"

Why, I never, when I have a mind to swallow anything, carry it to your mouth, but my own. I never, when I wanted bread, took sweepings instead, but went directly to the bread. You who deny all evidence of the senses, do you act otherwise? Which of you, when he wished to go into a bath, ever went into a mill?

"Why, then, must not we, to the utmost, defend these points; stand by common sense; be fortified against everything that opposes it?"[1]

Who denies that? But it must be done by him who has

---

[1] This seems to be said by one of the hearers, who wanted to have the absurdities of the skeptics confuted and guarded against by regular argument.

ability and leisure to spare; but he who is full of trembling and perturbation and inward disorders of heart must first employ his time about something else.

CHAPTER TWENTY-EIGHT

That We Ought Not to Be Angry with Men, and What Things Are Little, What Great, Among Men

WHAT is the basis of assent to anything? Its appearing to be true. It is not possible, therefore, to assent to what appears to be not true. Why? Because it is the very nature of the understanding to agree to truth, to be dissatisfied with falsehood, and to suspend its belief in doubtful cases.

"What is the proof of this?"

Persuade yourself, if you can, that it is now night. Impossible. Dissuade yourself from the belief that it is day. Impossible. Persuade yourself that the number of the stars is even or odd. Impossible.

When anyone, then, assents to what is false, be assured that he does not willfully assent to it as false—for, as Plato affirms, the soul is unwillingly deprived of truth[1]—but what is false appears to him to be true. Well, then; have we, in actions, anything correspondent to this distinction between true and false? There are right and wrong; advantageous and disadvantageous; desirable and undesirable, and the like.

---

[1] This is not a literal quotation from Plato, but similar passages are to be found in his *Laws,* ix. 5; *Sophist,* § 29.

"A person, then, cannot think a thing truly advantageous to him, and not choose it?"

He cannot. But how says Medea?—

> *I know what evils wait upon my purpose;*
> *But wrath is stronger than this will of mine.*[1]

Was it that she thought the very indulgence of her passion, and the punishing her husband, more advantageous than the preservation of her children? Yes; but she is deceived. Show clearly to her that she is deceived, and she will forbear; but, till you have shown it, what has she to follow but what appears to herself? Nothing.

Why, then, are you angry with her, that the unhappy woman is deceived in the most important points, and instead of a human creature, becomes a viper? Why do you not rather, as we pity the blind and lame, so likewise pity those who are blinded and lamed in their superior faculties? Whoever, therefore, duly remembers, that the appearance of things to the mind is the standard of every action to man—that this is either right or wrong, and if right, he is without fault; if wrong, he himself suffers punishment; for that one man cannot be the person deceived, and another the only sufferer—such a person will not be outrageous and angry at anyone; will not revile, or reproach, or hate, or quarrel with anyone.

"So, then, have all the great and dreadful deeds that have been done in the world no other origin than semblances?"

Absolutely no other. The *Iliad* consists of nothing but such semblances and their results. It seemed to Paris that he should carry off the wife of Menelaus. It seemed to Helen that she should follow him. If, then, it had seemed to Menelaus that it was an advantage to be robbed of such a wife, what could have happened? Not only the *Iliad* had been lost, but the *Odyssey* too.

---

[1] Euripides, *Medea*, 1087.

"Do such great events, then, depend on so small a cause?"
What events, then, call you great?

"Wars and seditions, the destruction of numbers of men,
and the overthrow of cities."

And what in all this is great? Nothing. What is great in the
death of numbers of oxen, numbers of sheep, or in the burning
or pulling down numbers of nests of storks or swallows?

"Are these things then similar?"

They are. The bodies of men are destroyed, and the bodies
of sheep and oxen. The houses of men are burnt, and the nests
of storks. What is there so great or fearful in all this? Pray,
show me what difference there is between the house of a man
and the nest of a stork, considered as a habitation, except that
houses are built with beams and tiles and bricks, and nests
with sticks and clay?

"What, then; are a stork and a man similar? What do you
mean?"

Similar in body.

"Is there no difference, then, between a man and a stork?"
Yes, surely; but not in these things.

"In what, then?"

Seek and you will find that the difference lies in something
else. See whether it be not in rationality of action, in social
instincts, fidelity, honor, providence, judgment.

"Where, then, is the real good or evil of man?"

Just where this difference lies. If this distinguishing trait
is preserved, and remains well fortified, and neither honor,
fidelity, nor judgment is destroyed, then he himself is likewise saved; but when any one of these is lost or demolished, he
himself is lost also. In this do all great events consist. Was
Paris undone because the Greeks invaded Troy, and laid it
waste, and his family were slain in battle? By no means; for
no one is undone by an action not his own. All that was only
like laying waste the nests of storks. But his true undoing was
when he lost decency, faith, honor, virtue. When was Achilles

undone—when Patroclus died? By no means. But when he gave himself up to rage; when he wept over a girl; when he forgot that he came there, not to win mistresses, but to fight. This is human undoing; this is the siege, this the overthrow, when right principles are ruined and destroyed.

"But when wives and children are led away captives, and the men themselves killed, are not these evils?"

Whence do you conclude them such? Pray inform me, in my turn.

"Nay; but whence do you affirm that they are not evils?"

Recur to the rules. Apply your principles. One cannot sufficiently wonder at what happens among men. When we would judge of light and heavy, we do not judge by guess, nor when we judge of straight and crooked; and, in general, when it concerns us to know the truth on any special point, no one of us will do anything by guess. But where the first and principal source of right or wrong action is concerned, of being prosperous or unprosperous, happy or unhappy— there only do we act rashly, and by guess. Nowhere anything like a balance; nowhere anything like a rule; but something seems thus or so to me, and I at once act accordingly. For am I better than Agamemnon or Achilles; that they, by following what seemed best to them, should do and suffer so many things, and yet that seeming should not suffice me? And what tragedy has any other origin? The *Atreus* of Euripides, what is it? Seeming. The *Oedipus* of Sophocles? Seeming. The *Phoenix*? The *Hippolytus*? All seeming. Who then, think you, can escape this influence? What are they called who follow every seeming? Madmen. Yet do we, then, behave otherwise?

CHAPTER TWENTY-NINE

Of Courage

THE essence of good and evil is a certain kind of moral purpose.

What are things outward, then?

Materials on which the moral purpose may act, in attaining its own good or evil.

How, then, will it attain good?

If it be not dazzled by its own materials; for right principles concerning these materials keep the moral purpose in a good state; but perverse and distorted principles, in a bad one. This law hath God ordained, who says, "If you wish for good, receive it from yourself." You say, No; but from another. "Nay; but from yourself."

Accordingly, when a tyrant threatens, and sends for me, I say, Against what is your threatening pointed? If he says, "I will chain you," I answer, It is my hands and feet that you threaten. If he says, "I will cut off your head," I answer, It is my head that you threaten. If he says, "I will throw you into prison," I answer, It is the whole of this paltry body that you threaten; and if he threatens banishment, just the same.

"Does he not threaten *you*, then?"

If I am persuaded that these things are nothing to me, he does not; but if I fear any of them, it is me that he threatens. Who is it, after all, that I fear? The master of what? Of things in my own power? Of these no one is the master. Of things not in my power? And what are these to me?

"What, then! do you philosophers teach us a contempt of kings?"

By no means. Which of us teaches anyone to contend with them about things of which they have the command? Take dy; take my possessions; take my reputation; take away my friends. If I persuade anyone to claim these things is own, you may justly accuse me. "Ay; but I would command your principles too." And who hath given you that power? How can you conquer the principle of another? "By applying terror, I will conquer it." Do not you see that what conquers itself is not conquered by another? And nothing but itself can conquer the will. Hence, too, the most excellent and equitable law of God, that the better should always prevail over the worse. Ten are better than one.

"For what purpose?"

For chaining, killing, dragging where they please; for taking away an estate. Thus ten conquer one, in the cases wherein they are better.

"In what, then, are they worse?"

When the one has right principles, and the others have not. For can they conquer in this case? How should they? If we were weighed in a scale, must not the heavier outweigh?

"How then came Socrates to suffer such things from the Athenians?"

O foolish man! what mean you by Socrates? Express the fact as it is. Are you surprised that the paltry body of Socrates should be carried away, and dragged to prison, by such as were stronger; that it should be poisoned by hemlock and die? Do these things appear wonderful to you; these things unjust? Is it for such things as these that you accuse God? Had Socrates, then, no compensation for them? In what, then, to him, did the essence of good consist? Whom shall we regard, you or him? And what says he? "Anytus and Melitus may indeed kill; but hurt me they cannot." And again, "If it so pleases God, so let it be."

But show me that he who has the worse principles can get the advantage over him who has the better. You never will show it, nor anything like it; for the law of nature and of God is this: let the better always prevail over the worse.

"In what?"

In that wherein it is better. One body may be stronger than another; many, than one; and a thief, than one who is not a thief. Thus I, for instance, lost my lamp because the thief was better at keeping awake than I. But for that lamp he paid the high price of becoming a thief; for that lamp he lost his virtue and became like a wild beast. This seemed to him a good bargain; and so let it be!

But someone takes me by the collar, and drags me to the forum; and then all the rest cry out, "Philosopher, what good do your principles do you? See, you are being dragged to prison; see, you are going to lose your head!" And, pray, what rule of philosophy could I contrive, that when a stronger than myself lays hold on my collar, I should not be dragged; or that, when ten men pull me at once, and throw me into prison, I should not be thrown there? But have I learned nothing, then? I have learned to know, whatever happens, that if it concerns not my moral purpose, it is nothing to me. Have my principles, then, done me no good? What then; do I seek for anything else to do me good, but what I have learned? Afterwards, as I sit in prison, I say, He who has made all this disturbance neither recognizes any guidance, nor heeds any teaching, nor is it any concern to him to know what philosophers say or do. Let him alone.

"Come forth again from prison." If you have no further need for me in prison, I will come out; if you want me again, I will return. "For how long?" Just so long as reason requires I should continue in this body; when that is over, take it, and fare ye well. Only let us not give up life irrationally, nor from cowardice, nor on slight grounds, since that would be contrary to the will of God; for he hath need of such a world, and such beings to live on earth. But, if he sounds a retreat, as he did to Socrates, we are to obey him when he sounds it, as our general.

"Well; but can these things be explained to the multitude?"

To what purpose? Is it not sufficient to be convinced one's self? When children come to us clapping their hands, and saying, "Tomorrow is the good feast of Saturn," do we tell them that good does not consist in such things? By no means; but we clap our hands also. Thus, when you are unable to convince anyone, consider him as a child, and clap your hands with him; or, if you will not do that, at least hold your tongue.

These things we ought to remember; and when we are called to any trial, to know that an opportunity is come of showing whether we have been well taught. For he who goes from a philosophical lecture to a difficult point of practice is like a young man who has been studying to solve syllogisms. If you propose an easy one, he says, "Give me rather a fine intricate one, that I may try my strength." Thus athletic champions are displeased with a slight antagonist. "He cannot lift me," says one. Is this a youth of spirit? No; for when the occasion calls upon him, he may begin crying, and say, "I wanted to keep on learning." Learning what? If you did not learn these things to show them in action, why did you learn them?

I trust there must be someone among you, sitting here, who feels secret pangs of impatience, and says, "When will such a trial come to my share, as hath now fallen to his? Must I sit wasting my life in a corner, when I might be crowned at Olympia? When will anyone bring the news of such a combat for me?" Such should be the disposition of you all. Even among the gladiators of Caesar, there are some who bear it very ill that they are not brought upon the stage and matched; and who offer vows to God, and address the officers, begging to fight. And will none among you appear such? I would willingly take a voyage on purpose to see how a champion of mine acts; how he meets his occasion.

This is not the contest I would choose, say you. Is it in your power, then, to make the selection? Such a body is given you, such parents, such brothers, such a country, and such a rank in it; and then you come to me, asking me to change the conditions! Have you not abilities to manage that which is given you? You should say to me, "It is your business to propose; mine, to treat the subject well." No; but you say, "Do not meet me with such a syllogism, but such a one; do not offer such an obstacle to me, but such a one." There will be a time, I suppose, when tragedians will fancy themselves to be mere masks, and buskins, and long robe. These things are your materials, man, and your stage properties. Speak something; that we may know whether you are a tragedian or a buffoon; for both have all the rest in common. Suppose anyone should take away his buskins and his mask, and bring him upon the stage in his common dress, is the tragedian lost, or does he remain? If he has a voice, he remains.

And so in life. "Here, this instant, take upon you the governorship." I take it; and taking it, I show how a skillful man performs the part. "Now lay aside your toga; put on rags, and come upon the stage in that character." What then? Is it not in my power to express the character by a suitable voice?

"In what character do you now appear?" As a witness summoned by God. "Come you, then, and bear witness for me; for you are a witness worthy to be produced by me. Is anything which is inevitable to be classed as either good or evil? Do I hurt anyone? Have I made the good of each individual to rest on anyone but himself? What evidence do you bear for God?"

"I am in a miserable condition, O Lord; I am undone: no mortal cares for me; no mortal gives me anything; all blame me; all speak ill of me."

Is this the evidence you are to give? And will you bring disgrace upon his summons, who hath conferred such an honor upon you, and thought you worthy of being produced as a witness in such a cause?

But someone in authority has given a sentence. "I judge you to be impious and profane." What has befallen you? "I have been judged to be impious and profane." Anything else? "Nothing." Suppose he had passed his judgment upon any process of reasoning, and had questioned the conclusion that, if it be day, it is light; what would have befallen the proposition? In this case, who is judged, who is condemned—the proposition, or he who cannot understand it? Does he know, who claims the power of ruling in your case, what pious or impious means? Has he made it his study or learned it? Where? From whom? A musician would not regard him, if he pronounced bass to be treble; nor a mathematician, if he passed sentence, that lines drawn from the center to the circumference are not equal. And shall he who is instructed in the truth respect an ignorant man, when he pronounces upon pious and impious, just and unjust?

"Oh, the persecutions to which the wise are exposed!" Is it *here* that you have learned this talk? Why do not you leave such pitiful discourse to idle, pitiful fellows; and let them sit in a corner, and receive some little mean pay, or grumble that nobody gives them anything? But do you come, and make some use of what you have learned. It is not reasonings that are wanted now, for there are books stuffed full of stoical reasonings.

"What is wanted, then?"

The man who shall apply them; whose actions may bear testimony to his arguments. Assume this character for me, that we may no longer make use in the schools of the examples of the ancients, but may have some examples of our own.

"To whom, then, does the contemplation of these abstractions belong?"

To anyone who has leisure for them; for man is a being fond of contemplation. But it is shameful to take only such view of things as truant slaves take of a play. We ought to sit calmly, and listen, whether to the actor or to the musician; and not do like those poor fellows, who come in and admire the actor, constantly glancing about them, and then, if anyone happens to mention their master, run frightened away. It is shameful for a philosopher thus to contemplate the works of nature. What, in this parallel case, stands for the master? Man is not the master of man; but death is, and life, and pleasure, and pain; for without these, bring even Caesar to me, and you will see how intrepid I shall be. But, if he comes thundering and lightening with these, and these are the objects of my terror, what do I else but, like the runaway slave, acknowledge my master? While I have only a respite from these, I am as the truant in the theater; I bathe, drink, sing, but all with terror and anxiety. But if I free myself from my masters, that is, from such things as render a master terrible, what trouble, what master have I remaining?

"Shall we then insist upon these things with all men?"

No, but make allowance for the ignorant, and say, This poor man advises me to what he thinks good for himself. I excuse him; for Socrates, too, excused the jailer, who wept when he was to drink the poison, and said, "How generously he sheds tears for us!" Was it to him that Socrates said, "For this reason we sent the women out of the way"? No, but to his friends—to such as were capable of hearing it; while he humored the jailer, as a child.

CHAPTER THIRTY

Weapons Ready for Difficult Occasions

WHEN you are going before any of the great, remember that there is another who sees from above what passes, and whom you ought to please, rather than man. He therefore asks you:

"In the schools, what did you use to call exile, and prison, and chains, and death, and calumny?"

"I? Indifferent things."

"What, then, do you call them now? Are they at all changed?"

"No."

"Are you changed, then?"

"No."

"Tell me, then, what things are indifferent."

"Things not dependent on our own moral purpose."

"What is the inference?"

"Things not dependent on my own moral purpose are nothing to me."

"Tell me, likewise, what appeared to be the good of man."

"Rectitude of moral purpose and a proper use of appearances."

"What was the end?"

"To follow thee."

"Do you say the same things now, too?"

"Yes. I do say the same things even now."

Well, go in then boldly, and mindful of these things; and you will show the difference between the instructed and the ignorant. I imagine, indeed, that you will have such thoughts as these: "Why do we make such elaborate preparations for nothing? Is the power, the antechamber, the attendants, the guards, no more than this? Is it for these that I have listened to so many dissertations? These are nothing; and yet I had prepared myself as for some great encounter."

BOOK II

CHAPTER ONE

That Courage Is Not Inconsistent
with Caution

THERE is an assertion of the philosophers which may perhaps appear a paradox to many; yet let us fairly examine whether it be true: that it is possible, in all things, to act at once with caution and courage. For caution seems, in some measure, contrary to courage; and contraries are by no means consistent. The appearance of a paradox in the present case seems to me to arise as follows. If indeed we assert that courage and caution are to be used in the same instances, we might justly be accused of uniting contradictions; but in the way that we affirm it, where is the absurdity? For if what has been so often said, and so often demonstrated, be certain, that the essence of good and evil consists in the use of things as they appear, and that things inevitable are not to be classed either as good or evil, what paradox do the philosophers assert, if they say, "Where events are inevitable, meet them with courage, but otherwise with caution"? For in these last cases only, if evil lies in a perverted moral purpose, is caution to be used; and if things inevitable and uncontrollable are nothing to us, in these we are to make use of courage. Thus we shall be at once cautious and courageous, and, indeed, courageous on account of this very caution; for by using caution with regard to things really evil, we shall gain courage with regard to what are not so.

But we are in the same condition with deer; when these in a fright fly from the plumes [which hunters wave], whither do they turn, and to what do they retire for safety? To the nets. And thus they are undone, by confusing the objects of fear and confidence. And so it is with us also. When do we yield to fear? About things inevitable. When, on the other hand, do we behave with courage, as if there were nothing to be dreaded? About things that might be controlled by will. To be deceived, then, or to act rashly or imprudently, or to indulge a scandalous desire, we treat as of no importance, in our effort to bring about things which we cannot, after all, control. But where death, or exile, or pain, or ignominy, is concerned, then comes the retreat, the flutter, and the fright. Hence, as it must be with those who err in matters of the greatest importance, we turn what should be courage into rashness, desperation, recklessness, effrontery; and what should be caution becomes timid, base, and full of fears and perturbations. Let one apply his spirit of caution to things within the reach of his own will, then he will have the subject of avoidance within his own control; but if he transfers it to that which is inevitable, trying to shun that which he cannot control and others can, then he must needs fear, be harassed, and be disturbed. For it is not death or pain that is to be dreaded, but the fear of pain or death. Hence we commend him who says:

Death is no ill, but shamefully *to die.*[1]

Courage, then, ought to be opposed to death, and caution to the *fear* of death; whereas we, on the contrary, oppose to

---

[1] Euripides, Fragments.

death, flight; and to these our false convictions concerning it, recklessness, and desperation, and assumed indifference.

Socrates used, very properly, to call these things masks; for as masks appear shocking and formidable to children from their inexperience, so we are thus affected with regard to things for no other reason. For what constitutes a child? Ignorance. What constitutes a child? Want of instruction; for they are our equals, so far as their degree of knowledge permits. What is death? A mask. Turn it on the other side and be convinced. See, it does not bite. This paltry body and spirit must be again, as once, separated, either now or hereafter; why, then, are you displeased if it be now? For if not now it will be hereafter. Why? To fulfill the course of the universe; for that has need of some things present, others to come, and others already completed.

What is pain? A mask. Turn it and be convinced. This weak flesh is sometimes affected by harsh, sometimes by smooth impressions. If suffering be beyond endurance, the door is open; till then, bear it. It is fit that the final door should be open against all accidents, since thus we escape all trouble.

What, then, is the fruit of these principles? What it ought to be; the most noble, and the most suitable to the wise—tranquillity, security, freedom. For in this case we are not to give credit to the many, who say that none ought to be educated but the free; but rather to the philosophers, who say that the wise alone are free.

"How so?"

Thus: is freedom anything else than the power of living as we like?

"Nothing else."

Well; tell me then, do you like to live in error?

"We do not. No one who lives in error is free."

Do you like to live in fear? Do you like to live in sorrow? Do you like to live in perturbation?

"By no means."

No one, therefore, in a state of fear, or sorrow, or per-turbation, is free; but whoever is delivered from sorrow, fear, and perturbation, by the same means is delivered like-wise from slavery. How shall we believe you, then, good legis-lators, when you say, "We allow none to be educated but the free"? For the philosophers say, "We allow none to be free but the wise"; that is, God doth not allow it.

"What, then; when any person has turned his slave about before the consul,[1] has he done nothing?"

Yes, he has.

"What?"

He has turned his slave about before the consul.

"Nothing more?"

Yes. He pays a tax of five per cent of the slave's value.

"Well, then; is not the man who has gone through this cere-mony rendered free?"

Only so far as he is emancipated from perturbation. Pray, have you, who are able to give this freedom to others, no master of your own? Are you not a slave to money; to a girl; to a boy; to a tyrant; to some friend of a tyrant? Else why do you tremble when any one of these is in question? Therefore, I so often repeat to you, let this be your study and constant pursuit, to learn in what it is necessary to be courageous, and in what cautious; courageous against the inevitable, cautious so far as your will can control.

"But have I not read my essay to you? Do not you know what I am doing?"

In what?

"In my essays."

Show me in what state you are as to desires and aversions; whether you do not fail of what you wish, and incur what you would avoid; but, as to these commonplace essays, if you are wise, you will take them, and destroy them.

---

[1] The prescribed form for the freeing of a slave.

"Why? Did not Socrates write?"

Yes; who so much? But how? As he had not always one at hand to argue against his principles, or be argued against in his turn, he argued with and examined himself, and always made practical application of some one great principle at least. These are the things which a philosopher writes; but such commonplaces as those of which I speak he leaves to the foolish, or to the happy creatures whom idleness furnishes with leisure, or to such as are too weak to regard consequences. And yet will you, when opportunity offers, come forward to exhibit and read aloud such things, and take a pride in them?

"Pray, see how I compose dialogues."

Talk not of that, man, but rather be able to say, See how I accomplish my purposes; see how I avert what I wish to shun. Set death before me; set pain, a prison, disgrace, doom, and you will know me. This should be the pride of a young man come out from the schools. Leave the rest to others. Let no one ever hear you waste a word upon them, nor suffer it, if anyone commends you for them; but admit that you are nobody, and that you know nothing. Appear to know only this, never to fail or fall. Let others study lawsuits, problems, and syllogisms. Do you rather contemplate death, change, torture, exile; and all these with courage, and reliance upon him who has called you to them, and judged you worthy a post in which you may show what reason can do when it encounters the inevitable. And thus this paradox ceases to be a paradox, that we must be at once cautious and courageous; courageous against the inevitable, and cautious when events are within our own control.

CHAPTER TWO

Of Tranquillity

CONSIDER, you who are going to court, what you wish to preserve, and in what to succeed. For if you wish to preserve a mind in harmony with nature, you are entirely safe; everything goes well; you have no trouble on your hands. While you wish to preserve that freedom which belongs to you, and are contented with that, for what have you longer to be anxious? For who is the master of things like these? Who can take them away? If you wish to be a man of modesty and fidelity, who shall prevent you? If you wish not to be restrained or compelled, who shall compel you to desires contrary to your principles; to aversions contrary to your opinion? The judge, perhaps, will pass a sentence against you, which he thinks formidable; but can he likewise make you receive it with shrinking? Since, then, desire and aversion are in your own power, for what have you to be anxious? Let this be your introduction; this your narration; this your proof; this your conclusion; this your victory; and this your applause. Thus said Socrates to one who reminded him to prepare himself for his trial: "Do you not think that I have been preparing myself for this very thing my whole life long?" "By what kind of preparation?" "I have attended to my own work." "What mean you?" "I have done nothing unjust, either in public or in private life."

But if you wish to retain possession of outward things too, your body, your estate, your reputation, I advise you immediately to prepare yourself by every possible preparation; and besides, to consider the disposition of your judge and of your adversary. If it be necessary to embrace his knees, do so; if to weep, weep; if to groan, groan. For when you have once made yourself a slave to externals, be a slave wholly; do not struggle, and be alternately willing and unwilling, but be simply and thoroughly the one or the other—free, or a slave; instructed, or ignorant; a game-cock, or a craven; either bear to be beaten till you die, or give in at once; and do not be soundly beaten first, and then give in at last.

If both alternatives be shameful, learn immediately to distinguish where good and evil lie. They lie where truth likewise lies. Where truth and nature dictate, there exercise caution or courage. Why, do you think that if Socrates had concerned himself about externals, he would have said, when he appeared at his trial, "Anytus and Melitus may indeed kill me, but they cannot harm me"? Was he so foolish as not to see that this way did not lead to safety, but the contrary? What, then, is the reason that he not only disregarded, but defied, his judges? Thus my friend Heraclitus, in a trifling suit about a little estate at Rhodes, after having proved to the judges that his cause was good, when he came to the conclusion of his speech, "I will not entreat you," said he; "nor be anxious as to what judgment you give; for it is rather you who are to be judged, than I." And thus he lost his suit. What need was there of this?

Be content not to entreat; yet do not proclaim that you will not entreat; unless it be a proper time to provoke the judges designedly, as in the case of Socrates. But if you too are preparing such a speech as his, what do you wait for? Why do you consent to be tried? For if you wish to be hanged, have patience, and the gibbet will come. But if you choose rather to consent, and make your defense as well as you can, all the rest is to be ordered accordingly, with a due regard, however, to the preservation of your own proper character.

For this reason it is absurd to call upon me for specific advice. How should I know what to advise you? Ask me rather to teach you to accommodate yourself to whatever may happen. The former is just as if an illiterate person should say,

"Tell me how to write down some name that is proposed to me"; and I show him how to write the name of Dion; and then another comes, and asks him to write the name, not of Dion, but of Theon. What will be the consequence? What will he write? Whereas, if you have practiced writing, you are ready prepared for whatever word may be dictated; if not, how can I advise you? For if circumstances dictate something different, what will you say, or how will you act? Remember, then, the general rule, and you will need no special suggestions; but if you are absorbed in externals, you must necessarily be tossed up and down, according to the inclination of your master.

Who is your master? Whosoever controls those things which you seek or shun.

CHAPTER THREE

To Those Who Recommend Persons to the Philosopher

DIOGENES rightly answered one who desired letters of recommendation from him: "At first sight he will know you to be a man; and whether you are a good or a bad man, if he has any skill in distinguishing, he will know likewise; and if he has not, he will never know it, though I should write a thousand times." Just as if you were a piece of coin, and should desire to be recommended to any person as good, in order to be tried; if it be to an assayer, he will know your value, for you will recommend yourself.

We ought, therefore, in life also to have something analogous to this skill in gold; that one may be able to say, like the assayer, Bring me whatever piece you will, and I will find out its value; or, as I would say with regard to syllogisms, Bring me whomsoever you will, and I will distinguish for you whether he knows how to solve syllogisms, or not. Why? Because I can do that myself, and have that faculty which is necessary for one who can discern persons skilled in such solutions. But how do I act in life? I sometimes call a thing good, at other times bad. What is the cause of this? Something contrary to what occurs to me in syllogisms—ignorance and inexperience.

CHAPTER FOUR

Concerning a Man Who Had Been Guilty of Adultery

JUST as he was once saying that man is made for fidelity, and that whoever subverts this subverts the peculiar property of man, there entered one of the so-called literary men, who had been caught in adultery in that city. But, continued Epictetus, if, laying aside that fidelity for which we were born, we form designs against the wife of our neighbor, what are we doing? What, but destroying and ruining? Whom? The man of fidelity, honor, and sanctity of manners. Only this? And do not we ruin neighborly feeling, friendship, the country? In what rank do we then place ourselves? How am I to consider you, sir, as a neighbor, a friend? What sort of one? As a citizen? How shall I trust you? Indeed, if you were some potsherd, so cracked that no use could be made of you, you might be thrown on a dunghill, and no mortal would take the trouble to pick you up; but if, being a man, you cannot fill any one place in human society, what shall we do with you? For, suppose you cannot hold the place of a friend, can you hold even that of a slave? And who will trust you? Why, then, should you not also be contented to be thrown upon some dunghill, as a useless vessel, and indeed as worse than that? Will you say, after this, Has no one any regard for me, a man of letters? Why, you are wicked and useless. Just as if wasps should complain that no one has any regard for them, but all shun, and whoever can, beats them down. You have such a sting that whoever you strike with it is thrown into troubles and sorrows. What would you have us do with you? There is nowhere to place you.

"What, then, are not women by nature common property?"

I admit it; and so is food at table common to those who are invited. But, after it is distributed, will you go and snatch away the share of him who sits next you, or slyly steal it, or stretch out your hand, and taste; and if you cannot tear away any of the meat, dip your fingers and lick them? A fine companion! A Socratic guest indeed! Again, is not the theater common to all the citizens? Therefore come, when all are seated, if you dare, and turn any one of them out of his place. In this sense only are women common property by nature; but when the laws, like a good host, have distributed them, cannot you, like the rest of the company, be contented with your own share, but must you pilfer, and taste what belongs to another?

"But I am a man of letters, and understand Archedemus."

With all your understanding of Archedemus, then, you will be an adulterer and a rogue; and instead of a man, a wolf or an ape. For where is the difference?

CHAPTER FIVE

How Nobility of Mind May Be Consistent with Prudence

THE materials of action are variable, but the use we make of them should be constant.

How, then, shall one combine composure and tranquillity with energy; doing nothing rashly, nothing carelessly?

By imitating those who play at games. The dice are variable; the pieces are variable. How do I know what will fall out? But it is my business to manage carefully and dexterously, whatever happens. Thus in life too, this is the chief business, to consider and discriminate things, and say, "Externals are not in my power; choice is. Where shall I seek good and evil? Within; in what is my own." But in what is controlled by others, count nothing good or evil, profitable or hurtful, or any such thing.

What, then; are we to treat these in a careless way?

By no means; for this, on the other hand, would be a perversion of the will, and so contrary to nature. But we are to act with care, because the use of our materials is not indifferent; and at the same time with calmness and tranquillity, because the materials themselves are uncertain. For where a thing is not uncertain, there no one can restrain or compel me. Where I am capable of being restrained or compelled, the acquisition does not depend upon me; nor is it either good or evil. The use of it, indeed, is either good or evil; but that *does* depend upon me. It is difficult, I own, to blend and unite tranquillity in accepting, and energy in using, the facts of life; but it is not impossible; if it be, it is impossible to be happy. How do we act in a voyage? What is in my power? To choose the pilot, the sailors, the day, the hour. Afterwards comes a storm. What have I to care for? My part is performed. This matter belongs to another, to the pilot. But the ship is sinking; what then have I to do? That which alone I can do; I submit to being drowned, without fear, without crying out, accusing God, but as one who knows that what is born must likewise die. For I am not eternity, but a man—a part of the whole, as an hour is of the day. I must come like an hour, and like an hour must pass away. What signifies it whether by drowning or by a fever? For, in some way or other, pass I must.

This you may see to be the practice of those who play ball skillfully. No one strives for the ball itself, as either a good or an evil; but how he may throw and catch it again. Here lies the address, here the art, the nimbleness, the skill; lest I fail to catch it, even when I spread out my cloak for it, while another catches it whenever I throw it. But if we catch or throw it in fear and trembling, what kind of play will this be? How shall we keep ourselves steady, or how see the order of the game? One will say, throw; another, do not throw; a third, you have thrown once already. This is a mere quarrel, not a game. Therefore Socrates well understood how to play ball.

"What do you mean?"

When he joked at his trial. "Tell me," said he, "Anytus, how can you say that I do not believe in a God? What do you think demons are? Are they not either the offspring of the gods, or compounded of gods and men?" "Yes." "Do you think, then, that one can believe there are mules, and not believe that there are asses?" This was just as if he had been playing ball. And what was the ball he had to play with? Life, chains, exile, a draught of poison, separation from a wife, and leaving his children orphans. These were what he had to play with; and yet he did play, and threw the ball with skill. Thus we should be careful as to the play, but indifferent as to the ball. We are by all means to manage our materials with art—

not taking them for the best, but showing our art about them, whatever they may happen to be. Thus a weaver does not make the wool, but employs his art upon what is given him. It is another who gives you food and property, and may take them away, and your paltry body too. Do you, however, work upon the materials you have received; and then, if you come off unhurt, others, no doubt, who meet you, will congratulate you on your escape. But he who has a clearer insight into such things will praise and congratulate you if he sees you to have done well; but if you owe your escape to any unbecoming action, he will do the contrary. For where there is a reasonable cause for rejoicing, there is cause likewise for congratulation.

How, then, are some external circumstances said to be according to nature; others contrary to it?

Only when we are viewed as isolated individuals I will allow that it is natural for the foot (for instance) to be clean. But if you take it as a foot, and not as a mere isolated thing, it will be fit that it should walk in the dirt, and tread upon thorns; and sometimes that it should even be cut off, for the good of the whole body; otherwise it is no longer a foot. We should reason in some such manner concerning ourselves. Who are you? A man. If then, indeed, you consider yourself isolatedly, it is natural that you should live to old age, should be prosperous and healthy; but if you consider yourself as a man, and as a part of the whole, it will be fit, in view of that whole, that you should at one time be sick; at another, take a voyage, and be exposed to danger; sometimes be in want; and possibly die before your time. Why, then, are you displeased? Do not you know that otherwise, just as the other ceases to be a foot, so you are no longer a man? For what is a man? A part of a commonwealth; first and chiefly of that which includes both gods and men; and next, of that to which you immediately belong, which is a miniature of the universal city.

What, then; must I, at one time, go before a tribunal; must

another, at another time, be scorched by a fever; another be exposed to the sea; another die; another be condemned?

Yes, for it is impossible, in such a body, in such a world, and among such companions, but that some one or other of us must meet with such circumstances. Your business, then, is simply to say what you ought, to arrange things as the case requires. After this comes a judge who says, "I pronounce you guilty." "May it be well with you. I have done my part. You are to look to it, whether you have done yours." For you may as well understand that the judge too runs a risk; do not forget that.

CHAPTER SIX

Of Circumstances [1]

A PROCESS of reasoning may be an indifferent thing; but our judgment concerning it is not indifferent; for it is either knowledge, or opinion, or mistake. So the events of life occur indifferently, but the use of it is not indifferent. When you are told, therefore, that these things are indifferent, do not, on that account, ever be careless; nor yet, when you are governed by prudence, be abject, and dazzled by material things. It is good to know your own qualifications and powers; that, where you are not qualified, you may be quiet, and not angry that others have there the advantage of you. For you too will think it reasonable, that you should have the advantage in the

---

[1] This discourse is supposed to have been addressed to a pupil, who feared to remain at Rome, because of the persecutions aimed by Domitian at the philosophers.

art of reasoning; and, if others should be angry at it, you will tell them, by way of consolation, "This I have learned, and you have not." Thus too, wherever practice is necessary, do not pretend to what can only be attained by practice; but leave the matter to those who are practiced, and be content in your own serenity.

"Go and pay your court to such a person," I am told. How? I will not do it abjectly. So I find myself shut out; for I have not learned to get in at the window, and finding the door shut, I must necessarily either go back, or get in at the window. "But speak to him at least." I am willing. "In what manner?" Not basely at any rate. "Well, you have failed." This is not my business, but his. Why must I claim what belongs to another? Always remember what is your own, and what is another's, and you will never be disturbed.

Hence Chrysippus rightly says: "While consequences are uncertain, I will keep to those things which will bring me most in harmony with nature; for God himself hath formed me to choose this. If I knew that it was inevitable for me to be sick, I would conform my inclinations that way; for even the foot, if it had understanding, would be inclined to get into the dirt." For why are ears of corn produced, if not to ripen? And why do they ripen, if not to be reaped? For they are not isolated, individual things. If they were capable of sense, do you think they would wish never to be reaped? It would be a curse upon ears of corn not to be reaped, and we ought to know that it would be a curse upon man not to die; like that of not ripening, and not being reaped.

Since, then, it is necessary for us to be reaped, and we have at the same time understanding to know it, are we angry at it? This is only because we neither know what we are, nor have we studied what belongs to man, as jockeys do what belongs to horses. Yet Chrysantas, when he was about to strike an enemy, on hearing the trumpet sound a retreat, drew back his hand; for he thought it more profitable to obey the command of his general than his own inclination.[1] But not one of us, even when necessity calls, is ready and willing to obey it; but we weep and groan over painful events, calling them our "circumstances." What circumstances, man? For if you call what surrounds you circumstances, everything is a circumstance; but if by this you mean hardships, where is the hardship, that whatever is born must die? The instrument is either a sword, or a wheel, or the sea, or a tile, or a tyrant; and what does it signify to you by what way you descend to Hades? All are equal; but, if you would hear the truth, the shortest is that by which a tyrant sends you. No tyrant was ever six months in cutting any man's throat; but a fever often takes a year. All these things are mere sound, and the rumor of empty names.

"My life is in danger from Caesar."

And am I not in danger, who dwell at Nicopolis, where there are so many earthquakes? And when you yourself recross the Adriatic, what is then in danger? Is it not your life?

"Ay, and my convictions also."

What, your own? How so? Can anyone compel you to have any convictions contrary to your own inclination?

"But the convictions of others too."

And what danger is it of yours, if others have false convictions?

"But I am in danger of being banished."

What is it to be banished? Only to be somewhere else than at Rome.

"Yes; but what if I should be sent to Gyaros?"[2]

If it be thought best for you, you will go; if not, there is another place than Gyaros whither you are sure to go—where he who now sends you to Gyaros must go likewise, whether

---

[1] In a speech which Cyrus made to his soldiers, after the battle with the Assyrians, he mentioned Chrysantas, one of his captains, with particular honor, for this instance of obedience. Xenoph. *Cyrop.* iv. 1.

[2] See note on p. 65.

he will or not. Why, then, do you come to these, as to great trials? They are not equal to your powers. So that an ingenuous young man would say, it was not worth while for this to have read and written so much, and to have sat so long listening to this old man. Only remember the distinction between what is your own and what is not your own, and you will never claim what belongs to others. Judicial bench or dungeon, each is but a place—one high, the other low; but your will is equal to either condition, and if you have a mind to keep it so, it may be so kept. We shall then become imitators of Socrates, when, even in a prison, we are able to write hymns of praise;[1] but as we now are, consider whether we could even bear to have another say to us in prison, "Shall I read you a hymn of praise?" "Why do you trouble me; do you not know my sad situation? In such circumstances, am I able to hear hymns?" What circumstances? "I am going to die." And are all other men to be immortal?

Of Divination

FROM an unseasonable regard to divination, we omit many duties; for what can the diviner contemplate besides death, danger, sickness, and such matters? When it is necessary, then, to risk my life for a friend, or even a duty to die for him, what occasion have I for divination? Have I not a diviner

---

[1] Diogenes Laertius in his life of Socrates gives the first verse of a hymn thus composed by him.

within, who has told me the essence of good and evil, and who explains to me the indications of both? What further need, then, have I of signs or auguries? Can I tolerate the other diviner, when he says, "This is for your interest"? For does he know what is for my interest? Does he know what good is? Has he learned the indications of good and evil, as he has those of the victims? If so, he knows the indications likewise of fair and base, just and unjust. You may predict to me, sir, what is to befall me—life or death, riches or poverty. But whether these things are for my interest or not, I shall not inquire of you. "Why?" Because you cannot even give an opinion about points of grammar; and do you give it here, in things about which all men differ and dispute? Therefore the lady who was going to send a month's provision to Gratilla,[1] in her banishment, made a right answer to one who told her that Domitian would seize it. "I had rather," said she, "that he should seize it, than I not send it."

What, then, is it that leads us so often to divination? Cowardice; the dread of events. Hence we flatter the diviners. "Pray, sir, shall I inherit my father's estate?" "Let us see; let us offer a sacrifice about that matter." "Nay, sir, just as fortune pleases." Then if he predicts that we shall inherit it, we give him thanks, as if we received the inheritance from *him*. The consequence of this is, that they go on fooling us.

What, then, is to be done?

We should come without previous desire or aversion; as a traveler inquires the road of the person he meets, without any desire for that which turns to the right hand, more than for that to the left; for he wishes for neither of these, but only for that road which leads to his destination. Thus we should come to God as to a guide, just as we make use of our eyes; not persuading them to show us one object rather than an-

---

[1] A lady of high rank at Rome, banished from Italy, among many noble persons, by Domitian.

other, but receiving such as they present to us. But now we conduct the augury with fear and trembling, and in our invocations to God, entreat him: "Lord, have mercy upon me, suffer me to come off safe." Foolish man! would you have anything then but what is best? And what is best but what pleases God? Why would you then, so far as in you lies, corrupt your judge and seduce your adviser?

What Is the Essence of the Good?

GOD is beneficial. Good is also beneficial. It would seem, then, that where the essence of God is, there too is the essence of good. What then is the essence of God—flesh? By no means. An estate? Fame? By no means. Intelligence? Knowledge? Right reason? Certainly. Here, then, without more ado, seek the essence of good. For do you seek that quality in a plant? No. Or in a brute? No. If, then, you seek it only in a rational subject, why do you seek it anywhere but in what distinguishes that from things irrational? Plants make no voluntary use of things, and therefore you do not apply the term of *good* to them. *Good*, then, implies such use. And nothing else? If so, you may say that good and happiness and unhappiness belong to mere animals. But this you do not say, and you are right; for, even if they have the use of things in the highest degree they have not the intelligent use, and with good reason; for they are made to be subservient to others, and are not themselves of primary importance. Why was an ass made? Was it as being of primary importance? No; but because we

had need of a back able to carry burdens. We had need too
that he should be capable of walking; therefore he had the
voluntary use of things added, otherwise he could not have
moved. But here his endowments end; for, if an understanding of that use had been likewise added, he would not, in
reason, have been subject to us, nor have done us these services,
but would have been like and equal to ourselves. Why will
you not, therefore, seek the essence of good in that without
which you cannot say that there is good in anything?

What then? Are not all these likewise the works of the
gods? They are; but not primary existences, nor parts of the
gods. But you are a primary existence. You are a distinct portion of the essence of God, and contain a certain part of him
in yourself. Why then are you ignorant of your own kinship?
Why do you not consider the source from which you came?
Why do you not remember, when you are eating, who you
are who eat, and whom you feed? When you are in the company of women, when you are conversing, when you are
exercising, when you are disputing, do you not know that it
is the Divine you feed, the Divine you exercise? You carry
a God about with you, poor wretch, and know nothing of it.
Do you suppose I mean some external god made of gold or
silver? It is within yourself that you carry him; and you do
not observe that you profane him by impure thoughts and
unclean actions. If the mere external image of God were present, you would not dare to act as you do; and when God
himself is within you, and hears and sees all, are you not
ashamed to think and act thus, insensible of your own nature,
and subject to God's wrath?

Why, then, are we afraid, when we send a young man from
the school into active life, that he should behave indecently,
eat indecently, behave indecently with women; that he should
either be debased if he is dressed in rags, or conceited if
he has clothed himself too finely? Knows he not the God
within him? Knows he not in what company he goes? It is

provoking to hear him say [to his instructor], "I wish to have *you* with me." Have you not God? Do you seek any other, while you have him? Or will he tell you any other things than these? If you were a statue of Phidias, as Zeus or Athene, you would remember both yourself and the artist; and if you had any sense, you would endeavor to be in no way unworthy of him who formed you, nor of yourself; nor to appear in an unbecoming manner to spectators. And are you now careless how you appear when you are the workmanship of Zeus himself? And yet, what comparison is there, either between the artists, or the things they have formed? What work of any artist has conveyed into its structure those very faculties which are shown in shaping it? Is it anything but marble, or brass, or gold, or ivory? And the Athene of Phidias, when its hand is once extended, and a *Victory* placed in it, remains in that attitude forever.

But the works of God are endowed with motion, breath, the powers of use and judgment. Being, then, the work of such an artist, will you dishonor him, especially when he has not only formed you, but given your guardianship to yourself? Will you not only be forgetful of this, but, moreover, dishonor the trust? If God had committed some orphan to your charge, would you have been thus careless of him? He has delivered yourself to your care; and says, "I had no one fitter to be trusted than you; preserve this person for me, such as he is by nature—modest, faithful, noble, unterrified, dispassionate, tranquil." And will you not preserve him?

But it will be said: "What need of this lofty look, and dignity of face?"

I answer that I have not yet so much dignity as the case demands; for I do not yet trust to what I have learned, and accepted. I still fear my own weakness. Let me but take courage a little, and then you shall see such a look, and such an appearance, as I ought to have. Then I will show you the statue when it is finished and polished. Do you think I will show you a supercilious countenance? Heaven forbid! For Olympian Zeus does not haughtily lift his brow, but keeps a steady gaze, as becomes him who is about to say,

My promise is irrevocable, sure.[1]

Such will I show myself to you; faithful, modest, noble, tranquil.

"What, and immortal too, and exempt from age and sickness?"

No. One who dies like a god or bears disease like a god. This is in my power; this I can do. The other is not in my power, nor can I do it. Shall I show you the muscular training of a philosopher?

"What muscles are those?"

A will undisappointed, evils avoided, powers duly exerted, careful resolutions, unerring decisions. These you shall see.

CHAPTER   NINE

That Some Persons, Failing to Fulfill What the Character of a Man Implies, Assume That of a Philosopher

It were no slight attainment, could we merely fulfill what the nature of man implies. For what is man? A rational and mortal being. Well; from what are we distinguished by reason? From wild beasts. From what else? From sheep, and the like.

Take care, then, to do nothing like a wild beast; otherwise

---

[1] Homer, *Iliad*. See Classics Club edition, p. 19.

you have destroyed the man; you have not fulfilled what your nature promises. Take care too, to do nothing like cattle; for thus likewise the man is destroyed.

In what do we act like cattle?

When we act gluttonously, lewdly, rashly, sordidly, inconsiderately, into what are we sunk? Into cattle. What have we destroyed? The rational being.

When we behave contentiously, injuriously, passionately, and violently, into what have we sunk? Into wild beasts.

And further, some of us are wild beasts of a larger size; others little mischievous vermin, such as suggest the proverb, "Let me rather be eaten by a lion."

By all these means, the nature of man is destroyed.

For when is a complex thing sustained? When it fulfills what its nature implies. So then the sustaining of such a proposition consists in this, that its several parts remain a series of truths.

When is a separate entity sustained? When it fulfills what its nature implies.

When is a flute, a harp, a horse, or a dog, preserved in existence? While each fulfills what its nature implies.

Where is the wonder, then, that manhood should be preserved or destroyed in the same manner? All things are preserved and improved by exercising their proper functions; as a carpenter, by building; a grammarian, by grammar; but if he permit himself to write ungrammatically, his art will necessarily be spoiled and destroyed. Thus modest actions preserve the modest man, and immodest ones destroy him; faithful actions preserve the faithful man, and the contrary destroy him. On the other hand, the contrary actions heighten the contrary characters. Thus the practice of immodesty develops an immodest character; knavery, a knavish one; slander, a slanderous one; anger, an angry one; and fraud, a covetous one.

For this reason, philosophers advise us not to be contented

with mere learning, but to add meditation likewise, and then practice. For we have been long accustomed to perverse actions, and have practiced upon wrong opinions. If, therefore, we do not likewise put into practice right opinions, we shall be nothing more than expositors of the abstract doctrines of others. For who among us is not already able to discourse, according to the rules of art, upon good and evil?—"That some things are good, some evil, and others indifferent; the good include the virtues and all things appertaining; the evil comprise the contrary; and the indifferent include riches, health, reputation"; and then, if while we are saying all this, there should happen some more than ordinary noise, or one of the bystanders should laugh at us, we are disconcerted. Philosopher, what is become of what you were saying? Whence did it proceed—merely from your lips? Why, then, do you confound the remedies which might be useful to others? Why do you trifle on the most important subjects? It is one thing to hoard up provision in a storehouse, and another to eat it. What is eaten is assimilated, digested, and becomes nerves, flesh, bones, blood, color, breath. Whatever is hoarded is ready indeed, whenever you desire to show it; but is of no further use to you than in the mere knowledge that you have it.

For what difference does it make whether you discourse on these doctrines, or on other schools of thought? Sit down and comment skillfully on Epicurus, for instance; perhaps you may comment more profitably than Epicurus himself. Why then do you call yourself a Stoic? Why do you act like a Jew, when you are a Greek? Do you not see on what terms each is called a Jew, a Syrian, an Egyptian? And when we see anyone wavering, we are wont to say, "This is not a Jew, but only acts like one." But, when he assumes the sentiments of one who has been baptized and circumcised, then he really is a Jew and is called one. Thus we, falsifying our profession, may be Jews in name, but are in reality something else. We are inconsistent with our own reasoning; we are far from practicing what we teach, and what we pride ourselves on knowing. Thus, while we are unable to fulfill what the character of a man implies, we take on the additional burden of being a philosopher. As if a person, incapable of lifting ten pounds, should endeavor to heave the same stone with Ajax.

CHAPTER TEN

How We May Discover Man's Duties from His Nominal Functions

CONSIDER who you are. In the first place, a man; that is, one who recognizes nothing superior to the faculty of free will, but all things as subject to this; and this itself as not to be enslaved or subjected to anything. Consider, then, from what you are distinguished by reason. You are distinguished from wild beasts; you are distinguished from cattle. Besides, you are a citizen of the universe, and a part of it; not a subordinate, but a principal part. You are capable of comprehending the divine economy, and of considering the connections of things. What then does the character of a citizen imply? To hold no private interest; to deliberate of nothing as a separate individual, but rather like the hand or the foot, which, if they had reason, and comprehended the constitution of nature, would never pursue, or desire, but with a reference to the whole. Hence the philosophers rightly say, that, if it were possible for a wise and good man to foresee what was to happen, he might co-operate in bringing on himself sickness, and death, and mutilation, being sensible that these things are appointed in the order of the universe; and that the whole is superior to a part, and the city to the citizen. But, since we do not foreknow what is to happen, it becomes our duty to hold to what is more agreeable to our choice, since we are born for this purpose.

Remember next, that perhaps you are a son, and what does this character imply? To esteem everything that is his, as belonging to his father; in every instance to obey him; not to revile him to anyone; not to say or do anything injurious to him; to give way and yield in everything, co-operating with him to the utmost of his power.

After this, know likewise, that you are a brother too; and that to this character it belongs to make concessions, to be easily persuaded, to use gentle language, never to claim for yourself any non-essential thing, but cheerfully to give up these to be repaid by a larger share of things essential. For consider what it is, instead of a lettuce, for instance, or a chair, to procure for yourself his good will. How great an advantage gained!

If, beside this, you are a senator of any city, demean yourself as a senator; if a youth, as a youth; if an old man, as an old man. For each of these names, if it comes to be considered, always points out the proper duties; but, if you go and revile your brother, I tell you that you have forgotten who you are, and what is your name. If you were a smith, and made an ill use of the hammer, you would have forgotten the smith; and if you have forgotten the brother, and are become, instead of a brother, an enemy, do you imagine you have made no change of one thing for another, in that case? If, instead of a man—a gentle, social creature—you have become a wild beast, mischievous, insidious, biting, have you lost nothing? Is it only the loss of money which is reckoned damage; and is there no other thing, the loss of which damages a man? If you were to part with your skill in grammar or in music, would you think the loss of these a damage; and yet, if you part with honor,

decency, and gentleness, do you think that no matter? Yet the
first may be lost by some external cause beyond the power of
our will; but the latter only by our own fault. There is no
shame in not having or in losing the one; but either not to
have or to lose the other is equally shameful and reproachful
and unhappy. What does the debauchee lose? Manhood. What
does he lose who made him such? Many things, but manhood
also. What does an adulterer lose? The qualities of a modest
man, the chaste character, the good neighbor. What does an
angry person lose? A coward? Each loses his portion. No one
is wicked without some loss or damage. Now if, after all, you
treat the loss of money as the only damage, all these are unhurt and uninjured. Nay, they may be even gainers; as, by
such practices, their money may possibly be increased. But
consider; if you refer everything to money, then a man who
loses his nose is not hurt. Yes, say you; he is maimed in his
body. Well, but does he who loses his sense of smell itself
lose nothing? Is there, then, no faculty of the soul which
benefits the possessor, and which it is an injury to lose?

"Of what sort do you mean?"

Have we not a natural sense of honor?

"We have."

Does he who loses this suffer no damage? Is he deprived of
nothing? Does he part with nothing that belongs to him? Have
we no natural fidelity; no natural affection; no natural disposition to mutual usefulness, to mutual forbearance? Is he,
then, who carelessly suffers himself to be damaged in these
respects still safe and uninjured?

"What, then; shall not I injure him who has injured me?"

Consider first what injury is; and remember what you have
heard from the philosophers. For, if both good and evil lie in
the will, see whether what you say does not amount to this:
"Since he has hurt himself by injuring me, shall I not hurt
myself by injuring him?" Why do we not make to ourselves
some such representation as this? Are we hurt when any det-

riment happens to our bodily possessions, and are we not at all hurt when our will is depraved? He who has erred, or injured another, has indeed no pain in his head; nor loses an eye, nor a leg, nor an estate; and we wish for nothing beyond these. Whether our will be habitually humble and faithful, or shameless and unfaithful, we regard as a thing indifferent, except only in the discussions of the schools. In that case, all the improvement we make reaches only to words; and beyond them is absolutely nothing.

CHAPTER ELEVEN

The Beginning of Philosophy

THE beginning of philosophy, at least to such as enter upon it in a proper way, and by the door, is a consciousness of our own weakness and inability in necessary things. For we came into the world without any concept of a right-angled triangle; of a diesis, or a semitone, in music; but we learn each of these things by some systematic method of instruction. Hence, they who do not understand them do not assume to understand them. But who ever came into the world without an innate idea of good and evil, fair and base, becoming and unbecoming, happiness and misery, proper and improper; what ought to be done, and what not to be done? Hence, we all make use of the terms, and endeavor to apply our impressions to particular cases. "Such a one hath acted well, not well; right, not right; is unhappy, is happy; is just, is unjust." Which of us refrains from these terms? Who defers the use of them till he has learned it, as those do who are ignorant of lines and sounds? The reason is, that we come instructed in some degree by nature upon these subjects; and from this beginning, we add our own ideas. "For why," say you, "should I not know what fair or base is? Have I not the idea of it?" You have. "Do I not apply this idea to the particular instance?" You do. "Do I not apply it rightly, then?" Here lies the whole question; and here arises the opinion. Beginning from these acknowledged points, men proceed, by applying them improperly, to reach the very position most questionable. For, if they knew how to apply them also, they would be all but perfect.

If you think that you know how to apply your general principles to particular cases, tell me on what you base this application.

"Upon its seeming so to me."

But it does not seem so to another; and does not he too think that he makes a right application?

"He does."

Is it possible, then, that each of you should rightly apply your principles, on the very subjects about which your opinions conflict?

"It is not."

Have you anything to show us, then, for this application, beyond the fact of its seeming so to you? And does a madman act any otherwise than seems to him right? Is this, then, a sufficient criterion for him too?

"It is not."

Come, therefore, to some stronger ground than seeming. "What is that?"

The beginning of philosophy is this: the being sensible of the disagreement of men with each other; an inquiry into the cause of this disagreement; and a disapprobation and distrust of what merely seems; a careful examination into what seems, whether it seem rightly; and the discovery of some rule which shall serve like a balance, for the determination of weights; like a square, for distinguishing straight and crooked. This is the beginning of philosophy.

Is it possible that all things which seem right to all persons are so? Can things contradictory be right? We say not all things; but all that seem so to *us*. And why more to *you* than to the Syrians or Egyptians; than to me, or to any other man? Not at all more.

Therefore, what seems true to each man is not sufficient to determine the reality of a thing; for even in weights and measures we are not satisfied with the bare appearance, but for everything we find some rule. And is there, then, in the present case no rule preferable to opinion? Is it possible that what is of the greatest necessity in human life should be left incapable of determination and discovery?

There must be some rule. And why do we not seek and discover it, and, when we have discovered, ever after make use of it, without fail, so as not even to move a finger without it? For this, I conceive, is what, when found, will cure those of their madness who make use of no other measure but their own perverted way of thinking. Afterwards, beginning from certain known and determinate points, we may make use of general principles, properly applied to particulars.

Thus, what is the subject that falls under our inquiry? Pleasure. Bring it to the rule. Throw it into the scale. Must good be something in which we can properly have confidence and trust? Yes. Is it fit to trust to anything unstable? No. Is pleasure, then, a stable thing? No. Take it, then, and throw it out of the scale, and drive it far away from the place of good things.

But, if you have not keen eyesight, and one balance is insufficient, bring another. Is it fit to be elated by good? Yes. Is it fit, then, to be elated by a present pleasure? See that you do not say it is; otherwise I shall not think you so much as worthy to use a scale. Thus are things judged and weighed, when we have the rules ready. This is the part of philosophy, to examine, and fix the rules; and to make use of them, when they are known, is the business of a wise and good man.

CHAPTER TWELVE

Of Disputation

WHAT things are to be learned, in order to know how to conduct an argument, the philosophers of our sect have accurately taught; but we are altogether unpracticed in the proper application of them. Only give to any one of us whom you will some illiterate person for an antagonist, and he will not find out how to treat him. But when he has moved the man a little, if he happens to answer at cross purposes, the questioner knows not how to deal with him any further, but either reviles or laughs at him, and says: "He is an illiterate fellow; there is no making anything of him." Yet a guide, when he perceives his charge going out of the way, does not revile and ridicule and then leave him, but leads him into the right path. Do you also show your antagonist the truth, and you will see that he will follow. But till you show it, do not ridicule him; but rather recognize your own incapacity.

How, then, did Socrates use to act? He obliged his antagonist himself to bear testimony to him; and wanted no other witness. Hence he might well say,[1] "I give up all the rest, and am always satisfied with the testimony of my opponent; and I call in no one to vote, but my antagonist alone." For he rendered the arguments drawn from natural impressions so clear, that everyone saw and avoided the contradiction. "Does an envious man rejoice?" "By no means; he rather grieves." (This he moves him to say by proposing the contrary.) "Well, and do you think envy to be a grief caused by evils?" "And who ever envied evils?" (Therefore he makes the other say, that envy is a grief caused by things good.) "Does anyone envy

[1] Plato, *Gorgias*, § 69, and elsewhere.

115

those things which are nothing to him?" "No, surely." Having thus fully drawn out his idea, he then leaves that point, not saying, "Define to me what envy is"; and after he has defined it, "You have defined it wrong; for the definition does not correspond to the thing defined."

There are phrases which are obscure to the illiterate, which yet we cannot dispense with. But we have no capacity at all to move them, by such arguments as might lead them, in following the methods of their own minds, to admit or abandon any position. And from a consciousness of this incapacity, those among us who have any modesty give the matter entirely up; but the greater part, rashly entering upon these debates, mutually confound and are confounded, and at last, reviling and reviled, walk off. Whereas it was the principal and most peculiar characteristic of Socrates, never to be provoked in a dispute, nor to throw out any reviling or injurious expression; but to bear patiently with those who reviled him, and thus put an end to the controversy. If you would know how great abilities he had in this particular, read Xenophon's *Symposium*, and you will see how many controversies he ended. Hence, even among the poets, this is justly mentioned with the highest commendation,

Wisely at once the greatest strife to still.[1]

But what then? This is no very safe affair now, and especially at Rome. For he who does it must not do it in a corner, but go to some rich person of consular rank, for instance, and question him. "Pray, sir, can you tell me to whom you intrust your horses?" "Yes, certainly." "Is it then to anyone at all, though he be ignorant of horsemanship?" "By no means." "To whom do you intrust your gold or your silver or your clothes?" "Not to any stranger." "And did you ever consider to whom you committed the care of your body?" "Yes,

---

[1] Hesiod, *Theogony*, 87.

surely." "To one skilled in exercise or medicine, I suppose?"
"Without doubt." "Are these things your chief good, or are
you possessed of something better than all of them?" "What
do you mean?" "Something which makes use of these, and
deliberates and counsels about each of them." "What, then;
do you mean the soul?" "You have guessed rightly; for indeed
I do mean that." "I do really think it a much better possession
than all the rest."

Can you show us, then, in what manner you have taken care
of this soul? For it is not probable that a person of your wisdom and approved character in the state would carelessly
suffer the most excellent thing that belongs to you to be neglected and lost. "No, certainly." But do you take care of it
yourself; and is it done by the instructions of another, or by
your own ability?—Here, now, comes the danger that he may
first say, "Pray, good sir, what business is that of yours? What
are you to me?" Then if you persist in troubling him, he may
lift up his hand and give you a box on the ear. I myself was
once a great admirer of this method of instruction, before I
fell into my present condition.

CHAPTER THIRTEEN

Of Anxiety

WHEN I see anyone anxious, I say, what does this man want?
Unless he wanted something or other not in his own power,
how could he still be anxious? A musician, for instance, feels
no anxiety while he is singing by himself; but when he appears
upon the stage he does, even if his voice be ever so good, or
he plays ever so well. For what he wishes is not only to sing

well, but likewise to gain applause. But this is not in his own power. In short, where his skill lies, there is his courage. Bring any ignorant person, and he does not mind him; but in the point which he neither understands nor has studied, there he is anxious.

"What point is that?"

He does not understand what a multitude is, nor what the applause of a multitude. He has learned, indeed, how to sound bass and treble; but what the applause of the many is, and what force it has in life, he neither understands nor has studied. Hence he must necessarily tremble and turn pale. I cannot indeed say that a man is no musician, when I see him afraid; but I can say something else, and indeed many things. And first of all I call him a stranger, and say, this man does not know in what country he is; and though he has lived here so long, he is ignorant of the laws and customs of the state, and what is permitted and what not; nor has he ever consulted any legal adviser, who might tell and explain to him the laws. But no man writes a will without knowing how it ought to be written, or consulting someone who knows; nor does he rashly sign a bond, or give security. Yet he indulges his desires and aversions, exerts his pursuits, intentions, and resolutions, without consulting any legal adviser about the matter.

"How do you mean, without a legal adviser?"

He knows not when he chooses what is not allowed him, and does not choose what is necessary; and he knows not what is his own, and what belongs to others; for if he did know he would never be hindered, would never be restrained, would never be anxious.

"How so?"

Why, does anyone fear things that are not evils?

"No."

Does anyone fear things that seem evils indeed, but which it is in his own power to prevent?

"No, surely."

If, then, the things independent of our will are neither good nor evil, and all things that do depend on will are in our own power, and can neither be taken away from us nor given to us unless we please, what room is there left for anxiety? But we are anxious about this paltry body or estate of ours, or about what Caesar thinks, and not at all about anything internal. Are we ever anxious not to take up a false opinion? No; for this is within our own power. Or not to follow any pursuit contrary to nature? No, nor this. When, therefore, you see anyone pale with anxiety, just as the physician pronounces from the complexion that such a patient is disordered in the spleen, and another in the liver, so do you likewise say, this man is disordered in his desires and aversions; he cannot walk steadily; he is in a fever. For nothing else changes the complexion, or causes trembling, or sets the teeth chattering.

He crouching walks, or squats upon his heels.[1]

Therefore Zeno,[2] when he was to meet Antigonus, felt no anxiety. For over that which he prized, Antigonus had no power; and those things over which he had power, Zeno did not regard. But Antigonus felt anxiety when he was to meet Zeno, and with reason, for he was desirous to please him; and this was external ambition. But Zeno did not care about pleasing Antigonus; for no one skillful in any art cares about pleasing a person unskillful.

"I am anxious to please you."

For what? Do you know the rules by which one man judges of another? Have you studied to understand what a good and

---

[1] Homer, *Iliad*. See Classics Club edition, p. 198.

[2] Antigonus Gonatas, king of Macedon, had so great an esteem for Zeno, that he often took a journey to Athens to visit him, and endeavored, by magnificent promises, to allure him to his court, but without success. He gave it as a reason for the distinguished regard which he paid him, that, though he had made him many and very considerable offers, Zeno never appeared either mean or insolent.

what a bad man is, and how each becomes such? Why, then, are not you yourself a good man?

"In what respect am I not?"

Because no good man laments or sighs or groans; no good man turns pale and trembles and says, "How will such a one receive me; how will he hear me?" As he thinks fit, foolish man. Why do you trouble yourself about what belongs to others? Is it not his fault if he receives you ill?

"Yes, surely."

And can one person be in fault and another the sufferer?

"No."

Why, then, are you anxious about what belongs to others?

"Well; but I am anxious how I shall speak to him."

What, then; cannot you speak to him as you will?

"But I am afraid I shall be disconcerted."

If you were going to write down the name of Dion, should you be afraid of being disconcerted?

"By no means."

What is the reason? Is it because you have learned how to write?

"Yes."

And if you were going to read, would it not be exactly the same?

"Exactly."

What is the reason?

"Because every art gives a certain assurance and confidence on its own ground."

Have you not learned, then, how to speak? And what else did you study at school?

"Syllogisms and convertible propositions."

For what purpose? Was it not in order to argue skillfully? And what is that but to talk seasonably and discreetly and intelligently, and without flutter or hesitation, and, by means of all this, with courage?

"Very true."

When, therefore, you go into the field on horseback, are you anxious on being matched against one who is on foot—you being practiced and he unpracticed?

"Yes, but Caesar has power to kill me."

Then speak the truth, O unfortunate! and be not arrogant, nor take the philosopher upon you, nor conceal from yourself who are your masters; but while you are thus to be held by the body, follow the strongest. Socrates, indeed, had studied how to speak, who talked in such a manner to tyrants and judges, and in prison. Diogenes[1] had studied how to speak, who talked in such a manner to Alexander, to Philip, to the pirates, to the person who bought him. This is a matter for those who have studied, those who have courage. But you should go where you belong and stay there; retire into some corner, and there sit and weave syllogisms, and propound them to others. For there is not in you a man who can rule the city.

---

[1] When Diogenes was sailing to Aegina, he was taken by pirates, and carried to Crete, and there exposed to sale. Being asked what he could do, he answered, "Govern men"; and pointing to a well-dressed Corinthian who was passing by, "Sell me," said he, "to him; for he wants a master." The Corinthian, whose name was Xeniades, bought him, and appointed him the tutor to his children; and Diogenes perfectly well discharged his trust.

CHAPTER FOURTEEN

Concerning Naso

WHEN a certain Roman came to him with his son, and had heard one lesson,—This, said Epictetus, is the method of teaching; and ceased. When the other desired him to go on, he answered, Every art seems tedious, when it is delivered to a person ignorant and unskillful in it. The things performed by the common arts quickly manifest the use for which they were made; and most of them have something attractive and agreeable. Thus the trade of a shoemaker, as one seeks to learn it, is an unpleasant thing; but the shoe is useful, and not unpleasing to the eye. The trade of a smith is extremely unattractive to an ignorant observer; but the work shows the usefulness of the art. You will see this much more strongly in music; for if you stand by while a person is learning, it will appear to you of all sciences the most unpleasant; but the effects are agreeable and delightful, even to those who do not understand it.

So, in our own case, we take it to be the work of one who studies philosophy to bring his will into harmony with events; so that none of the things which happen may happen against our inclination, nor those which do not happen be desired by us. Hence they who have settled this point have it in their power never to be disappointed in what they seek, nor to incur what they shun; but to lead their own lives without sorrow, fear, or perturbation, and in society to preserve all the natural or acquired relations of son, father, brother, citizen, husband, wife, neighbor, fellow traveler, ruler, or subject. Something like this is what we take to be the work of a philosopher. It remains to inquire how it is to be effected. Now we see that a carpenter becomes a carpenter by learning certain things; and a pilot, by learning certain things, becomes a pilot. Probably, then, it is not sufficient, in the present case, merely to be willing to be wise and good; but it is moreover necessary that certain things should be learned. What these things are, is the question. The philosophers say that we are first to learn that there is a God, and that his providence directs the whole; and that it is not merely impossible to conceal from him our actions, but even our thoughts and emotions. Next we are to learn what the gods are; for whatever they are found to be, this must he who would please and obey them try his best to resemble. If the Deity is faithful, he too must be faithful; if free, beneficent, and noble, he must be free, beneficent, and noble likewise, in all his words and actions behaving as an imitator of God.

"Where, then, are we to begin?"

If you will give me leave, I will tell you. It is necessary, in the first place, that you should understand words.

"So then! I do not understand them now?"

No, you do not.

"How is it, then, that I use them?"

Just as the illiterate use the words of the learned, and as brutes use the phenomena of nature. For use is one thing, and understanding another. But if you think you understand them, bring whatever words you please, and let us see whether we understand them or not.

"Well; but it is a grievous thing for a man who has grown old, to be confuted, and has perhaps served through his three campaigns to a senatorship."

I know it very well. For you now come to me, as if you wanted nothing. And how can it enter into your imagination that there should be anything in which you are deficient? You are rich; and perhaps have a wife and children, and a great number of domestics. Caesar takes notice of you; you have many friends at Rome; you render to all their dues; you know how to requite a favor, and revenge an injury. In what are

you deficient? Suppose, then, I should prove to you that you
are deficient in what is most necessary and important to happiness; and that hitherto you have taken care of everything,
rather than your duty; and to complete all, that you understand not what God or man, or good or evil, means? That
you are ignorant of all the rest, perhaps, you may bear to be
told; but if I prove to you that you are ignorant even of
yourself, how will you bear with me, and will you have
patience to stay and be convinced? Not at all. You will immediately be offended, and go away. And yet what injury
have I done you? None, unless a mirror injures a person not
handsome, when it shows him to himself as he is; or unless a
physician can be thought to affront his patient, when he says
to him: "Do you think, sir, that you are not ill? You have a
fever. Eat no meat today, and drink water." Nobody cries
out here, "What an intolerable affront!" But if you say to
anyone: "You exhibit feverishness in your desires, and low
habits in what you shun; your aims are contradictory, your
pursuits not conformable to nature, your opinions rash and
mistaken,"—he presently goes away, and complains that he is
affronted.

This is the position we assume. As, in a crowded fair, the
horses and cattle are brought to be sold, and most men come
either to buy or sell; but there are a few who come only to
look at the fair, and inquire how it is carried on, and why in
that manner, and who appointed it, and for what purpose—
thus, in this fair [of the world] some, like cattle, trouble themselves about nothing but fodder. To all of you who busy yourselves about possessions and farms and domestics and public
posts, these things are nothing else but mere fodder. But there
are some few men among the crowd who are fond of looking
on, and considering: "What then, after all, is the world? Who
governs it? Has it no governor? How is it possible, when
neither a city nor a house can remain, ever so short a time,
without someone to govern and take care of it, that this vast

and beautiful system should be administered in a fortuitous and disorderly manner? Is there then a governor? Of what sort is he, and how does he govern? And what are we who are under him, and for what designed? Have we some connection and relation to him, or none?" In this manner are the few affected, and apply themselves only to view the fair, and then depart. Well; and they are laughed at by the multitude? Why, so are the lookers-on, by the buyers and sellers; and if the cattle had any apprehension, they too would laugh at such as admired anything but fodder.

CHAPTER FIFTEEN

Concerning Those Who Obstinately Persist in Judgments Which They Have Once Formed

SOME, when they hear such discourses as these, "That we ought to be steadfast; that the will is by nature free and unconstrained; and that all else is liable to restraint, compulsion, slavery, and tyranny," imagine that they must remain immutably fixed to everything which they have determined. But it is first necessary that the judgment formed should be a wise one. I agree that there should be strength in the body, but it must be the strength of a healthy and athletic body; for if you show me that you have the strength of a lunatic, and boast about it, I will say to you, Seek a physician, man; this is not strength but weakness. Such is the distemper of mind in those who hear these discourses in a wrong manner; like an acquaintance of mine, who, for no reason, had determined to starve himself to death. I went the third day, and inquired what was the matter. He answered, "I am determined." Well; but what is your motive? For if your determination be right, we will stay, and assist your departure; but, if unreasonable, change it. "We should abide by our decisions." What do you mean, sir? Not all of them; but only such as are right. Else, if you should fancy that it is night, if this be your principle, do not change, but persist, and say, "We ought to abide by our decisions." What do you mean, sir? Not by all of them.

Why do you not begin by first laying the foundation, inquiring whether your decision be a sound one or not, and then build your firmness and constancy upon it. For if you lay a rotten and crazy foundation, you must not build; since the greater and more weighty the superstructure, the sooner will it fall. Without any reason, you are withdrawing from us, out of life, a friend, a companion, a fellow citizen both of the greater and the lesser city; and while you are committing murder, and destroying an innocent person, you say, "We must abide by our decisions." Suppose, by any means, it should ever come into your head to kill me; must you keep such a determination?

With difficulty this person was, however, at last convinced; but there are some at present who cannot be convinced. So that now I think I understand, what before I did not, the meaning of that common saying, that a fool will neither bend nor break. May it never fall to my lot to have a wise, that is, an untractable, fool for my friend. "It is all to no purpose; I am determined." So are madmen too; but the more strongly they are determined upon absurdities, the more need have they of hellebore.[1] Why will you not act like a sick person, and apply yourself to a physician? "Sir, I am sick. Give me your assistance; consider what I am to do. It is my part to follow your

---

[1] A poisonous herb used in ancient times as a remedy for insanity.

directions." So say in the present case: "I know not what I ought to do; and I am come to learn." "No; but talk to me about other things; for upon *this* I am determined." What other things? What is of greater consequence, than to convince you that it is not sufficient to be determined, and to refuse to change? This is the vigor of a madman; not of one in health. "I will die, if you compel me to this." Why so, man; what is the matter? "I am determined." It is fortunate that you decided not to kill me. "I will not be bribed." Why so? "I am determined." Be assured, that with that very vigor which you now employ to refuse the bribe, you may hereafter have as unreasonable a propensity to take it; and again to say, "I am determined." As, in a sick and rheumatic body, the disease tends sometimes to one part, sometimes to another; this is also true of the sick mind. But if obstinacy is added to this inclination and bent, the evil then becomes desperate and incurable.

CHAPTER   SIXTEEN

That We Do Not Study to Make Use of the Established Principles Concerning Good and Evil

WHERE lies good? In the will. Where evil? In the will. Where lies that which is neither good nor evil? In things inevitable. What then? Does any one of us remember these lessons out of the schools? Does any one of us study how to answer for himself in the affairs of life, as in common questions? "Is it day?" "Yes." "Is it night, then?" "No." "Is the number of stars even?" "I cannot tell." When a bribe is offered you, have you learned to make the proper answer, that it is not a good? Have you exercised yourself in such answers as, these, or only in sophistries? Why do you wonder, then, that you improve in points which you have studied; while in those which you have not studied, there you remain the same? When an orator knows that he has written well, that he has committed to memory what he has written, and that he brings an agreeable voice with him, why is he still anxious? Because he is not contented with what he has studied. What does he want then? To be applauded by the audience. He has studied the power of speaking, then; but he has not studied censure and applause. For when did he hear from anyone what applause, what censure is? What is the nature of each? What kind of applause is to be sought, and what kind of censure to be shunned? And when did he ever apply himself to study what follows from these lessons? Why do you wonder, then, if, in what he has learned, he excels others; but where he has not studied, he is the same with the rest of the world? Just as a musician knows how to play, sings well, and has the proper dress of his profession, yet trembles when he comes upon the stage. For the first he understands; but what the multitude is, or what the clamor and laughter of the multitude means, he does not understand. Nor does he even know what anxiety itself is; whether it be our own affair, or that of others; or whether it is possible to suppress it, or not. Hence, if he is applauded, he is puffed up when he makes his exit; but if he is laughed at, his conceit is punctured, and subsides.

Thus are we too affected. What do we admire? Externals. For what do we strive? Externals. And are we then in any doubt why we fear and are anxious? What is the consequence, then, when we esteem the things that are brought upon us to be evils? We cannot but fear; we cannot but be anxious. And then we say, "O Lord God, how shall I avoid anxiety!" Have you not hands, foolish man? Has not God made them for you?

You might as well kneel and pray to be cured of your catarrh. Take care of your disease, rather, and wipe your nose. Well; and has he given you nothing in the present case? Has he not given you patience? Has he not given you magnanimity? Has he not given you fortitude? When you have such hands as these, do you still seek help in wiping your nose? But we neither study nor regard these things. For give me but one who cares how he does anything, who does not regard the mere success of anything, but his own manner of acting. Who, when he is walking, regards his own action? Who, when he is deliberating, prizes the deliberation itself, and not the success that is to follow it? If it happens to succeed, he is elated, and cries, "How prudently have we deliberated! Did not I tell you, my dear friend, that it was impossible, when we considered about anything, that it should not happen right?" But if it miscarries, the poor wretch is dejected, and knows not what to say about the matter. Who among us ever, for such a purpose, consulted a seer? Who of us ever slept in a temple, to be instructed [in a dream] concerning his manner of acting? I say, who? Show me one who is truly noble and ingenuous, that I may see what I have long sought. Show me either a young or an old man.

Why, then, are we still surprised, if, when we waste all our attention on the mere materials of action, we are, in the manner of action itself, low, sordid, unworthy, timid, wretched, and altogether failures? For we do not care about these things, nor make them our study. If we had feared, not death or exile, but fear itself, we should have studied not to fall into what appears to us to be evil. But as the case now stands, we are eager and loquacious in the schools; and when any little question arises about any of these things, we are prepared to trace its consequences; but drag us into practice, and you will find us miserably shipwrecked. Let something of alarming aspect attack us, and you will perceive what we have been studying.

and in what we are trained for. Besides, through this negligence we always exaggerate, and represent things greater than the reality.

In a voyage, for instance, casting my eyes down upon the ocean below, and looking round me, and seeing no land, I am beside myself, and imagine that, if I should be shipwrecked, I must swallow all that ocean; nor does it occur to me, that three pints are enough for me. What is it, then, that alarms me —the ocean? No; my own impressions. Again, in an earthquake I imagine the city is going to fall upon me; but is not one little stone enough to knock my brains out? What is it, then, that oppresses and makes us beside ourselves? Why, what else but our own impressions? For what is it, but mere impressions, that distress him who leaves his country, and is separated from his acquaintance and friends and place and usual manner of life? When children cry, if their nurse happens to be absent for a little while, give them a cake, and they forget their grief. Shall we compare you to these children, then?

"No, indeed. For I do not desire to be pacified by a cake, but by right impressions. And what are they?"

Such as a man ought to study all day long, so as not to be absorbed in what does not belong to him—neither friend, place, nor academy, nor even his own body; but to remember the law, and to have that constantly before his eyes. And what is the divine law? To preserve inviolate what is properly our own; not to claim what belongs to others; to use what is given us, and not desire what is not given us; and when anything is taken away, to restore it readily, and to be thankful for the time you have been permitted the use of it; and not cry after it, like a child for its nurse and its mamma. For what does it signify what gets the better of you, or on what you depend? Which is the worthier, one crying for a doll, or for an academy? You lament for the portico and the assembly of young people, and such entertainments. Another comes la-

menting that he must no longer drink the water of Dirce.[1]
Why, is not the Marcian water as good? "But I was used to
that." And in time you will be used to the other. And when
you are attached to this too, you may weep again, and set
yourself, in imitation of Euripides, to celebrate, in verse,

The baths of Nero, and the Marcian water.

Hence see the origin of Tragedy, when trifling accidents
befall foolish men. "Ah, when shall I see Athens and the citadel
again?" Foolish man, are not you contented with what you
see every day? Can you see anything better than the sun, the
moon, the stars, the whole earth, the sea? But if, besides, you
comprehend him who administers the whole, and carry him
about within yourself, do you still long after certain stones
and a fine rock? [2] What will you do then, when you are to
leave even the sun and moon? Will you sit crying, like an
infant? What, then, have you been doing in the school? What
did you hear? What did you learn? Why have you written
yourself down a philosopher, instead of writing the real fact?
"I have prepared some abstracts, and read over Chrysippus;
but I have not so much as approached the door of philosophy.
For what pretensions have I in common with Socrates, who
died and who lived in such a manner; or with Diogenes?" Do
you observe either of these crying, or out of humor, that he
is not to see such a man, or such a woman; nor to live any
longer at Athens nor at Corinth; but at Susa, for instance, or
Ecbatana? For does he stay and repine, who may at any time,
if he will, quit the banquet, and play no longer? Why does he
not stay, as children do, so long as he is amused? Such a one,
no doubt, will bear perpetual banishment and a sentence of
death wonderfully well! Why will not you be weaned, as

---

[1] The fountain of Dirce was in Boetia. The Marcian aqueduct brought
water to Rome.

[2] This refers to the Acropolis, with its marble temples.

children are, and take more solid food? Will you never cease to cry after your mammas and nurses, whom the old women about you have taught you to bewail? "But if I go away, I shall trouble them also." You trouble them! No; it will not be you, but that which troubles you too—a mere impression. What have you to do then? Rid yourself of that impression; and if they are wise, they will do the same for theirs; or if not, they must lament for themselves.

Boldly make a desperate push, man, as the saying is, for prosperity, for freedom, for magnanimity. Lift up your head at last, as being free from slavery. Dare to look up to God, and say, "Make use of me for the future as thou wilt. I am of the same mind; I am one with thee. I refuse nothing which seems good to thee. Lead me whither thou wilt. Clothe me in whatever dress thou wilt. Is it thy will that I should be in a public or a private condition; dwell here, or be banished; be poor, or rich? Under all these circumstances I will testify unto thee before men. I will explain the nature of every dispensation." No? Rather sit alone, then, in safety, and wait till your mamma comes to feed you. If Hercules had sat loitering at home, what would he have been? Eurystheus,[1] and not Hercules. Besides, by traveling through the world, how many acquaintances and how many friends he made. But none more his friend than God; for which reason he was believed to be the son of God, and was so. In obedience to him, he went about extirpating injustice and lawless force. But you are not Hercules, nor able to extirpate the evils of others; nor even Theseus, to extirpate the evils of Attica. Extirpate your own then. Expel, instead of Procrustes and Sciron,[2] grief, fear, desire, envy, malevolence, avarice, effeminacy, intemperance. But these cannot be expelled save by looking up to God alone,

---

[1] The king for whom Hercules performed his labors.
[2] Two famous robbers who infested Attica, and were at last killed by Theseus.

as your pattern; by attaching yourself to him alone, and being consecrated to his commands. If you wish for anything else, you will, with sighs and groans, follow what is stronger than you; always seeking prosperity without, and never able to find it. For you seek it where it is not, and neglect to seek it where it is.

CHAPTER SEVENTEEN

How to Apply General Principles to Particular Cases

WHAT is the first business of one who studies philosophy? To part with self-conceit. For it is impossible for anyone to begin to learn what he thinks that he already knows. We all go to the philosophers, talking at random upon negative and positive duties; good and evil; fair and base. We praise, censure, accuse; we judge and dispute about fair and base enterprises. And yet for what do we go to the philosophers? To learn what we suppose ourselves not to know. And what is this? General principles. We are desirous to hear what the philosophers say, for its elegance and acuteness; and some with a view only to gain. Now it is ridiculous to suppose that a person will learn anything but what he desires to learn; or make an improvement, in what he does not learn. But most are deceived, in the same manner as Theopompus, the orator, when he blames Plato for defining everything. "For," he says, "did none of us, before you, use the word 'good' and 'just'; or did we utter them as empty sounds, without understanding what each of them meant?" Why, who tells you, Theo-

pompus, that we had not natural ideas and general principles
as to each of these? But it is not possible to apply principles
in detail, without having minutely distinguished them, and
examined what details appertain to each. You may make the
same objection to the physicians. For who of us did not use
the words "wholesome" and "unwholesome," before Hippocrates was born; or did we utter them as empty sounds? For
we have some general conception of what is wholesome too,
but we cannot apply it. Hence one says, let the patient abstain
from meat; another, give it to him. One says, let him be bled;
another, cup him. And what is the reason, but not being able
to adapt the general conception of wholesomeness to particular cases? Thus, too, in life; who of us does not talk of good
or evil, advantageous and disadvantageous; for who of us has
not a general conception of each of these? But is it then a
distinct and perfect one? Show me this.

"How shall I show it?"

Apply it properly in detail. Plato, to go no further, puts
definitions under the general head of useful; but you, under
that of useless. Can both of you be right? How is it possible?
Again, does not one man adapt the general conception of good
to riches; another not to riches, but to pleasure or health? In
general, unless we who use words employ them vaguely, or
without proper care in discrimination, why do we differ?
Why do we wrangle? Why do we censure each other? But
what occasion have I to mention this mutual contradiction?
If you yourself apply your principles properly, how comes it
to pass that you do not prosper? Why do you meet with any
hindrance? Let us for the present omit our second point concerning the *pursuits* and the duties relative to them; let us
omit the third too, concerning *assent*. I waive all these for you.
Let us insist only on the first,[1] which affords almost a palpable
proof that you do not properly apply your principles. You

---

[1] The topic of the *Desires* and *Aversions*.

desire what is possible in itself, and possible for you. Why then are you hindered? Why are you not in a prosperous way? You do not shrink from the inevitable. Why then do you incur anything undesirable? Why are you unfortunate? When you desire anything, why does it not happen? When you do not desire it, why does it happen? For this is the greatest proof of ill success and trouble: "I desire something and it does not happen; and what is more wretched than I?" From such impatience Medea came to murder her own children—a lofty action in this point of view alone, that she had a proper conception of what it means to fail of one's aim. "Thus I shall punish him who has injured and dishonored me; and what is so wicked a wretch good for? But how is this to be effected? I will murder the children; but that will be punishing myself. And what do I care?"

This is the error of a powerful soul. For she knew not where the fulfillment of our desires is to be found; that it is not to be had from without, nor by altering the appointment of things. Give up wanting to keep your husband, and then nothing which you want will fail to happen. Do not desire to keep him to yourself. Do not desire to stay at Corinth, and, in a word, have no will but the will of God, and who shall restrain you; who shall compel you, any more than Zeus?

When you have such a guide, and conform your will and inclinations to his, why need you fear being disappointed? Fix your desire and aversion on riches or poverty; the one will be disappointed, the other incurred. Fix them on health, power, honors, your country, friends, children—in short, on anything beyond the control of your will—you will be unfortunate. But fix them on Zeus, on the gods; give yourself up to these; let these govern; let your powers be ranged on the same side with these, and how can you be troubled any longer? But if, poor wretch, you envy, and pity, and are jealous, and tremble, and never cease a single day from complaining of yourself and the gods, why do you boast of your education?

What education, man—that you have labored over syllogisms?

Why do not you, if possible, unlearn all these, and begin again, convinced that hitherto you have not even touched upon the essential point? And for the future, beginning from this foundation, proceed in order to the superstructure; that nothing may happen which you do not wish, and that everything may happen which you desire. Give me but one young man who brings this intention with him to the school, who is a champion for this point, and says, "I yield up all the rest; it suffices me, if once I become able to pass my life free from hindrance and grief, to stretch out my neck to all events as freely, and to look up to heaven as the friend of God, fearing nothing that can happen." Let any one of you show himself of such a disposition, that I may say, "Come into the place, young man, that is of right your own; for you are destined to be an ornament to philosophy. Yours are these possessions; yours these books; yours these discourses." Then, when he has thoroughly mastered this first class, let him come to me again and say, "I desire indeed to be free from passion and turmoil; but I desire too, as a pious, a philosophic, and a diligent man, to know what is my duty to God, to my parents, to my relations, to my country, and to strangers." Come into the second class too; for this likewise is yours. "But I have now sufficiently studied the second class too; and I would willingly be secure and unshaken by error and delusion, not only when awake, but even when asleep; when warmed with wine; when I am melancholy." You are becoming as a god, man; your aims are sublime!

"No, but I, for my part, desire to understand what Chrysippus says, in his logical treatise of the Pseudomenos." [1] Go hang yourself, pitiful man, with only such an aim as this! What

---

[1] The "Pseudomenos" was a famous problem among the Stoics, and it is this. When a person says, *I lie*, does he lie, or does he not? If he lies, he speaks truth; if he speaks truth, he lies.

good will it do you? You will read the whole, lamenting all the while; and say to others, trembling, "Do as I do. Shall I read to you, my friend, and you to me? You write amazingly well; and you very finely imitate the style of Plato; and you, of Xenophon; and you, of Antisthenes." And thus, having related your dreams to each other, you return again to the same state. Your desires and aversions, your pursuits, your intentions, your resolutions, your wishes, and endeavors are just what they were. You do not so much as seek for one to advise you, but are offended when you hear such things as these, and cry, "An ill-natured old man! He never wept over me, when I was setting out, nor said, To what a danger are you going to be exposed? If you come off safe, child, I will illuminate my house. This would have been the part of a man of feeling." Truly it will be a mighty happiness if you do come off safe; it will be worth while to make an illumination. For you ought to be immortal and exempt from sickness, to be sure.

Throwing away, then, I say, this self-conceit, by which we fancy we have gained some knowledge of what is useful, we should come to philosophic reasoning as we do to mathematics and music; otherwise we shall be far from making any improvement, even if we have read over all the treatises and commentaries, not only of Chrysippus, but of Antipater, and Archedemus too.

CHAPTER EIGHTEEN

How to Struggle Against the Semblances of Things

EVERY habit and faculty is preserved and increased by the corresponding actions; as the habit of walking, by walking; of running, by running. If you would be a reader, read; if a writer, write. But if you do not read for a month together, but do something else, you will see what will be the consequence. So after sitting still for ten days, get up and attempt to take a long walk, and you will find how your legs are weakened. Upon the whole, then, whatever you would make habitual, practice it; and if you would not make a thing habitual, do not practice it, but habituate yourself to something else.

It is the same with regard to the operations of the soul. Whenever you are angry, be assured that it is not only a present evil, but that you have increased a habit, and added fuel to a fire. When you are overcome by the seductions of a woman, do not consider it as a single defeat alone, but that you have fed, that you have increased, your incontinence. For it is impossible but that habits and faculties must either be first produced, or strengthened and increased, by corresponding actions. Hence the philosophers derive the growth of all maladies. When you once desire money, for example, if reason be applied to produce a sense of the evil, the desire ceases, and the governing faculty of the mind regains its authority; whereas, if you apply no remedy, it returns no more to its former state, but being again similarly excited, it kindles at the desire more quickly than before; and by frequent repetitions at last becomes callous, and by this weakness is the love of money established. For he who has had a fever, even after it has left him, is not in the same state of health as before, unless he was perfectly cured; and the same thing happens in distempers of the soul likewise. There are certain traces and blisters left in it, which, unless they are well effaced, whenever a new hurt is received in the same part, instead of blisters will become sores.

If you would not be of an angry temper, then, do not feed the habit. Give it nothing to help its increase. Be quiet at first and reckon the days in which you have not been angry. I used to be angry every day; now every other day; then every third and fourth day; and if you miss it so long as thirty days, offer a sacrifice of thanksgiving to God. For habit is first weakened and then entirely destroyed. "I was not vexed today, nor the next day, nor for three or four months after; but restrained myself under provocation." Be assured that you are in an excellent way. "Today, when I saw a handsome person, I did not say to myself, Oh, that I could possess her! and how happy is her husband (for he who says this, says too, how happy is her lover), nor did I go on to fancy her in my arms." On this I pat myself on the head and say, Well done, Epictetus; thou hast solved a hard problem, harder than the chief syllogism. But if the lady herself should happen to be willing and give me intimations of it, and send for me and press my hand and place herself next to me, and I should then forbear and get the victory—that would be a triumph beyond all the forms of logic. This is the proper subject for exultation, and not one's power in handling the syllogism.

How then is this to be effected? Be willing to approve yourself to yourself. Be willing to appear beautiful in the sight of God; be desirous to converse in purity with your own pure mind, and with God; and then, if any such semblance comes upon you, Plato directs you: "Have recourse to expiations; go a suppliant to the temples of the deities who ward off evil deities." It is sufficient, however, if you set before yourself the example of wise and good men, whether alive or dead, and compare your conduct with theirs. Go to Socrates, and see him placed beside his beloved, yet not seduced by youth and beauty. Consider what a victory he was conscious of obtaining; what an Olympic triumph! How near does he rank to Hercules![1] So that, by heaven! one might justly salute him, "Hail, wondrous man!"[2] instead of those sorry boxers and wrestlers, and the gladiators who resemble them.

By placing such an example before you, you will conquer any alluring semblance, and not be drawn away by it. But in the first place, be not hurried away by excitement; but say, "Semblance, wait for me a little. Let me see what you are, and what you represent; let me try you." Then, afterwards, do not let it go on drawing gay pictures of what will follow; if you do, it will lead you wherever it pleases. But rather oppose to it some good and noble semblance, and banish this base one. If you are habituated to this kind of exercise, you will see what shoulders, what nerves, what sinews, you will have. But now it is mere trifling talk, and nothing more. He is the true athlete who trains himself to deal with such semblances as these. Stay, wretch, do not be hurried away. The combat is great, the achievement divine—for empire, for freedom, for prosperity, for tranquillity. Remember God. Invoke him for your aid and protector, as sailors do Castor and Pollux, in a storm. For what storm is greater than that which arises from these perilous semblances, contending to overturn our reason? Indeed what is the storm itself, but a semblance? For do but take away the fear of death, and let there be as many thunders and lightnings as you please, you will find that to the reason

[1] Hercules is said to have been the author of the gymnastic games, and the first victor. Those who afterwards conquered in wrestling, and the pancratium, were numbered from him.

[2] This pompous title was given to those who had been victors in all the Olympic games.

all is serenity and calm; but if you are once defeated, and say, you will get the victory another time, and then the same thing over again; assure yourself that you will at last be reduced to so weak and wretched a condition, you will not so much as know when you do wrong; but you will even begin to make defenses for your behavior, and thus verify the saying of Hesiod:

With constant ills, the dilatory strive.[1]

CHAPTER   NINETEEN

Concerning Those Who Embrace Philosophy Only in Words

THE science of "the ruling argument"[2] appears to have developed from such principles as these: of the following propositions, any two imply a contradiction to the third. They are these: "That everything past is necessarily true"; "that an impossibility is not the consequence of a possibility"; and, "that something is a possibility, which neither is nor will be true." Diodorus, perceiving this contradiction, combined the first two, to prove that nothing is possible, which neither is nor will be true. Some again hold the second and third—"that something is possible, which neither is nor will be true"; and "that an impossibility is not the consequence of a possibility"; and consequently assert, "that not everything past is neces-

---

[1] *Works and Days*, v. 383.
[2] So-called because it was supposed to be unanswerable.

sarily true." This way Cleanthes and his followers took; whom
Antipater stoutly defends. Others, lastly, maintain the first
and third—"that something is possible, which neither is nor
will be true"; and "that everything past is necessarily true";
but then, "that an impossibility may be the consequence of a
possibility." But all these three propositions cannot be at once
maintained, because of their mutual contradiction.

If anyone should ask me, then, which of them I maintain, I
answer him, that really I cannot tell. But I have heard it related that Diodorus held one opinion about them; the followers of Panthaedes, I think, and Cleanthes, another; and
Chrysippus a third.

"What then is your opinion?"

I express none. I was born to examine things as they appear
to my own mind; to compare what is said by others, and
thence to form some conviction of my own on any topic. Of
these things I had merely technical knowledge. Who was the
father of Hector? Priam. Who were his brothers? Paris and
Deiphobus. Who was his mother? Hecuba. This I have heard
related. From whom? Homer. But I believe Hellanicus, and
other authors, have written on the same subject. And what
better account have I of "the ruling argument"? But, if I
were vain enough, I might, especially at some entertainment,
astonish all the company by an enumeration of authors relating to it. Chrysippus has written wonderfully, in his first
Book of Possibilities. Cleanthes and Archedemus have each
written separately on this subject. Antipater too has written,
not only in his Treatise of Possibilities, but especially in a
discourse on "the ruling argument." Have you not read the
work? "No." Read it then. And what good will it do him?
He will be more trifling and impertinent than he is already.
For what else have you gained by reading it? What conviction have you formed upon this subject? But you tell us of
Helen, and Priam, and the isle of Calypso, something which

never was, nor ever will be.[1] And in these matters, indeed, it is of no great consequence if you retain the story, without forming any principle of your own. But we commit this error much more in dealing with moral questions, than upon such subjects as these.

"Talk to me concerning good and evil."

Hear:

Winds blew from Ilium to Ciconian shores.[2]

Some things are good, some evil, and some indifferent. Now the good are the virtues, and whatever partakes of them; and the evil are vices, and what partakes of vice; the indifferent lie between these, as riches, health, life, death, pleasure, pain.

"How do you know this?"

[Suppose I say] Hellanicus says it, in his Egyptian History. For what does it signify, whether one quotes the history of Hellanicus, or the ethics of Diogenes, or Chrysippus, or Cleanthes? Have you then examined any of these things, and formed convictions of your own? How, for instance, would you conduct yourself on shipboard? Remember these distinctions, when the mast rattles, and some idle fellow stands by you while you are screaming, and says: "For heaven's sake! talk as you did a little while ago. Is it vice to suffer shipwreck; or does it partake of vice?" Would you not take up a piece of wood, and throw it at his head? "What have we to do with you, sir? We are perishing, and you come and make jokes." Again, if Caesar should summon you to answer an accusation, remember these distinctions. If, when you are going in, pale and trembling, anyone should meet you and say, "Why do you tremble, sir? What is this affair you are engaged in? Does Caesar, inside the palace, give virtue and vice to those who ap-

---

[1] In other words you are repeating what you have heard from others rather than expressing your own convictions.

[2] Homer, *Odyssey*, ix. 39. A proverbial expression, signifying "from bad to worse." See Classics Club edition, p. 104.

proach him?" "What, do *you* too insult me, and add to my evils?" "Nay, but tell me, philosopher, why you tremble. Is there any other danger, but death, or a prison, or bodily pain, or exile, or slander?" "Why, what else should there be?" "Are any of these vice; or do they partake of vice? What, then, did you yourself use to say of these things?" "What have you to do with me, sir? My own evils are enough for me." You say rightly. Your own evils are indeed enough for you; your baseness, your cowardice, and that arrogance which you displayed, as you sat in the schools. Why did you assume plumage not your own? Why did you call yourself a Stoic?

Observe yourselves thus in your actions, and you will find of what sect you are. You will find that most of you are Epicureans; a few are Peripatetics, and those without convictions. For by what action will you prove that you think virtue equal, and even superior, to all other things? Show me a Stoic, if you have one. Where? Or how should you? You can show, indeed, a thousand who repeat the Stoic reasonings. But do they repeat the Epicurean less well? Are they not just as perfect in the Peripatetic? Who then is a Stoic? As we call that a Phidian statue which is formed according to the art of Phidias, so show me some one person formed according to the principles which he professes. Show me one who is sick, and happy; in danger, and happy; dying, and happy; exiled, and happy; disgraced, and happy. Show him to me; for, by heaven! I long to see a Stoic. But you have not one fully developed? Show me then one who is developing; one who is approaching towards this character. Do me this favor. Do not refuse an old man a sight which he has never yet seen.

Do you suppose that you are to show the Zeus or Athene of Phidias, a work of ivory or gold? Let any of you show me a human soul desiring to be in unity with God; not to accuse either God or man; not to be disappointed of its desire, nor incur its aversion; not to be angry; not to be envious; not to be jealous; in a word, desiring from a man to become a god;

and, in this poor mortal body, aiming to have fellowship with Zeus. Show him to me. But you cannot.

Why then do you impose upon yourselves, and play tricks with others? Why do you put on a dress not your own, and walk about in it, mere thieves and pilferers of names and things which do not belong to you? I am now your teacher, and you come to be instructed by me. And indeed my aim is to secure you from being restrained, compelled, hindered; to make you free, prosperous, happy; looking to God upon every occasion, great or small. And you come to learn and study these things. Why then do you not finish your work, if you have the proper aims, and I, besides the aim, the proper qualifications? What is wanting? When I see a craftsman, and the materials lying ready, I await the finished work. Now here is the craftsman; here are the materials; what is it we lack? Is not the thing capable of being taught? It is. Is it not in our own power, then? The only thing of all others that is so. Neither riches nor health nor fame nor, in short, anything else is in our power except a right use of the semblances of things. This alone is, by nature, not subject to restraint, not subject to hindrance.

Why then do not you finish it? Tell me the cause. It must be my fault, or yours, or from the nature of the thing. The thing itself is practicable, and the only thing in our power. The fault then must be either in me or in you, or, more truly, in both. Well, then, shall we at length begin to carry such an aim with us? Let us lay aside all that is past. Let us begin. Only believe me, and you shall see.

CHAPTER TWENTY

Against the Epicureans and Academics

THINGS true and evident must, of necessity, be recognized even by those who would contradict them. And perhaps one of the strongest proofs that there is such a thing as evidence is the necessity which compels even those who contradict it to make use of it. If a person, for instance, should deny that anything is universally true, he will be obliged to assert the contrary, that nothing is universally true. Foolish man, not so. For what is this but a universal statement? Again, suppose anyone should come and say, "Know that there is nothing to be known; but all things are uncertain"; or another, "Believe me, for your good, that no man ought to be believed in anything"; or a third, "Learn from me that nothing is to be learned; I tell you this, and will teach the proof of it, if you please." Now what difference is there between such as these, and those who call themselves Academics, who say to us, "Be convinced that no one ever is convinced; believe us, that nobody believes anybody"?

Thus also, when Epicurus would destroy the natural tie between mankind, he makes use of the very thing he is destroying. For what says he? "Be not deceived; be not seduced and mistaken. There is no natural tie between reasonable beings. Believe me. Those who say otherwise mislead and impose upon you." Why are you concerned for us then? Let us be deceived. You will fare never the worse, if all the rest of us are persuaded that there is a natural tie between mankind, and that it is by all means to be preserved. Nay, it will be much safer and better. Why do you give yourself any trouble about us, sir? Why do you break your rest for us? Why do you light your lamp? Why do you rise early? Why do you compose so many volumes? Is it that none of us should be deceived concerning the gods, as if they took any care of men; or that we may not suppose the essence of good consists in anything but in pleasure?

For if these things be so, lie down and sleep, and lead the life of which you judge yourself worthy—that of a mere worm. Eat, drink, debauch, snore. What is it to you, whether others think rightly or wrongly about these things? For what have you to do with us? You take care of sheep, because they afford their milk, their wool, and at last their flesh. And would it not be a desirable thing that men might be so lulled and enchanted by the Stoics as to give themselves up to be milked and fleeced by you, and such as you? Should not these doctrines be taught to your brother Epicureans only, and concealed from the rest of the world; who should by all means, above all things, be persuaded that we have a natural tie with each other, and that self-command is a good thing, in order that all may be kept safe for *you?* Or is this tie to be preserved towards some and not towards others? Towards whom, then, is it to be preserved—towards such as mutually preserve, or such as violate it? And who violate it more than you, who teach such doctrines?

What was it, then, that waked Epicurus from his sleep, and compelled him to write what he did; what else, but that which is of all influences the most powerful among mankind, Nature; which draws every one, however unwilling and reluctant, to its own purposes. For since, she says, you think that there is no tie between mankind, write out this doctrine, and leave it for the use of others; and break your sleep upon that account; and by your own practice confute your own principles. Do we say that Orestes was roused from sleep because driven by the Furies; and was not Epicurus waked by sterner furies and avengers, which would not allow him to rest, but compelled him to utter his own ills, as wine and madness do the priests of Cybele?[1] So strong and unconquerable a thing is human nature! For how can a vine have the properties not of a vine, but of an olive tree; or an olive tree not those of an olive tree, but of a vine? It is impossible. It is inconceivable. Neither, therefore, is it possible for a human creature entirely to lose human affections. But even those who have their organs cut off cannot rid themselves of man's desires; and so Epicurus, when he had cut himself off from the duties of a man, of a master of a family, of a citizen, and of a friend, did not rid himself of human desires; for this he could not do, any more than the idle Academics can throw away or blind their own senses, though this be the point they chiefly labor. What a misfortune is it, when anyone, after having received from Nature standards and rules for the knowledge of truth, does not strive to add to these, and make up their deficiencies; but, on the contrary, endeavors to take away and destroy whatever truth may be known even by them.

What do you say, philosopher? What do you think of piety and sanctity? "If you please, I will prove that they are good." Pray do prove it; that our citizens may be converted, and honor the Deity, and may no longer neglect what is of the highest importance. "Do you accept these proofs, then?" I have, and I thank you. "Since you are so well pleased with this, then, learn these contrary propositions: that there are no gods, or, if there are, that they take no care of mankind, neither have we any concern with them; that this piety and sanctity, so much talked of by many, are only a lie told by boasters and sophists, or perhaps by legislators, to frighten and check wrongdoers." Well done, philosopher. Our citizens are much the better for you. You have already brought back all the youth to a contempt of the Deity. "What! does not this please you, then? Learn next, that justice is nothing; that shame is folly; that the paternal relation is nothing; the filial,

---

[1] These priests were supposed to mutilate themselves.

nothing." Well said, philosopher; persist, convince the youth; that we may have many more to think and talk like you. By such doctrines as these, no doubt, have our well-governed states flourished! Upon these was Sparta founded! Lycurgus, by his laws and method of education, introduced such persuasions as these: that it is not base to be slaves, rather than honorable; nor honorable to be free, rather than base! They who died at Thermopylae, died for such principles as these! And for what principles but these did the Athenians give up their city?[1]

And yet they who talk thus marry, and produce children, and engage in public affairs, and get themselves made priests and prophets. Of whom? Of gods that have no existence. And they consult the Pythian priestess, only to hear falsehoods, and interpret the oracles to others. Oh, monstrous impudence and imposture!

What are you doing, man?[2] You contradict yourself every day; and you will not give up these paltry cavils. When you eat, where do you put your hand—to your mouth, or to your eye? When you bathe, where do you go? Do you ever call a kettle a dish, or a spoon a spit? If I were a slave to one of these gentlemen, were it at the hazard of being flayed every day, I would plague him. "Throw some oil into the bath, boy." I would take pickle sauce and pour it on his head. "What is this?" Really, sir, I was impressed by a certain semblance so like oil as not to be distinguished from it. "Give me the soup." I would carry him a dish full of vinegar. "Did I not ask for the soup?" Yes, sir; this is the soup. "Is not this vinegar?" Why so, more than soup? "Take it and smell it, take it and

---

[1] When in 480 B.C. and again in 479, the Athenians found themselves unable to resist the forces of the Persians, they left their city for Troezen and Salamis, where they boarded their ships and defended the liberty of Greece by their fleet.

[2] There is an abrupt transition here from a discussion of the Epicureans to the Academics who denied the evidence of the senses.

taste it." How do you know, then, but our senses deceive us? If I had three or four fellow-slaves to join with me, I would make him either choke with passion and burst, or change his opinions.

But now they insult us by making use of the gifts of nature, while in words they destroy them. Those must be grateful and modest men, at least, who, while eating their daily bread, dare to say, "We do not know whether there be any such beings as Demeter, or Core, or Pluto." Not to mention that while they possess the blessings of night and day, of the annual seasons, of the stars, the earth, and the sea, they are not the least affected by any of these things; but only study to belch out some trivial problem, and when they have thus relieved themselves, go and bathe; but take not the least care what they say, nor on what subjects, nor to whom, nor what may be the consequence of their talk—whether any well-disposed young man, on hearing such doctrines, may not be affected by them, and so affected as entirely to lose the seeds of his good disposition; whether they may not furnish an adulterer with occasions of growing shameless in his guilt; whether a public plunderer may not find excuses from these doctrines; whether he, who neglects his parents, may not gain additional audacity from this teaching.

"What things, then, in your opinion, are good and evil, fair and base—these things, or those things?" But why should one argue any more with such as these, or interchange opinions, or endeavor to convince them? By Zeus! one might sooner hope to convince the most unnatural debauchees, than those who are thus deaf and blind to their own ills.

CHAPTER TWENTY-ONE

Of Inconsistency

THERE are some things which men confess with ease, and others with difficulty. No one, for instance, will confess himself a fool or a blockhead; but, on the contrary, you will hear everyone say, "I wish my fortune were in proportion to my abilities." But they easily confess themselves fearful, and say, "I am somewhat timorous, I confess; but in other respects you will not find me a fool." No one will easily confess himself intemperate in his desires, upon no account dishonest, nor indeed envious or meddlesome; but many confess themselves to have the weakness of being compassionate. What is the reason of all this? The principal reason is an inconsistency and confusion in what relates to good and evil. But different people have different motives, and in general, whatever they imagine to be base, they do not absolutely confess. Fear and compassion they imagine to belong to a well-meaning disposition; but stupidity, to a slave. Offenses against society they do not own; but in most faults they are brought to a confession chiefly from imagining that there is something involuntary in them, as in fear and compassion. And though a person should in some measure confess himself intemperate in his desires, he accuses his passion, and expects forgiveness, as for an involuntary fault. But dishonesty is not imagined to be, by any means, involuntary. In jealousy too there is something they suppose involuntary and this likewise, in some degree, they confess.

Conversing therefore with such men, thus confused, thus ignorant what they say, and what are or are not their ills, whence they have them, and how they may get rid of them, it is worth while, I think, to ask oneself continually, "Am

I too one of these? What do I imagine myself to be? How do I conduct myself—as a prudent, as a temperate man? Do I, too, ever talk at this rate—that I am prepared for anything that may come? Have I that persuasion that I know nothing which becomes one who knows nothing? Do I go to a master as to an oracle, prepared to obey; or do I also, like a mere driveler, enter the school only to learn and understand books which I did not understand before, or perhaps to explain them to others?"

You have been fighting at home with your slave; you have turned the house upside-down, and alarmed the neighborhood; and do you come to me with a pompous show of wisdom, and sit and criticize how I explain a sentence, how I prate whatever comes into my head? Do you come, envious and dejected that nothing has come from home for you, and in the midst of the disputations sit thinking on nothing but how your father or your brother may treat you? "What are they saying about me at home? Now they think I am improving, and say, He will come back with universal knowledge. I wish I could learn everything before my return; but this requires much labor, and nobody sends me anything. The baths are very bad at Nicopolis; and things go very ill both at home and here."

After all this, it is said, nobody is the better for the philosophic school. Why, who goes to the school? I mean, who comes to be reformed; who, to submit his principles to correction; who, with a sense of his wants? Why do you wonder, then, that you bring back from the school the very thing you carried there? For you do not come to lay aside, or correct, or change, your principles. How should you? Far from it. Rather consider this, therefore, whether you have not what you have come for. You have come to talk about theorems. Well; and are you not more impertinently talkative than you were? Do not these paltry theorems furnish you with matter for ostentation? Do you not solve convertible and hypothetical syllogisms? Why, then, are you still displeased, if you have the very thing for which you came?

"Very true; but if my child or my brother should die; or if I must die or be tortured myself, what good will these things do me?" Why, did you come for *this*? Did you sit with me for *this*? Was it for this that you lighted your lamp, or sat up at night? Or did you, when you went into the covered walk, propose any delusive semblance to your own mind to be discussed, instead of a syllogism? Did any of you ever go through such a subject jointly? And after all, you say, theorems are useless. To whom? To such as apply them ill. For medicines for the eyes are not useless to those who apply them when and as they ought. Fomentations are not useless, dumb-bells are not useless; but they are useless to some, and on the contrary, useful to others. If you should ask me, now, are syllogisms useful? I should answer that they are useful; and, if you please, I will show you how. "Will they be of service to me, then?" Why, did you ask, man, whether they would be useful to *you*, or in general? If anyone in a dysentery should ask me whether vinegar is useful, I should answer, it is. "Is it useful for *me*, then?" I say, no. First try to get the flux stopped, and the ulceration healed. Do you too first get your ulcers healed, your fluxes stopped. Quiet your mind, and bring it free from distraction to the school; and then you will know what power there is in reasoning.

CHAPTER TWENTY-TWO

Of Friendship

To whatever objects a person devotes his attention, these objects he probably loves. Do men ever devote their attention, then, to [what they think] evils? By no means. Or even to things indifferent? No, nor this. It remains, then, that good must be the sole object of their attention; and if of their attention, of their love too. Whoever, therefore, understands good, is capable likewise of love; and he who cannot distinguish good from evil, and things indifferent from both, how is it possible that he can love? The wise person alone, then, is capable of loving.

"How so? I am not this wise person, yet I love my child."

I protest it surprises me that you should, in the first place, confess yourself unwise. For in what are you deficient? Have not you the use of your senses? Do you not distinguish the semblances of things? Do you not provide such food and clothing and habitation as are suitable to you? Why then do you confess that you want wisdom? In truth, because you are often struck and disconcerted by semblances, and their speciousness gets the better of you; and hence you sometimes suppose the very same things to be good, then evil, and lastly, neither; and, in a word, you grieve, you fear, you envy, you are disconcerted, you change. Is it from this that you confess yourself unwise? And are you not changeable too in love? Riches, pleasure, in short, the very same things, you sometimes consider good, and at other times evil. And do you not consider the same persons too alternately as good and bad, at one time treating them with kindness, at another with enmity; at one time commending, and at another censuring them?

"Yes. This too is the case with me."

Well, then; can he who is deceived in another be his friend, think you?

"No, surely."

Or does he who loves him with a changeable affection bear him genuine good will?

"Nor he, neither."

Or he who now vilifies, then admires him?

"Nor he."

Do you not often see little dogs caressing and playing with each other, so that you would say nothing could be more friendly? But to learn what this friendship is, throw a bit of meat between them, and you will see. Do you too throw a bit of land between you and your son, and you will see that he will quickly wish you under ground, and you him; and then you, no doubt, on the other hand will exclaim, What a son have I brought up! He would bury me alive! Throw in a pretty girl, and the old fellow and the young one will both fall in love with her; or let fame or danger intervene, the words of the father of Admetus will be yours:

> *You love to see the light. Doth not your father?*
> *You fain would still behold it. Would not he?*[1]

Do you suppose that he did not love his own child when it was little; that he was not in agonies when it had a fever, and often wished to undergo that fever in its stead? But, after all, when the trial comes home, you see what expression he uses. Were not Eteocles and Polynices born of the same mother and of the same father? Were they not brought up, and did they not live and eat and sleep, together? Did they not kiss and fondle each other? So that anyone who saw them would have laughed at all the paradoxes which philosophers

---

[1] Euripides, *Alcestis*, v. 691. Pheres, the father of Admetus, is defending himself for not consenting to die in place of his son.

utter about love. And yet when a kingdom, like a bit of meat, was thrown between them, see what they say—

> *Polynices.* Where wilt thou stand before the towers?
> *Eteocles.* Why askest thou this of me?
> *Pol.* I will oppose myself to thee, to slay thee.
> *Et.* I too am seized by this desire.[1]

Such are the prayers they offer. Be not therefore deceived. No living being is held by anything so strongly as by its own needs. Whatever therefore appears a hindrance to these, be it brother or father or child or mistress or friend, is hated, abhorred, execrated; for by nature it loves nothing like its own needs. This motive is father and brother and family and country and God. Whenever, therefore, the gods seem to hinder this, we vilify even them, and throw down their statues, and burn their temples; as Alexander ordered the temple of Aesculapius to be burned, because he had lost the man he loved.

When, therefore, anyone identifies his interest with those of sanctity, virtue, country, parents, and friends, all these are secured; but whenever he places his interest in anything else than friends, country, family, and justice, then these all give way, borne down by the weight of self-interest. For wherever *I* and *mine* are placed, thither must every living being gravitate. If in body, that will sway us; if in our own will, that; if in externals, these. If, therefore, I rest my personality in the will, then only shall I be a friend, a son, or a father, such as I ought. For in that case it will be for my interest to preserve the faithful, the modest, the patient, the abstinent, the beneficent character; to keep the relations of life inviolate. But if I place my personality in one thing, and virtue in another, the doctrine of Epicurus will stand its ground, that virtue is nothing, or mere opinion.

---

[1] Euripides, *Phoenissae*, v. 630, 631.

From this ignorance it was that the Athenians and Lacedemonians quarreled with each other, and the Thebans with both; the Persian king with Greece, and the Macedonians with both; and now the Romans with the Getes. And in still remoter times the Trojan war arose from the same cause. Alexander [Paris] was the guest of Menelaus; and whoever had seen the mutual proofs of good will that passed between them would never have believed that they were not friends. But a tempting bait, a pretty woman, was thrown in between them; and over her arose a war. At present, therefore, when you see that dear brothers have, in appearance, but one soul, do not immediately pronounce upon their love; not though they should swear it, and affirm it was impossible to live apart. For the governing faculty of a bad man is faithless, unsettled, undiscriminating, successively vanquished by different semblances. Do not inquire, as others do, whether they were born of the same parents, and brought up together, and under the same teacher; but this thing only, in what they place their interest—in externals or in their own wills. If in externals, you can no more pronounce them friends, than you can call them faithful, or constant, or brave, or free; nay, nor even truly men, if you are wise. For it is no principle of humanity that makes them bite and vilify each other, and take possession of public assemblies, as wild beasts do of solitudes and mountains; and convert courts of justice into dens of robbers; that prompts them to be intemperate, adulterers, seducers; or leads them into other offenses that men commit against each other—all from that one single error, by which they risk themselves and their own concerns on things uncontrollable by will.

But if you hear that these men in reality suppose good to be placed only in the will, and in a right use of things as they appear, no longer take the trouble of inquiring if they are father and son, or old companions and acquaintances; but boldly pronounce that they are friends, and also that they are faithful and just. For where else can friendship be found, but where joined with fidelity and modesty, a devotion to virtue alone?

"Well; but such a one paid me the utmost regard for so long a time, and did he not love me?"

How can you tell, foolish man, if that regard be any other than he pays to his shoes, or his horse, when he cleans them? And how do you know but that when you cease to be a necessary utensil, he may throw you away, like a broken platter?

"Well; but it is my wife, and we have lived together many years."

And how long did Eriphyle live with Amphiaraus, becoming the mother of many children? But a necklace came between them. What does a necklace signify? One's conviction concerning such things. This turned her into a savage animal; this cut asunder all love, and, allowed her to remain neither the wife nor the mother.[1]

Whoever, therefore, among you studies either to be or to gain a friend, let him dig out all false convictions by the root, hate them, drive them utterly out of his soul. Thus, in the first place, he will be secure from inward reproaches and contests, from vacillation and self-torment. Then, with respect to others, to every like-minded person he will be without disguise; to such as are unlike he will be patient, mild, gentle, and ready to forgive them, as failing in points of the greatest importance; but severe to none, being fully convinced of Plato's doctrine, that the soul is never willingly deprived of truth. Without all this, you may, in many respects, live as friends do; and drink and lodge and travel together, and even be born

---

[1] Amphiaraus married Eriphyle, the sister of Adrastus, king of Argos, and was betrayed by her for a golden chain.

of the same parents; and so may serpents too; but neither they nor you can ever be really friends, while your accustomed principles remain brutal and execrable.

CHAPTER TWENTY-THREE

Of Eloquence

A BOOK will always be read with more pleasure and ease, if it be written in fair characters; and so everyone will the more easily attend to discourses likewise, if ornamented with proper and beautiful expressions. It ought not then to be said, that there is no such thing as the faculty of eloquence; for this would be at once the part of an impious and timid person—impious, because he dishonors the gifts of God; just as if he should deny any use in the faculties of sight, hearing, and speech itself. Has God then given you eyes in vain? Is it in vain that he has infused into them such a strong and active spirit as to be able to represent the forms of distant objects? What messenger is so quick and diligent? Is it in vain that he has made the intermediate air so yielding and elastic that sight penetrates through it? And is it in vain that he has made the light, without which all the rest would be useless? Man, be not ungrateful, nor, on the other hand, unmindful of your superior advantages; but for sight and hearing, and indeed for life itself, and the supports of it, as fruits and wine and oil, be thankful to God; but remember that he has given you another thing, superior to them all, which uses them, proves them, estimates the value of each. For what is it that pronounces upon the value of each of these faculties? Is it the

faculty itself? Did you ever perceive the faculty of sight or
hearing to say anything concerning itself; or wheat, or barley,
or horses, or dogs? No. These things are appointed as instruments and servants, to obey that which is capable of using
things as they appear.

If you inquire the value of anything, of what do you inquire? What is the faculty that answers you? How then can
any faculty be superior to this, which uses all the rest as instruments, and tries and pronounces concerning each of them?
For which of them knows what itself is, and what is its own
value? Which of them knows when it is to be used, and when
not? Which is it that opens and shuts the eyes, and turns
them away from improper objects? Is it the faculty of sight?
No; but that of moral purpose. Which is it that opens and
shuts the ears? By which faculty are they made curious and
inquisitive, or, on the contrary, deaf, and unaffected by what
is said? Is it the faculty of hearing? No; but that of moral
purpose. This, then, recognizing itself to exist amidst other
faculties, all blind and deaf, and unable to discern anything
but those offices in which they are appointed to minister and
serve, itself alone sees clearly, and distinguishes the value of
each of the rest. Will this, I say, inform us that anything is
supreme but itself? What can the eye, when it is opened, do
more than see? But whether we ought to look upon the wife
of anyone, and in what manner, what is it that decides us?
The faculty of moral purpose. Whether we ought to believe,
or disbelieve what is said; or whether, if we do believe, we
ought to be moved by it, or not, what is it that decides us? Is
it not the faculty of moral purpose?

Again, the very faculty of eloquence, and that which orna-
ments discourse, if any such peculiar faculty there be, what
else does it do than merely ornament and arrange expressions,
as curlers do the hair? But whether it be better to speak or to
be silent, or better to speak in this or in that manner, whether
this be decent or indecent, and the season and use of each,

what is it that decides for us, but the faculty of moral purpose?
What, then; would you have it appear, and bear testimony
against itself? What means this? If the case be thus, then that
which serves may be superior to that to which it is subservient; the horse to the rider, the dog to the hunter, the instrument to the musician, or servants to the king.[1] What is it that
makes use of all the rest? Moral purpose. What takes care of
all? Moral purpose. What destroys the whole man, at one time,
by hunger; at another, by a rope or a precipice? Moral purpose. Has man, then, anything stronger than this? And how
is it possible that what is liable to restraint should be stronger
than what is not? What has a natural power to restrain the
faculty of sight? Moral purpose and its workings. And it is
the same with the faculties of hearing and of speech. And
what natural power can restrain moral purpose? Nothing
beyond itself, only its own perversion. Therefore in moral
purpose alone is vice; in moral purpose alone is virtue.

Since, then, moral purpose is such a faculty, and placed in
authority over all the rest, suppose it to come forth and say
to us that the body is of all things the most excellent! If even
the body itself pronounced itself to be the most excellent, it
could not be borne. But now, what is it, Epicurus, that pronounces all this? What was it that composed volumes concerning "The End," "The Nature of Things," "The Rule";
that assumed a philosophic beard; that as it was dying wrote
that it was "then spending its last and happiest day"?[2] Was this
the body, or was it the faculty of moral purpose? And can
you, then, without madness, admit anything to be superior to
this? Are you in reality so deaf and blind? What, then; does
anyone dishonor the other faculties? Heaven forbid! Does

---

[1] This obscure passage was probably inserted here by an ancient
editor. Essentially, it repeats the preceding paragraph.

[2] These words are part of a letter written by Epicurus, when he was
dying, to one of his friends. The titles previously given are those of
treatises by Epicurus.

anyone assert that there is no use or excellence in the faculty of sight? Heaven forbid! It would be stupid, impious, and ungrateful to God. But we render to each its due. There is some use in an ass, though not so much as in an ox; and in a dog, though not so much as in a servant; and in a servant, though not so much as in the citizens; and in the citizens, though not so much as in the magistrates. And though some are more excellent than others, those uses which the last afford are not to be despised.

The faculty of eloquence has thus its value, though not equal to that of moral purpose. When therefore I talk thus, let not anyone suppose that I would have you neglect eloquence, any more than your eyes, or ears, or hands, or feet, or clothes, or shoes. But if you ask me what is the most excellent of things, what shall I say? I cannot say eloquence, but a right moral purpose; for it is this which makes use of that and of all the other faculties, whether great or small. If this be set right, a bad man becomes good; if it be wrong, a good man becomes wicked. By this we are unfortunate or fortunate; we disapprove or approve each other. In a word, it is this which, neglected, forms unhappiness; and, well cultivated, happiness.

But to take away the faculty of eloquence, and to say that it is in reality nothing, is not only ungrateful to those who gave it, but cowardly too. For such a person seems to me to be afraid that, if there be any such faculty, we may on occasion be compelled to respect it. Such are they too, who deny any difference between beauty and deformity. Was it possible, then, to be affected in the same manner by seeing Thersites, as by Achilles; by Helen, as by any other woman? These also are the foolish and clownish notions of those who are ignorant of the nature of things, and afraid that whoever perceives such a difference must presently be carried away and overcome. But the great point is to leave to each thing its own proper faculty, and then to see what the value of that faculty is; to learn what is the principal thing, and upon every occasion to follow that, and to make it the chief object of our attention; to consider other things as trifling in comparison with this, and yet, so far as we are able, not to neglect even these. We ought, for instance, to take care of our eyes; yet not as of the principal thing, but only on account of that which is principal; because that can no otherwise preserve its own nature, than by making a due estimate of the rest, and preferring some to others.

What is the usual practice, then? That of a traveler who, returning into his own country, and meeting on the way with a good inn, being pleased with the inn, should remain there. Have you forgotten your intention, man? You were not traveling to this place, but only through it. "But this is a fine place." And how many other fine inns are there, and how many pleasant fields, yet they are simply as a means of passage. What is the real business? To return to your country; to relieve the anxieties of your family; to perform the duties of a citizen; to marry, have children, and go through the public offices. For you did not travel in order to choose the finest places; but to return, to live in that where you were born, and of which you are appointed a citizen.

Such is the present case. Because, by speech and such instruction, we are to perfect our education and purify our own will and rectify that faculty which deals with things as they appear; and because, for the statement of theorems, a certain diction, and some variety and subtlety of discourse are needful, many, captivated by these very things—one by diction, another by syllogisms, a third by convertible propositions, just as our traveler was by the good inn—go no further, but sit down and waste their lives shamefully there, as if amongst the sirens. Your business, man, was to prepare yourself for such use of the semblances of things as nature demands; not to fail in what you seek, or incur what you shun; never to be disappointed or unfortunate, but free, unrestrained, uncompelled; conformed to the divine administration, obedient to that; finding fault with nothing, but able to say, from your whole soul, the verses which begin,

Conduct me, Zeus, and thou, O Destiny,[1]

While you have such a business before you, will you be so pleased with a pretty form of expression, or a few theorems, as to choose to stay and live with them, forgetful of your home, and say, "They are fine things!" Why, who says they are not fine things? But only as a means; as an inn. For what hinders one speaking like Demosthenes from being miserable? What hinders a logician equal to Chrysippus from being wretched, sorrowful, envious, vexed, unhappy? Nothing. You see, then, that these are merely unimportant inns, and what concerns you is quite another thing. When I talk thus to some, they suppose that I am setting aside all care about eloquence and about theorems; but I do not object to that, only the dwelling on these things incessantly, and placing our hopes there. If anyone, by maintaining this, hurts his hearers, place me amongst those hurtful people; for I cannot, when I see one thing to be the principal and most excellent, call another so to please you.

---

[1] A Fragment of Cleanthes, quoted in full in Enchiridion.

CHAPTER TWENTY-FOUR

To a Person Whom He Thought Unworthy

WHEN a certain person said to him, "I have often come to you with a desire of hearing you, and you have never given me any answer; but now, if possible, I entreat you to say something to me,"— Do you think, replied Epictetus, that as in other things, so in speaking, there is an art by which he who understands it speaks skillfully, and he who does not unskillfully?

"I do think so."

He, then, who by speaking both benefits himself, and is able to benefit others, must speak skillfully; but he who injures and is injured, must be unskillful in this art. For you may find some speakers injured, and others benefited. And are all hearers benefited by what they hear? Or will you find some benefited, and some hurt?

"Both."

Then those who hear skillfully are benefited, and those who hear unskillfully, hurt.

"Granted."

Is there any art of hearing, then, as well as of speaking?

"It seems so."

If you please, consider it thus. To whom think you that the practice of music belongs?

"To a musician."

To whom the proper formation of a statue?

"To a sculptor."

And do you not imagine some art necessary even to view a statue skillfully?

"I do."

If, therefore, to speak properly belongs to one who is skillful, do you not see that to hear profitably belongs likewise to
one who is skillful? For the present, however, if you please,
let us say no more of doing things perfectly and profitably,
since we are both far enough from anything of that kind; but
this seems to be universally admitted, that he who would hear
philosophers needs some kind of exercise in hearing. Is it not
so? Tell me, then, on what I shall speak to you. On what subject are you able to hear me?

"On good and evil."

The good and evil of what—of a horse?

"No."

Of an ox?

"No."

What, then; of a man?

"Yes."

Do we know, then, what man is; what his nature is, what
our idea of him, and how far our ears are open in this respect
to him? Nay, do you understand what nature is; or are you
able in any degree to comprehend me when I come to say,
"But I must use a demonstration for you"? How can I? Do
you know what a proof is, or how a thing is demonstrated,
or by what methods; or what resembles a demonstration, and
yet is not a demonstration? Do you know what true or false
is; what follows what, and what is contradictory or out of
agreement or out of harmony with what? But I must excite
you to study philosophy. How shall I show you that contradiction in the ideas of mankind, by which they differ concerning good and evil, profitable and unprofitable, when you
know not what *contradiction* means? Show me, then, what
I shall gain by discoursing with you. Excite an inclination in
me, as a proper pasture excites an inclination to eating, in a
sheep; for if you offer him a stone or a piece of bread, he will
not be excited.

Thus we too have certain natural inclinations to speaking, when the hearer appears to be somebody, when he gives us encouragement; but if he sits by like a stone or a tuft of grass, how can he excite any desire in a man? Does a vine say to an husbandman, "Take care of me"? No; but invites him to take care of it, by showing him that, if he does, it will reward him for his care. Who is there, whom bright and agreeable children do not attract to play, and creep, and prattle with them? But who ever wanted to divert himself by playing or braying with an ass; for be the creature ever so little, it is still a little ass.

"Why then do you say nothing to me?"

I have only this to say to you; that whoever is utterly ignorant of who he is and why he was born, and in what kind of a universe and in what society he lives; what things are good and what evil, what fair and what base; who understands neither discourse nor demonstration, nor what is true nor what is false, nor is able to distinguish between them; such a one will neither exert his desires, nor aversions, nor pursuits in accordance with Nature; he will neither aim, nor assent, nor deny, nor suspend his judgment conformably to Nature; but will wander up and down, entirely deaf and blind, supposing himself to be somebody, while he is nobody. Is there anything new in all this? Is not this ignorance the cause of all the errors that have happened, from the very origin of mankind? Why did Agamemnon and Achilles differ? Was it not for want of knowing what is advantageous, what disadvantageous? Does not one of them say it is advantageous to restore Chryseis to her father; the other, that it is not? Does not one say that he ought to take away the prize of the other; the other, that he ought not? Did they not by these means forget who they were, and for what purpose they had come there? Why, what did you come for, man—to win mistresses, or to fight? "To fight." With whom—Trojans or Greeks? "With the Trojans." Leaving Hector, then, do you draw your sword upon your own king? And do you, good sir, forgetting the duties of a king—

Intrusted with a nation and its cares,[1]—

go to squabbling about a girl with the bravest of your allies, whom you ought by every method to conciliate and preserve? And will you be inferior to a subtle priest who pays his court anxiously to you fine gladiators? You see the effects produced by ignorance of what is truly advantageous.

"But I am rich, as well as other people." What, richer than Agamemnon? "But I am handsome too." What, handsomer than Achilles? "But I have fine hair too." Had not Achilles finer and brighter? Yet he never combed it exquisitely, nor curled it. "But I am strong too." Can you lift such a stone, then, as Hector or Ajax? "But I am of a noble family too." Is your mother a goddess, or your father descended from Zeus? And what good did all this do Achilles, when he sat crying for a girl? "But I am an orator." And was not he? Do you not see how he treated the most eloquent of the Greeks— Odysseus and Phoenix—how he struck them dumb? This is all I have to say to you; and even this against my inclination.

"Why so?"

Because you have not excited me to it. For what can I see in you to excite me, as spirited horses their riders? Your person? That you disfigure. Your dress? That is effeminate. Your behavior? Your look? Absolutely nothing. When you would hear a philosopher, do not say to him, "What do you have to say to me?"; but only show yourself fit and worthy to hear; and you will find how you will move him to speak.

---

[1] Homer, *Iliad*. See Classics Club edition, p. 23.

CHAPTER TWENTY-FIVE

How Logic Is Necessary

WHEN one of the company said to him, "Convince me that logic is necessary,"—Would you have me demonstrate it to you? he said. "Yes." Then I must use a demonstrative form of argument. "Granted." And how will you know, then, whether my arguments mislead you? On this, the man being silent, Epictetus said, You see that even by your own confession, logic is necessary; since without it, you cannot even learn whether it is necessary or not.

CHAPTER TWENTY-SIX

What Is the Test of Error?

EVERY error implies a contradiction; for since he who errs does not wish to err, but to be in the right, it is evident that he acts contrary to his wish. What does a thief desire to attain? His own interest. If, then, thieving is really against his interest, he acts contrary to his own desire. Now, every rational soul naturally dislikes contradiction; but so long as anyone is ignorant that it is a contradiction, nothing restrains him from acting contradictorily; but whenever he discovers it, he must as necessarily renounce and avoid it, as anyone must dissent from a falsehood whenever he perceives it to be a falsehood; only while the falsehood is not evident, he assents to it as to a truth.

He, then, is gifted in speech, and excels at once in exhortation and conviction, who can disclose to each man the contradiction by which he errs, and prove clearly to him how he is not doing what he wishes and is doing what he does not wish. For, if that is shown, he will depart from it of his own accord; but, till you have shown it, do not be surprised that he remains where he is; for he proceeds on the semblance of acting rightly. Hence Socrates, relying on this faculty, used to say, "It is not my custom to cite any other witness for my assertions; but I am always contented with my opponent. I call and summon him for my witness; and his single evidence serves instead of all others." For he knew that if a rational soul is moved by anything, the scale must turn whether it will or no. Show the governing faculty of Reason a contradiction, and it will renounce it; but till you have shown it, rather blame yourself than him who remains unconvinced.

BOOK III

CHAPTER ONE

Of Personal Adornment

A CERTAIN young student of rhetoric coming to him with his hair too elaborately ornamented, and his dress very fine, Tell me, said Epictetus, whether you do not think some horses and dogs beautiful, and so of all other animals.

"I do."

Are some men, then, likewise beautiful, and others deformed?

"Certainly."

Do we pronounce all these beautiful the same way, then, or each in some way peculiar to itself? You will judge of it by this; since we see a dog naturally formed for one thing, a horse for another, and a nightingale, for instance, for another, therefore, in general, it will be correct to pronounce each of them beautiful so far as it is developed suitably to its own nature; but since the nature of each is different, I think each of them must be beautiful in a different way. Is it not so?

"Agreed."

Then what makes a dog beautiful makes a horse deformed, and what makes a horse beautiful makes a dog deformed, if their natures are different.

"So it seems."

For, I suppose, what makes a good pancratiast [1] makes no good wrestler, and a very ridiculous racer; and the very same person who appears well as pentathlete might make a very ill figure in wrestling.

"Very true."

What, then, makes a man beautiful? Is it on the same principle that a dog or a horse is beautiful?

"The same."

What is it, then, that makes a dog beautiful?

"That excellence which belongs to a dog."

What a horse?

"The excellence of a horse."

What a man? Must it not be the excellence belonging to a man? If, then, you would appear beautiful, young man, strive for human excellence.

"What is that?"

Consider whom you praise, when unbiased by partiality; is it the honest or dishonest?

"The honest."

The sober or the dissolute?

"The sober."

The temperate or the intemperate?

"The temperate."

Then, if you make yourself such a character, you know that you will make yourself beautiful; but while you neglect these things, though you use every contrivance to appear beautiful, you must necessarily be deformed.

I know not how to say anything further to you; for if I speak what I think, you will be vexed, and perhaps go away and return no more. And if I do not speak, consider what I

---

[1] These are the names of combatants in the Olympic games. A Pancratiast was one who united the exercises of wrestling and boxing. A Pentathlete, one who contended in all the five games of leaping, running, throwing the discus, darting, and wrestling.

am doing. You come to me to be improved, and I do not improve you; and you come to me as to a philosopher, and I do not speak like a philosopher. Besides, how could it be consistent with my duty towards yourself, to pass you by as incorrigible? If, hereafter, you should come to have sense, you will accuse me with reason: "What did Epictetus observe in me, that, when he saw me come to him in such a shameful condition, he overlooked it, and never said so much as a word about it? Did he so absolutely despair of me? Was I not young? Was I not able to hear reason? How many young men, at that age, are guilty of many such errors! I am told of one Polemo, who, from a most dissolute youth, became totally changed.[1] Suppose he did not think I should become a Polemo, he might nevertheless have set my hair to rights, he might have stripped off my bracelets and rings, he might have prevented my plucking my hairs. But when he saw me dressed like a— what shall I say?—he was silent." I do not say like what; when you come to your senses, you will say it yourself, and will know what it is, and who they are who adopt such a dress.

If you should hereafter lay this to my charge, what excuse could I make? "Yes, but if I do speak, he will not regard me." Why, did Laius regard Apollo? Did not he go and get intoxicated, and bid farewell to the oracle? What then? Did this hinder Apollo from telling him the truth? Now, I am uncertain whether you will obey me or not; but Apollo positively knew that Laius would not obey him, and yet he spoke.[2] And why did he speak? You may as well ask, why is he Apollo; why does he deliver oracles; why has he placed himself in such a post as a prophet, and the fountain of truth, to whom the inhabitants of the world should come? Why is KNOW

---

[1] By accidentally visiting the school of Xenocrates, Polemo became a philosopher, and eventually head of the Academy.

[2] Laius, king of Thebes, petitioned Apollo for a son. The oracle answered him, that if Laius became a father, he should perish by the hand of his son. The prediction was fulfilled by Oedipus.

THYSELF inscribed on the front of his temple, when no one heeds it?

Did Socrates prevail upon all who came to him, to take care of their own character? Not one in a thousand; but being, as he himself declares, divinely appointed to such a post, he never deserted it. What said he even to his judges? "If you would acquit me, on condition that I should no longer act as I do now, I would not accept it, nor desist; but I will accost all I meet, whether young or old, and interrogate them in just the same manner; but particularly you, my fellow citizens, since you are more nearly related to me." "Are you so curious and officious, Socrates? What is it to you, how we act?" "What say you? While you are of the same community and the same kindred with me, will you be careless of yourself, and show yourself a bad citizen to the city, a bad kinsman to your kindred, and a bad neighbor to your neighborhood?" "Why, who are you?" Here one ought nobly to say, "I am he who ought to take care of mankind." For it is not every little heifer that dares resist the lion; but if the bull should come up, and resist him, would you say to him, "Who are you? What business is it of yours?" In every species, man, there is some one quality which by nature excels—in oxen, in dogs, in bees, in horses. Do not say to the superior individual, "Who are you?" If you do, it will, somehow or other, find a voice to tell you, "I am like the purple thread in a garment. Do not expect me to be like the rest, nor find fault with my nature, which has distinguished me from others."

"What, then; am I such a one? How should I be?" Indeed, are you such a one as to be able to hear the truth? I wish you were. But, however, since I am condemned to wear a gray beard and a cloak, and you come to me as a philosopher, I will not treat you cruelly, nor as if I despaired of you; but will ask you, Who is it, young man, whom you would render beautiful? Know, first, who you are; and then adorn yourself accordingly.

You are a human being; that is, a mortal animal, capable of a rational use of things as they appear. And what is this rational use? A perfect conformity to nature. What have you, then, particularly excellent? Is it the animal part? No. The mortal? No. That which is capable of the mere use of these things? No. The excellence lies in the rational part. Adorn and beautify this; but leave your hair to him who formed it as he thought good.

Well, what other appellations have you? Are you a man or a woman? A man. Then adorn yourself as a man, not as a woman. A woman is naturally smooth and delicate, and if hairy, is a monster, and shown among the monsters at Rome. It is the same thing in a man *not* to be hairy; and if he is by nature not so, he is a monster. But if he plucks it out, what shall we do with him? Where shall we show him, and how shall we advertise him? "A man to be seen, who would rather be a woman." What a scandalous show! Who would not wonder at such an advertisement? I believe, indeed, that these very persons themselves would; not apprehending that it is the very thing of which they are guilty.

Of what have you to accuse your nature, sir, that it has made you a man? Why, were all to be born women, then? In that case what would have been the use of your finery? For whom would you have made yourself fine, if all were women? But the whole affair displeases you. Go to work upon the whole, then. Remove your manhood itself and make yourself a woman entirely, that we may no longer be deceived, nor you be half man, half woman. To whom would you be agreeable—to the women? Be agreeable to them as a man.

"Yes, but they are pleased with fops."

Go hang yourself. Suppose they were pleased with sexual perverts, would you be one? Is this your business in life? Were you born to please dissolute women? Shall we make such a one as you, in the Corinthian republic for instance, governor of the city, master of the youth, commander of the army, or director of the public games? Will you pursue the same practices when you are married? For whom, and for what? Will you be the father of children, and introduce them into the state, such as yourself? Oh, what a fine citizen, and senator, and orator! Surely, young man, we ought to pray for a succession of young men disposed and bred like you!

Now, when you have once heard this discourse, go home and say to yourself, It is not Epictetus who has told me all these things—for how should he?—but some propitious god through him; for it would never have entered the head of Epictetus, who is not used to dispute with anyone. Well, let us obey God then, that we may not incur the divine displeasure. If a crow gives you a sign by his croaking, it is not the crow that gives it, but God through him. And if you have any sign given to you through the human voice, does God not cause that man to tell it to you, that you may know the divine power which acts thus variously, and gives sign of the greatest and principal things through the noblest messenger? What else does the poet mean, when he says—

> *Since we forewarned him,*
> *Sending forth Hermes, watchful Argicide,*
> *Neither to slay, nor woo another's wife.*[1]

Hermes, descending from heaven, was to warn him; and the gods now, likewise, send a Hermes, the Argicide, as messenger to warn you not to overturn the well-appointed order of things, or be absorbed in fopperies; but suffer a man to be a man, and a woman to be a woman; a beautiful man to be beautiful as a man; a deformed man to be deformed as a man; for you are not flesh and hair, but moral purpose. If you take care to have this beautiful, you will be beautiful. But all this while, I dare not tell you that you are deformed; for I fancy you would rather hear anything than this. But consider what

---

[1] Homer, *Odyssey*. See Classics Club edition, p. 4.

Socrates says to the most beautiful and blooming of all men, Alcibiades. "Endeavor to make yourself beautiful." What does he mean to say to him—"Curl your locks, and pluck hairs from your legs"? Heaven forbid! But rather, "Regulate your moral purpose; throw away your wrong principles."

"What is to be done with the poor body, then?"

Leave it to nature. Another has taken care of such things. Give them up to him.

"What, then; must one be unclean?"

By no means; but act in conformity to your nature. A man should care for his body, as a man; a woman, as a woman; a child, as a child. If not, let us pluck out the mane of a lion, that he may not be slovenly; and the comb of a cock, for he too should be tidy. Yes, but let it be as a cock; and a lion, as a lion; and a hound, as a hound.

CHAPTER TWO

In What a Well-Trained Man Should
Exercise Himself, and That We
Neglect the Principal Things

THERE are three fields of study, in which he who would be wise and good must be exercised: that of the *desires* and *aversions*, that he may not be disappointed of the one, nor incur the other; that of the *pursuits* and *avoidances*, and, in general, the duties of life, that he may act with order and consideration, and not carelessly; the third includes integrity of mind and prudence, and, in general, whatever belongs to the judgment.

Of these points the principal and most urgent is that which reaches the passions; for passion is only produced by a disappointment of one's desires and an incurring of one's aversions. It is this which introduces perturbations, tumults, misfortunes, and calamities; this is the spring of sorrow, lamentation, and envy; this renders us envious and emulous, and incapable of hearing reason.

The next topic regards the duties of life. For I am not to be undisturbed by passions, as a statue is; but as one who preserves the natural and acquired relations—as a pious person, a son, a brother, a father, a citizen.

The third topic belongs to those scholars who are now somewhat advanced; and is a security to the other two, that no bewildering semblance may surprise us, either in sleep, or wine, or in depression. This, say you, is beyond us. Yet our present philosophers, leaving the first and second topics, employ themselves wholly about the third; dealing in the logical subtleties. For they say that we must, by engaging in these subjects, take care to guard against deception. Who must? A wise and good man. Is this really, then, the thing you need? Have you mastered the other points? Are you not liable to be deceived by money? When you see a fine girl, do you oppose the seductive influence? If your neighbor inherits an estate, do you feel no vexation? Is it not steadfastness which you chiefly need? You learn even these very things, slave, with trembling, and a solicitous dread of contempt; and are inquisitive to know what is said of you. And if anyone comes and tells you that, in a dispute as to which was the best of the philosophers, one of the company named a certain person as the only philosopher, immediately your one-inch soul shoots up a yard high. But if another comes and says, "You are mistaken, he is not worth hearing; for what does he know? He has the first rudiments, but nothing more," you are thunder-

struck; you presently turn pale, and cry out, "I will show
what I am; that I am a great philosopher." You show what a
man is by just such conduct. Do you not know that Diogenes
exhibited some sophist in this manner, by pointing with his
middle finger; [1] and when the man was mad with rage, Diogenes said, "This is the very man; I have exhibited him to you."
For a man is not shown by the finger in the same sense as a
stone or a piece of wood, but when one points out a man's
principles, one shows him as a man.

Let us see your principles too. For is it not evident that
you consider your own moral purpose as nothing, but are
always aiming at something beyond its reach? As, what such
a one will say of you, and what you shall be thought—
whether a man of letters; whether to have read Chrysippus
or Antipater; and if Archedemus too, you have everything.
Why are you still solicitous, lest you should not show us what
you are? Shall I tell you what you have shown yourself? A
mean, discontented, passionate, cowardly person, complaining of everything, accusing everybody, perpetually restless,
good for nothing. This you have shown us. Go now and read
Archedemus; and then, if you hear but the noise of a mouse,
you are a dead man; for you will die some such kind of death
as—who was it?—Crinis,[2] who was also very proud that he
understood Archedemus.

Wretch, why do you not let alone things that do not belong
to you? These things belong to such as are able to learn them
without perturbation; who can say, "I am not subject to anger,
or grief, or envy. I am not restrained; I am not compelled.
What do I yet lack? I am at leisure; I am at ease. Let us now
see how logical inversions are to be treated; let us consider,
when an hypothesis is laid down, how we may avoid a con-

---

[1] Extending the middle finger, with the ancients, was a mark of the
greatest contempt.

[2] Crinis was an obscure Stoic philosopher who is supposed to have
died of fright at the sight of a mouse.

tradition." To such persons do these things belong. Those who are prosperous may light a fire, go to dinner if they please, and sing and dance; but you are for spreading sail just when your ship is sinking.

CHAPTER THREE

What Is the Chief Concern of a Good Man, and in What We Chiefly Ought to Train Ourselves

THE chief concern of a wise and good man is his own reason. The body is the concern of a physician, and of a gymnastic trainer; and the fields, of the husbandman. The business of a wise and good man is to use the phenomena of existence conformably to nature. Now, every soul, just as it is naturally formed to assent to truth, dissent from falsehood, and to suspend judgment with regard to things uncertain, so it is moved by a desire of good, an aversion from evil, and an indifference to what is neither good nor evil. For as a money-changer, or a gardener, is not at liberty to reject Caesar's coin, but when once it is shown is obliged, whether he will or not, to deliver his wares in exchange for it, so is it with the soul. Apparent good at first sight attracts, and evil repels. Nor will the soul any more reject an evident appearance of good, than Caesar's coin.

Hence depends every movement, both of God and man; and hence good is preferred to every obligation, however near. My connection is not with my father; but with good.

Are you so hard-hearted? Such is my nature, and such is the coin which God has given me. If therefore good is interpreted to be anything but what is fair and just, away go father and brother and country and everything. What! Shall I overlook my own good, and give it up to you? For what? "I am your father." But not my good. "I am your brother." But not my good. But if we define the good as consisting in a right moral purpose, then the preservation of the several relations of life becomes a good; and then he who gives up mere externals acquires the good. Your father deprives you of your money; but he does not hurt you. He will possess more land than you, as much more as he pleases; but will he possess more honor, more fidelity, more affection? Who can deprive you of this possession? Not even Zeus; for he did not will it so, since he has put this good into my own power, and given it me, like his own, uncompelled, unrestrained, and unhindered. But when anyone deals in coin different from this, then whoever shows it to him, may have whatever is sold for it in return. A thievish proconsul comes into the province. What coin does he use? Silver. Offer it to him, and carry off what you please. An adulterer comes. What coin does he use? Women. Take the coin, says one, and give me this little wench. "Give it to me, and it is yours." Another is interested in boys; give him the coin, and take what you please. Another is fond of hunting; give him a fine pony or puppy, and he will sell you for it what you want, though it be with sighs and groans. For there is that within which controls him, and assumes this to be current coin.

In this manner ought everyone chiefly to train himself. When you go out in the morning, examine those whom you see or hear; and answer as to a question. What have you seen? A handsome person. Apply the rule. Is this a thing controllable by moral purpose or uncontrollable? Uncontrollable. Then discard it. What have you seen? One in agony for the death of a child. Apply the rule. Death is inevitable. Banish this de-

spair, then. Has a consul met you? Apply the rule. What kind
of thing is the consular office—controllable by moral purpose
or uncontrollable? Uncontrollable. Throw aside this too. It
will not pass. Cast it away; it is nothing to you.

If we acted thus, and practiced in this manner from morning till night, by heaven! something would be done. Whereas
now, on the contrary, we are allured by every semblance, half
asleep; and if we ever awake, it is only for a little while at the
lecture; but as soon as we go out, if we meet anyone grieving,
we say, "He is undone." If a consul, "How happy he is!" If
an exile, "How miserable!" If a poor man, "How wretched;
he has nothing to eat!"

These miserable prejudices, then, are to be lopped off; and
this is the end to which we should direct our efforts. For what
is weeping and groaning? Prejudice. What is misfortune?
Prejudice. What is sedition, discord, complaint, accusation,
impiety, levity? All these are prejudices, and nothing more;
and prejudices concerning things uncontrollable by moral
purpose, as if they could be either good or evil. Let anyone
transfer these convictions to things controllable by moral
purpose, and I will guarantee that he will preserve his constancy, whatever be the state of things about him.

The soul is like a bowl filled with water; while the semblances of things fall like rays upon its surface. If the water is
moved, the ray will seem to be moved likewise, though it is
in reality without motion. When, therefore, anyone is seized
with a giddiness in his head, it is not the arts and virtues that
are confused, but the mind in which they lie; when this re-
covers its composure, so they will too.

CHAPTER FOUR

Concerning One Who Made Himself Improperly Conspicuous in the Theater

WHEN the governor of Epirus had exerted himself with improper eagerness in favor of a comedian, and was upon that account publicly railed at, and, when he came to hear it, was highly displeased with those who railed at him, Why, what harm, said Epictetus, have these people done? They have shown favoritism; which is just what you did.

"Is this a proper manner, then, of expressing their favor?"

Seeing you, their governor, and the friend and procurator of Caesar, express it thus, was it not to be expected that they would express it thus too? For if this zealous favoritism is not right, do not show it yourself; and if it is, why are you angry at them for imitating you? For whom have the many to imitate, but you, their superiors? From whom are they to take example, when they come into the theater, but from you? "Look how Caesar's procurator acts in the theater! Has he cried out? I will cry out too. Has he leaped up from his seat? I too will leap up from mine. Do his slaves sit in different parts of the house, making an uproar? I have no slaves; but I will make as much uproar as I can unaided."

You ought to consider, then, that when you appear in the theater, you appear as a standard and example to others as to how they ought to behave in the theater. Why is it that they have railed at you? Because every man hates what stands in his way. They would have one actor crowned; you, another. They stood in your way, and you in theirs. You proved the stronger. They have done what they could; they have railed at the person who hindered them. What would you have, then? Would you do as you please, and not have them even talk as they please? Where is the wonder of all this? Does not the husbandman rail at Zeus when he is hindered by him? Does not the sailor? Do men ever cease railing at Caesar? What, then; is Zeus ignorant of this? Are not the things that are said reported to Caesar? How then does he act? He knows that, if he were to punish all railers, he would have nobody left to command.

When you enter the theater, then, ought you to say, "Come, let Sophron be crowned"? No. But rather, "Come, let me at this time regulate my moral purpose in a manner conformable to nature. No one is dearer to me than myself. It is ridiculous, then, that because another man gains the victory as a player, I should be hurt. Whom do I wish to gain the victory? Him who does gain it; and thus he will always be victorious whom I wish to be so." "But I would have Sophron crowned." Why, celebrate as many games as you will at your own house, Nemean, Pythian, Isthmian, Olympic, and proclaim him victor in all; but in public do not arrogate more than your due, nor seek to monopolize what belongs to all; or if otherwise, bear to be railed at, for if you act like the mob, you put yourself on their level.

CHAPTER FIVE

To Those Who Leave School
Because of Illness

"I AM ill here," said one of the scholars. "I will return home."

Were you never ill at home, then? Consider whether you are doing anything here conducive to the regulation of your Will; for if you make no improvement, it was to no purpose that you came. Go home, then, and take care of your domestic affairs. For if your reason cannot be brought into conformity to nature, your land may. You may increase your money, support the old age of your father, mix in the public assemblies, and being bad you will do badly whatever you have to do. But if you understand yourself, namely that you are casting off some of your wrong principles, and taking up different ones in their place; and that you have transferred your scheme of life from things not controllable by will to those controllable; and that if you do sometimes cry *alas*, it is not for what concerns your father or your brother, but yourself—why do you still plead illness? Do you not know that both illness and death must overtake us? No matter what we are doing? The husbandman at his plow, the sailor on his voyage. What do you wish to be doing when you are taken? For, no matter what you do you will have to be overtaken by death.

If there is any better employment at which you can be taken, follow that. For my own part, I would be found engaged in nothing but in the regulation of my own will; how to make it undisturbed, unrestrained, uncompelled, free. I would be found studying this, that I may be able to say to God, "Have I transgressed thy commands? Have I perverted

185

the powers, the senses, the instincts which thou hast given me? Have I ever accused thee, or censured thy dispensations? I have been ill, because it was thy pleasure, like others; but I willingly. I have been poor, it being thy will; but with joy. I have not been in power, because it was not thy will; and power I have never desired. Hast thou ever seen me saddened because of this? Have I not always approached thee with a cheerful countenance, prepared to execute thy commands and the indications of thy will? Is it thy pleasure that I should depart from this assembly? I depart. I give thee all thanks that thou hast thought me worthy to have a share in it with thee; to behold thy works, and to join with thee in comprehending thy administration." Let death overtake me while I am thinking, while I am writing, while I am reading such things as these.

"But I shall not have my mother to hold my head when I am ill."

Get home then to your mother; for you are the sort of person who deserves to have your head held when you are ill.

"But at home I used to lie on a fine couch."

Get to this couch of yours; for you are fit to lie upon such a one, even in health; so do not miss doing that for which you are qualified. But what says Socrates? "As one man rejoices in the improvement of his estate, another of his horse, so do I daily rejoice in perceiving myself to grow better."

"In what—in pretty speeches?"

Use courteous words, man.

"In trifling theorems? What do they signify? Yet, indeed, I do not see that the philosophers are employed in anything else."

Do you think it nothing, to accuse and censure no one, God nor man; always to wear the same expression whether going out or coming in? These were the things which Socrates knew; and yet he never professed to know, or to teach anything; but if anyone wanted pretty speeches, or little theorems, he brought him to Protagoras, to Hippias; just as, if anyone had come for potherbs, he would have taken him to a gardener. Which of you, then, earnestly sets his heart on this? If you had, you would bear illness and hunger and death with cheerfulness. If anyone of you has truly loved a pretty girl, he knows that I speak truth.

CHAPTER   SIX

Miscellaneous

WHEN he was asked how it came to pass, that though the art of logic might be studied more now, yet there was more progress made in former times, Epictetus answered, In what respect is it now more studied; and in what respect were the improvements greater then? For in that which is now more cultivated, in that will more progress be found. The present study is the solution of syllogisms, and in this improvements are made. But formerly the study was to harmonize the reason with nature; and improvement was made in that. Therefore do not confound things, nor, when you study one thing, expect improvement in another; but see whether any one of us who applies himself to think and act in conformity with nature ever fails of improvement. Depend upon it, you will not find one.

A good man is invincible; for he does not contend where he is not superior. If you would have his land, take it; take his servants, take his office, take his body. But you will never frustrate his desire, nor make him incur his aversion. He engages in no combat but what concerns objects within his own control. How then can he fail to be invincible?

Being asked what common sense was, he answered: As that may be called a common ear which distinguishes only sounds, but that which distinguishes tones may be called a technical ear; so there are some things which men, not totally perverted, discern by their common natural powers; and such a disposition is called common sense.

It is not easy to gain the attention of effeminate young men —for you cannot take up custard by a hook—but the ingenuous, even if you discourage them, are the more eager for learning. Hence Rufus, for the most part, did discourage them; and made use of that as a criterion of the gifted and those who were not. For, he used to say, as a stone, even if you throw it up, will by its own nature be carried downward, so a gifted mind, the more it is forced from its natural bent, will incline towards it the more strongly.

CHAPTER SEVEN

Concerning a Certain Governor Who Was an Epicurean

WHEN the governor, who was an Epicurean, came to him saying, "It is fit that we ignorant people should inquire of you philosophers what is the most valuable thing in the world; as those who come into a strange city do of the citizens and such as are acquainted with it; that after this inquiry we may go and take a view of it, as they do in cities. Now, almost everyone admits that there are three things belonging to man —soul, body, and externals. It belongs to such as you to answer which is the best. What shall we tell mankind? Is it the flesh?"

And was it for this that Maximus took a voyage in winter as far as Cassiope to accompany his son? Was it to gratify the flesh?

"No, surely."

Is it not fit, then, to study what is best?

"Yes, beyond all other things."

What have we, then, better than flesh?

"The soul."

Are we to prefer the good of the better, or of the worse?

"Of the better."

Does the good of the soul consist in things controllable. by will or uncontrollable?

"In things controllable."

Does the pleasure of the soul, then, depend on the will?

"It does."

And whence does this pleasure arise—from itself. But that is inconceivable. For there must exist some principal essence of good, in the attainment of which we shall enjoy this pleasure of the soul.

"This too is granted."

In what, then, consists this pleasure of the soul? If it be in mental objects, the essence of good is found. For it is impossible that good should lie in one thing, and rational enjoyment in another; or that, if the cause is not good, the effect should be good. For, to make the effect reasonable, the cause must be good. But this you cannot reasonably allow, for it would be to contradict both Epicurus and the rest of your principles. It remains, then, that the pleasures of the soul must be the cause and the essence of good.

Maximus, therefore, acted foolishly, if he took a voyage for the sake of anything but his body; that is, for the sake of what is best. A man acts foolishly too, if he refrains from what is another's, when he is a judge and able to take it. We should consider only this, if you please, how it may be done secretly and safely, and so that no one may know it. For Epicurus himself does not pronounce stealing to be evil, only being found out in it; and prohibits it for no other reason, but because it is impossible to insure ourselves against discovery. But I say to you that, if it be done adroitly and cautiously, we shall not be discovered. Besides, we have powerful friends of both sexes at Rome; and the Greeks are weak; and nobody will dare to go up to Rome on such an affair. Why do you refrain from your own good? It is madness; it is folly. But if you were to tell me that you do refrain, I would not believe you. For, as it is impossible to assent to an apparent falsehood, or to deny an apparent truth, so it is impossible to abstain from an apparent good.

Now, riches are a good, and, indeed, the chief instrument of pleasures. Why do you not acquire them? And why do we not corrupt the wife of our neighbor, if it can be done secretly? And if the husband should happen to be annoyed, why not cut his throat too, if you have a mind to be such a philosopher as you ought to be—a complete one—to be consistent with your own principles. Otherwise you will not differ from us who are called Stoics. For we, too, say one thing and do another; we talk well and act ill; but you will be perverse in a contrary way, teaching bad principles, and acting well.

For heaven's sake represent to yourself a city of Epicureans. "I do not marry." "Nor I; for we are not to marry nor have children, nor to engage in public affairs." What will be the consequence of this? Whence are the citizens to come? Who will educate them? Who will be the governor of the youth? Who is the gymnasium director? What then will he teach them? Will it be what used to be taught at Athens, or Lacedemon? Take a young man; bring him up according to your principles. These principles are wicked, subversive of a state, destructive to families, not becoming even to women. Give them up, sir. You live in a capital city. You are to govern and judge uprightly, and to refrain from what belongs to others. No one's wife or child, or silver or gold plate, is to have any charms for you, except your own. Provide yourself with principles consonant to these truths; and setting out thence, you will with pleasure refrain from things so persuasive to mislead and conquer. But if to their own persuasive force we can add such a philosophy as hurries us upon them and gives them additional strength, what will be the consequence?

In a sculptured vase, which is the best—the silver, or the workmanship? The substance of the hand is flesh; but its operations are the principal thing. Accordingly, its functions are threefold—relating to its existence, to the manner of its existence, and to its principal operations. Thus, likewise, do not set a value on the mere materials of man, the flesh; but on the principal operations which belong to him.

"What are these?"

Engaging in public business, marrying, the production of children, the worship of God, the care of parents, and, in general, the regulation of our desires and aversions, our pursuits and avoidances, in accordance with our nature.

"What is our nature?"

To be free, noble-spirited, modest. For what other animal blushes? What other has the idea of shame? But pleasure must be subjected to these, as an attendant and handmaid, to call forth our activity, and to keep us acting in accordance with nature.

"But I am rich and want nothing."

Then why do you pretend to philosophize? Your gold and silver plate is enough for you. What need do you have of principles?

"Yes, but I am also judge of the Greeks."

Do you know how to judge? Who has imparted this knowledge to you?

"Caesar has given me a commission."

Let him give you a commission to judge of music; what good will it do you? But how were you made a judge? Whose hand have you kissed—that of Symphorus, or Numenius?[1] Before whose door have you slept?[2] To whom have you sent presents? After all, do you not perceive that the office of judge puts you in the same rank with Numenius?

"But I can throw whom I please into a prison."

So you may a stone.

"But I can beat whom I will too."

So you may an ass. This is not a government over men. Govern us like reasonable creatures. Show us what is best for us, and we will pursue it; show us what is otherwise, and we will avoid it. Like Socrates, make us imitators of yourself. He was properly a governor of men, who controlled their desires and aversions, their pursuits, their avoidances. "Do this; do not that, or I will throw you into prison." This is not a government for reasonable creatures. But "Do as Zeus has commanded, or you will be punished, and be a loser."

"What shall I lose?"

Simply your own right action, your fidelity, honor, decency. You can find no losses greater than these.

---

[1] Probably persons then influential at court.
[2] In order to salute him the first thing in the morning.

CHAPTER EIGHT

How We Are to Deal with the Semblances of Things

In the same manner as we exercise ourselves against sophistical questions, we should exercise ourselves likewise in relation to such semblances as every day occur; for these, too, offer questions to us. Such a one's son is dead. What think you of it? Answer: It is a thing inevitable, and therefore not an evil. Such a one is disinherited by his father. What think you of it? It is inevitable; and so not an evil. Caesar has condemned him. This is inevitable, and so not an evil. He has been afflicted by it. This is controllable by will; it is an evil. He has supported it bravely. This is within the control of will; it is a good.

If we train ourselves in this manner we shall make improvement; for we shall never assent to anything but what the semblance itself includes. A son is dead. What then? A son is dead. Nothing more? Nothing. A ship is lost. What then? A ship is lost. He is carried to prison. What then? He is carried to prison. That he is *unhappy* is an addition which everyone must make for himself. "But Zeus does not order these things rightly." Why so? Because he has made you to be patient? Because he has made you to be brave? Because he has made them to be no evils? Because it is permitted you, while you suffer them, to be happy? Because he has opened the door for you whenever they do not suit you? Go out, man, and do not complain!

If you would know how the Romans treat philosophers, hear. Italicus, esteemed one of the greatest philosophers among them, being in a passion with his own people when I was near by, said, as if he had suffered some intolerable evil, "I cannot bear it; you are the ruin of me; you will make me just like *him*," pointing to me.[1]

CHAPTER NINE

Concerning a Certain Orator, Who Was Going to Rome on a Lawsuit

A PERSON came to him who was going to Rome on a lawsuit in which his dignity was concerned; and after telling him the occasion of his journey, asked him what he thought of the affair. If you ask me, says Epictetus, what will happen to you at Rome, and whether you shall gain or lose your case, I have no suggestion as to that. But if you ask me how you shall fare, I can answer, If you have right principles, well; if wrong ones, ill. For every action turns upon its principle. What was the reason that you so earnestly desired to be chosen governor of the Gnossians?[2] Principle. What is the reason that you are now going to Rome? Principle. And in winter too, and with danger and expense? Why, because it is necessary. What tells you so? Your principle. If, then, principles are the source of all our actions, wherever anyone has bad principles

---

1 The sense of this anecdote seems to be that Italicus, when urged by his friends to submit to some hardship in a philosophical manner, resented the implication that he actually *was* a philosopher. Roman popular feeling about philosophy is probably well represented in the words of Ennius: "Taste of philosophy, but do not gorge yourself in it."

2 Gnossus was the chief city of Crete.

the effect will correspond to the cause. Well, then; are all our principles sound? Are both yours and your antagonist's? How then do you differ? Or are yours better than his? Why? You think so, and so thinks he of his, and so do madmen. This is a bad criterion.

But show me that you have given some attention and care to your principles. As you now take a voyage to Rome for the government of the Gnossians, and are not contented to stay at home with the honors you before enjoyed, but desire something greater and more illustrious, did you ever take such a voyage in order to examine your own principles and to throw away the bad ones, if you happened to have any? Did you ever approach anyone for this purpose? What time did you ever appoint to yourself for it? What age? Run over your years. If you are ashamed of me, do it for yourself. Did you examine your principles when you were a child? Did you not act then as now? When you were a youth, and fre- quented the schools of the orators, and yourself made decla- mations, did you ever imagine that you were deficient in any- thing? And when you became a man and entered upon public business, pleaded cases, and acquired credit, whom did you then recognize as your equal? How would you have tolerated that anyone should examine whether your principles were bad? What, then, would you have me say to you?

"Assist me in this affair."

I have no suggestion to offer for that. Neither are you come to me, if it be upon that account you came, as to a philosopher; but as you would come to an herb-seller or a shoemaker.

"For what purposes, then, can the philosophers give sug- gestions?"

For preserving and conducting the reason in accord with nature, whatever happens. Do you think this a small thing?

"No, but the greatest."

Well, and does it require but a short time, and may it be taken as you pass by? If you can, take it then; and so you will say, "I have visited Epictetus." Yes; just as you would visit a stone or a statue. For you have seen me, and nothing more. But he visits a man, as a man, who learns his principles, and, in return, shows his own. Learn my principles; show me yours. Then say you have visited me. Let us confute each other. If I have any bad principle, take it away. If you have any, bring it forth. This is visiting a philosopher. No, but "It lies in our way, and while we are hiring a ship, we may call on Epictetus. Let us see what he says." And then when you are gone, you say, "Epictetus is nothing. His language was inaccurate, was barbarous." For what else did you come to criticize? "Well; but if I employ myself in these things, I shall be without an estate, like you, without plate, without fine cattle, like you." Nothing, perhaps, is necessary to be said to this, but that I do not want them. But if you possess many things, you still want others; so that whether you will or not, you are poorer than I.

"What then do I need?"

What you do not have—constancy, a mind in accord with nature, and a freedom from perturbation. Patron or no patron, what do I care? But you do. I am richer than you; I am not anxious what Caesar will think of me; I flatter no one on that account. This I have, instead of silver and gold plate. You have your vessels of gold; but your discourse, your principles, your opinions, your pursuits, your desires, are of mere earthenware. When I have all these in conformity with nature, why should not I bestow some study upon my reasoning too? I am at leisure. My mind is under no distraction. In this freedom from distraction, what shall I do? Have I anything more becoming a man than this? You, when you have nothing to do, are restless; you go to the theater, or perhaps to bathe. Why should not the philosopher polish his reasoning? You have fine crystal and myrrhine vases;[1] I have acute forms of

---

[1] Myrrhine cups were probably a kind of agate described by Pliny, which, when burnt, had the smell of myrrh.

arguing. To you, all you have appears little; to me all I have
seems great. Your appetite is insatiable; mine is satisfied. When
children thrust their hand into a narrow jar of nuts and figs,
if they fill it, they cannot get it out again; then they begin
crying. Drop a few of them, and you will get out the rest.
And do you too drop your desire; do not demand much, and
you will attain.

CHAPTER TEN

How We Should Bear Illness

WE should have all our principles ready for use on every
occasion—at dinner, such as relate to dinner; in the bath, such
as relate to the bath; in the bed, such as relate to the bed.

> *Let not the stealing god of sleep surprise,*
> *Nor creep in slumbers on thy weary eyes,*
> *Ere every action of the former day*
> *Strictly thou dost, and righteously survey.*
> *What have I done? In what have I transgressed?*
> *What good, or ill, has this day's life expressed?*
> *Where have I failed in what I ought to do?*
> *If evil were thy deeds, repent and mourn;*
> *If good, rejoice.*[1]

We should retain these verses so as to apply them to our
use; not merely to say them by rote, as we do with verses in
honor of Apollo.

Again, in a fever we should have such principles ready as

---

[1] Pythagoras, *Golden Verses*, 40-44.

relate to a fever; and not, as soon as we are taken ill, forget all. Provided I do but act like a philosopher, let what will happen. Some way or other I must depart and take care of this frail body whether a fever comes or not. What is it to be a philosopher? Is it not to be prepared against events? Do you not comprehend that you then say, in effect, "If I am but prepared to bear all events with calmness, let what will happen"? Otherwise you are like an athlete, who, after receiving a blow, should quit the combat. In that case, indeed, you might leave off without a penalty. But what shall we get by leaving off philosophy?

What, then; ought each of us to say upon every difficult occasion, "It was for this that I exercised; it was for this that I trained myself"? God says to you, Give me a proof if you have gone through the preparatory combats according to rule; if you have followed a proper diet and proper exercise;[1] if you have obeyed your master; and after this, do you faint at the very time of action?

Now is your time for a fever. Bear it well. For thirst; bear it well. For hunger; bear it well. Is it not in your power? Who shall restrain you? A physician may restrain you from drinking, but he cannot restrain you from bearing your thirst well. He may restrain you from eating, but he cannot restrain you from bearing hunger well. "But I cannot follow my studies." And for what end do you follow them, slave? Is it not that you may be prosperous, that you may be constant, that you may think and act in conformity with nature? What restrains you, but that, in a fever, you may keep your reason in harmony with nature?

Here is the test of the matter. Here is the trial of the philosopher; for a fever is a part of life, as is a walk, a voyage, or a journey. Do you read when you are walking? No, nor

---

[1] At Olympia, athletes were trained under supervision, adhering to a strict diet for a month before the games.

in a fever. But when you walk well, you attend to what belongs to a walker; so, if you bear a fever well, you have everything belonging to one in a fever. What is it to bear a fever
well? Not to blame either God or man, not to be afflicted at
what happens, to await death bravely, and to do what is to
be done. When the physician enters, not to dread what he
may say; nor, if he should tell you that you are doing well,
to be too much rejoiced; for what good has he told you?
When you were in health, what good did it do you? Not to
be dejected when he tells you that you are very ill; for what
is it to be very ill? To be near the separation of soul and body.
What harm is there in this, then? If you are not near it now,
will you not be near it hereafter? What, will the world be
quite overturned when you die? Why, then, do you flatter
your physician? Why do you say, "If you please, sir, I shall
do well"? Why do you give him occasion to put on airs? Why
not give him what is his due (with regard to an insignificant
body—which is not yours, but by nature mortal) as you do
a shoemaker about your foot, or a carpenter about a house?
It is the season for these things, to one in a fever. If he fulfills
these, he has what belongs to him. For it is not the business of
a philosopher to take care of these mere externals—of his wine,
his oil, or his body—but of his reason. And how with regard
to externals? Not to behave inconsiderately about them.

What occasion is there, then, for fear; what occasion for
anger, for desire, about things that belong to others, or are of
no value? For two rules we should always have ready—*that
there is nothing good or evil save in the will;* and *that we are
not to lead events, but to follow them.* "My brother ought
not to have treated me so." Very true; but he must see to that.
However he treats me, I am to act rightly with regard to him;
for the one is my own concern, the other is not; the one cannot be restrained, the other may.

CHAPTER ELEVEN

Miscellaneous

THERE are some punishments appointed, as by a law, for such as disobey the divine administration. Whoever shall esteem anything good, except what depends on the will, let him envy, let him covet, let him flatter, let him be full of perturbation. Whoever esteems anything else to be evil, let him grieve, let him mourn, let him lament, let him be wretched. And yet, though thus severely punished, we cannot desist.

Remember what the poet says of a guest,

> *It were not lawful to affront a guest,*
> *Even did the worst draw nigh.*[1]

This too you should be prepared to say with regard to a father, It is not lawful for me to affront you, father, even if a worse than you had come; for all are from Zeus, the God of Fathers. And so of a brother; for all are from kindred Zeus. And thus we shall find Zeus to be the superintendent of all the other relations.

---

[1] Homer, *Odyssey*. See Classics Club edition, p. 171.

CHAPTER TWELVE

Of Training

WE are not to carry our training beyond nature and reason; for in that case we, who call ourselves philosophers, shall not differ from jugglers. For it is no doubt difficult to walk upon a rope, and not only difficult, but dangerous. Ought we too, for that reason, to make it our study to walk upon a rope, or balance a pole,[1] or grasp a statue?[2] By no means. It is not everything difficult or dangerous that is a proper training, but such things as are conducive to what lies before us to do.

"And what is it that lies before us to do?"

To have our desires and aversions free from restraint.

"How is that?"

Not to be disappointed in our desire, nor fall into anything which we would avoid. To this ought our training to be directed. For without vigorous and steady training, it is not possible to preserve our desire undisappointed and our aversion unincurred; and therefore, if we allow it to be externally employed on things uncontrollable by will, be assured that your desire will neither gain its object, nor your aversion avoid it.

And because habit has a powerful influence, and we are accustomed to apply our desire and aversion to externals only, we must oppose one habit to another: and where the semblances are most treacherous, there oppose the force of train-

---

[1] A phrase occurs here which has greatly puzzled the commentators, but which evidently refers to the gymnastic exercises known as the "perche-pole," where a pole is balanced by one performer and ascended by another.

[2] Diogenes used, in winter, to grasp statues when they were covered with snow, as an exercise to inure himself to hardship.

202 THE DISCOURSES OF EPICTETUS

ing. I am inclined to pleasure. I will bend myself, even unduly, toward the other extreme, as a matter of training. I am averse to pain. I will strive and wrestle with these semblances, that I may cease to shrink from any such object. For who is truly in training? He who endeavors totally to control desire, and to apply aversion only to things controllable by will, and strives for it most in the most difficult cases. Hence different persons are to be trained in different ways. What is the point of balancing a pole, or going about with a leather tent and a mortar and pestle? [1] If you are hasty, man, let it be your training to bear ill language patiently; and when you are affronted, not to be angry. Thus, at length, you may arrive at such a proficiency as, when anyone strikes you, to say to yourself, "Let me suppose this to be like grasping a statue." Next train yourself to make but a moderate use of wine—not to drink a great deal, to which some are so foolish as to train themselves—but to abstain from this first; and then to abstain from women and from gluttony. Afterwards you will venture into the lists at some proper season, by way of trial, if at all, to see whether these semblances get the better of you as much as they used to do. But at first flee from what is stronger than you. The contest between a fascinating woman and a young man just initiated into philosophy is unequal. The brass pot and the earthen pitcher, as the fable says, are an unfair match.

After the desires and aversions comes the second topic, that of choices and refusals; that they may be obedient to reason; that nothing may be done improperly, in point of time and place, or in any other respect.

The third topic relates to the faculty of assent and to what is plausible and persuasive. As Socrates said that we are not to lead a life which is not tested, so neither are we to admit

---

[1] This is obscure, but the reference is probably to the Cynics, some of whom carried about with them all equipment which they required for life.

an untested semblance; but to say, "Stop, let me see what you are and whence you come," just as the police say, "Show me your pass."[1] "Have you that pass from nature which is necessary to the acceptance of every semblance?"

In short, whatever things are applied to the body by those who train it, so may these be used in our training if they any way affect desire or aversion. But if this be done for mere ostentation, it belongs to one who looks and seeks for something external, and strives for spectators to exclaim, "What a great man!" Hence Apollonius said well, "If you have a mind to train yourself for your own benefit, when you are choking with heat, take a little cold water in your mouth, and spit it out again, and hold your tongue."[2]

CHAPTER THIRTEEN

What Forlornness Is; and What a Forlorn Person

To be forlorn is the condition of a helpless person. For he who is alone is not therefore forlorn, any more than one in a crowd is the contrary. When, therefore, we lose a son, or a brother, or a friend, on whom we have been used to repose, we often say we are left forlorn, even in the midst of Rome, where such a crowd is continually meeting us; where we live among so many, and where we have, perhaps, a numerous

---

[1] A token of identification, such as is used in most European countries today.

[2] Said to be an exercise practiced by Plato.

train of servants. For he is understood to be forlorn who is helpless, and exposed to such as would injure him. Hence, in a journey especially, we call ourselves solitary when we fall among thieves; for it is not the sight of a man that removes our solitude, but of an honest man, a man of honor, and a helpful companion. If merely being alone is sufficient for forlornness, Zeus may be said to be forlorn at the world conflagration,[1] and bewail himself that he hath neither Hera, nor Athene nor Apollo, nor brother, nor son, nor descendant, nor relation. This, some indeed say, he does when he is alone at the conflagration. Such as these, moved by some natural principle, some natural desire of society and mutual love, and by the pleasure of conversation, do not rightly consider the state of a person who is alone. But none the less should we be prepared for this also, to be self-sufficient, and to bear our own company. For as Zeus communes with himself, is at peace with himself, and contemplates his own administration, and is employed in thoughts worthy of himself; so should we too be able to talk with ourselves, and not to need the conversation of others, nor suffer boredom; to attend to the divine administration; to consider our relation to other beings; how we have formerly been affected by events, how we are affected now; what are the things that still press upon us; how these too may be cured, how removed; if anything wants perfecting, to perfect it according to reason. You perceive that Caesar has procured us a profound peace; there are neither wars nor battles, nor great robberies nor piracies; but we may travel at all hours, and sail from east to west. But can Caesar procure us peace from a fever too; from a shipwreck; from a fire; from an earthquake; from a thunderstorm; nay, even from love? He cannot. From grief; from envy? No, not from any one of these. But the doctrine of philosophers

_____
[1] The Stoics believed that there were successive conflagrations at destined periods, in which all beings were reabsorbed into the Deity.

promises to procure us peace from these too. And what does it say? "If you will attend to me, O mortals! wherever you are, and whatever you are doing, you shall neither grieve, nor be angry, nor be compelled, nor restrained; but you shall live serene, and free from all disturbance." When a man enjoys this peace proclaimed, not by Caesar (for how should he have it to proclaim?), but by God, through reason, is he not contented when he is alone? When he reflects and considers, "Now no ill can happen to me; there is no thief, no earthquake. All is full of peace, all full of tranquillity; every road, every city, every assembly, neighbor, companion, is powerless to hurt me." Another,[1] whose care it is, provides you with food, with clothes, with senses, with ideas. Whenever he does not provide what is necessary, he sounds a retreat; he opens the door and says to you, "Come." Whither? To nothing dreadful; but back to that from which you came—to what is friendly and congenial, to the elements. What in you was fire goes away to fire; what was earth, to earth; what air, to air; what water, to water. There is no Hades, nor Acheron, nor Cocytus, nor Pyriphlegethon; but all is full of gods and divine beings. He who can have such thoughts, and can look upon the sun, moon, and stars, and enjoy the earth and sea, is no more forlorn than he is helpless. "Well; but suppose anyone should come and murder me when I am alone." Foolish man!—not you, but that insignificant body of yours.

What forlornness is there then left; what destitution? Why do we make ourselves worse than children? What do they do when they are left alone? They take up shells and dust; they build houses, then pull them down; then build something else; and thus never want amusement. Suppose you were all to sail away; am I to sit and cry because I am left alone and forlorn? Am I so unprovided with shells and dust? But children do this from folly; and shall we be wretched through wisdom?

---

[1] A reverent expression for God.

[1] Every great gift is dangerous to a beginner. Study first how to live like a person in sickness; that in time you may know how to live like one in health. Abstain from food. Drink water. Totally repress your desire for some time, that you may at length use it according to reason; and if so, when you are stronger in virtue, you will use it well. No; but we wish to live as wise men from the start, and be of service to mankind. Of what service? What are you doing? Why, have you been of so much service to yourself that you would exhort them? *You* exhort! Would you be of service to them, show them by your own example what kind of men philosophy makes, and do not trifle. When you eat, be of service to those who eat with you; when you drink, to those who drink with you. Be of service to them by giving way to all, yielding to them, bearing with them; and not by venting upon them your own ill-humor.

CHAPTER FOURTEEN

Miscellaneous

As bad performers cannot sing alone, but in a chorus, so some persons cannot walk alone. If you are anything, walk alone; talk by yourself; and do not skulk in the chorus. Laugh a little at yourself; look about you; stir yourself, that you may know what you are.

If a person drinks water, or does anything else for the sake of training, upon every occasion he tells all he meets, "I drink

---

[1] This abrupt change of subject suggests that a section of the manuscript is missing.

water." Why, do you drink water merely for the sake of drinking it? If it does you any good to drink it, do so; if not, you act ridiculously. But if it is for your advantage that you drink it, say nothing about it before those who would criticize. Yet can it be possible that these are the very people you wish to please?

Of actions, some are performed on their own account; others from circumstances, others from complaisance, others upon system.

Two things must be rooted out of men, conceit and diffidence. Conceit lies in thinking that you want nothing; and diffidence in supposing it impossible that under such adverse circumstances you should ever succeed. Now, conceit is removed by cross-examination, and of this Socrates set the example. And consider and ascertain that the undertaking is not impracticable. The inquiry itself will do you no harm; and it is almost being a philosopher to inquire how it is possible to employ our desire and aversion without hindrance.

"I am better than you, for my father has been consul." "I have been a tribune," says another, "and you not." If we were horses, would you say, "My father was swifter than yours; I have abundance of oats and hay and fine trappings"? What now, if, while you were saying this, I should answer: "Be it so. Let us run a race then"? Is there nothing in man analogous to a horse race, by which it may be decided which is better or worse? Is there not honor, fidelity, justice? Show yourself the better in these, that you may be the better as a man. But if you only tell me that you can kick violently, I will tell you again that you value yourself on what is the characteristic of an ass.

CHAPTER FIFTEEN

That Everything Is to Be Undertaken with Circumspection

IN every affair consider what precedes and follows, and then undertake it. Otherwise you will begin with spirit indeed, careless of the consequences, and when these are developed, you will shamefully desist. "I would conquer at the Olympic Games." But consider what precedes and follows, and then, if it be for your advantage, engage in the affair. You must conform to rules, submit to a diet, refrain from dainties; exercise your body, whether you choose it or not, at a stated hour, in heat and cold; you must drink no cold water, and sometimes no wine—in a word, you must give yourself up to your trainer as to a physician. Then, in the combat, you may be covered with sand,[1] dislocate your arm, turn your ankle, swallow abundance of dust, receive stripes [for any foul committed], and, after all, lose the victory. When you have reckoned up all this, if your inclination still holds, set about the combat. Otherwise, take notice, you will behave like children who sometimes play wrestlers, sometimes gladiators; sometimes blow a trumpet, and sometimes act a tragedy, when they happen to have seen and admired these shows. Thus you too will be at one time a wrestler, at another a gladiator; now a philosopher, now an orator; but nothing in earnest. Like an ape you mimic all you see, and one thing after another is sure to please you, but is out of favor as soon as it becomes familiar. For you have never entered upon anything considerately, nor after

---

1 It was part of the routine of a wrestler to cover himself with sand before a match.

having surveyed and tested the whole matter; but carelessly, and half-heartedly. Thus some, when they have seen a philosopher, and heard a man speaking like Euphrates[1]—though indeed who can speak like him?—have a mind to be philosophers too. Consider first, man, what the matter is, and what your own nature is able to bear. If you would be a wrestler, consider your shoulders, your back, your thighs; for different persons are made for different things. Do you think that you can act as you do and be a philosopher; that you can eat, drink, be angry, be discontented, as you are now? You must watch, you must labor, you must get the better of certain appetites; must quit your acquaintances, be despised by your servant, be laughed at by those you meet; come off worse than others in everything—in offices, in honors, before tribunals. When you have fully considered these drawbacks, approach philosophy, if you think best; that is, if at that price, you have a mind to purchase serenity, freedom, and tranquillity. If not, do not come hither; do not, like children, be now a philosopher, then a publican, then an orator, and then one of Caesar's officers. These things are not consistent. You must be one man either good or bad. You must cultivate either your own reason or else externals; apply yourself either to the inner man or to things outside; that is, be either a philosopher, or one of the mob.

When Galba was killed, somebody said to Rufus, "Now, indeed, the world is governed by Providence." "I had never thought," answered Rufus, "of extracting from Galba the slightest proof that the world was governed by Providence."

---

[1] A philosopher of Syria, whose character is described, with the highest praise, by Pliny.

CHAPTER SIXTEEN

Social Intercourse Should Be Entered into Cautiously

HE who frequently mingles with others, either in conversation or at entertainments, for social purposes in general, must necessarily either become like his companions, or bring them over to his own way. For if a dead coal be applied to a live one, either the first will quench the last, or the last kindle the first. Since, then, the danger is so great, caution must be used in entering into these familiarities with the crowd, remembering that it is impossible to touch a chimney-sweeper without picking up some soot. For what will you do if you have to discuss gladiators, horses, wrestlers, and, what is worse, men? "Such a one is good, another bad; this was well, that ill, done." Besides, what if anyone should sneer, or ridicule, or be ill-natured? Are any of you prepared, like a harpist, who, when he takes his harp and tries the strings, finds out which notes are discordant, and knows how to put the instrument in tune? Have any of you such a faculty as Socrates had, who in every conversation could bring his companions to his own purpose? How could you have it? You must therefore be carried along by the crowd. And why are they more powerful than you? Because they utter their corrupt discourses from sincere opinion, and you your good ones only from your lips. Hence they are without strength or life; and it is disgusting to hear your exhortations and your poor miserable virtue proclaimed up hill and down. Thus it is that the crowd gets the better of you; for sincere opinion is always strong, always invincible. Therefore before wise sentiments are fixed in you, and you have acquired some power of self-defense, I advise you to be

cautious in your associations with common persons; otherwise, if you have any impressions made on you in the schools,
they will melt away daily like wax before the sun. Get away
then, far from the sun, while you have these waxen opinions.

It is for this reason that the philosophers advise us to leave
our country; because habitual practices draw the mind aside
and prevent the formation of new habits. We cannot bear that
those who meet us should say, "Hey-day! such a one is turned
philosopher, who was formerly thus and so." Thus physicians
send patients with chronic disorders to another place and
another air; and they do right. Do you too import other manners instead of those you carry out. Fix your opinions, and
exercise yourself in them. No; but you go hence to the theater,
to the gladiators, to the walks, to the circus; then hither again,
then back again—just the same persons all the while! No good
habit, no criticism, no scrutiny upon ourselves. No observation of what use we make of the appearances presented to our
minds—whether they are in accord with, or contrary to nature; whether we interpret them rightly or wrongly. Can I
say to the inevitable that it is nothing to me? If this is not yet
your case, flee from your former habits; flee from the crowd
if you intend to begin to be somebody.

CHAPTER SEVENTEEN

Of Providence

WHENEVER you lay anything to the charge of Providence, do but reflect, and you will find that it has happened in accordance with reason.

"Well; but a dishonest man has the advantage."

In what?

"In money."

Here he ought to surpass you; because he flatters, he is shameless, he keeps awake. Where is the wonder? But look whether he has the advantage of you in fidelity or in honor. You will find he has not, but that wherever it is best for you to have the advantage of him, there you have it. I once said to one who was full of indignation at the good fortune of Philostorgus, "Why, would you be willing to sleep with Sura?" [1] "God forbid," said he, "that day should ever come!" Why then are you angry that he is paid for what he sells; or how can you call him happy in possessions acquired by means which you detest? Or what harm does Providence do in giving the best things to the best men? Is it not better to have a sense of honor than to be rich? "Granted." Why then are you angry, man, if you have what is best? Always remember, then, and have it in mind that a better man has the advantage of a worse in that direction in which he is better; and you will never be indignant.

"But my wife treats me badly."

Well; if you are asked what is the matter, answer, "My wife treats me badly."

"Nothing more?"

---

[1] Probably Palfurius Sura who had been expelled from the Senate.

Nothing.

"My father gives me nothing." To call this an evil, some external and false addition must be made. We are not therefore to get rid of poverty, but of our impressions concerning it; and we shall do well.

CHAPTER EIGHTEEN

That We Ought Not to Be Alarmed by Any News That Is Brought Us

WHEN any alarming news is brought you, always have it ready in mind that no news can be brought you concerning what is within the power of your own will. Can anyone bring you news that your opinions or desires are ill-conducted? By no means; only that such a person is dead. What is that to *you* then? That somebody speaks ill of you. And what is that to *you* then? That your father is perhaps forming some contrivance or other. Against what? Against your will? How can he? No; but against your body, against your estate? You are very safe; this is not against *you*. But the judge has pronounced you guilty of impiety. And did not the judges pronounce the same of Socrates? Is his pronouncing a sentence any business of yours? No. Then why do you any longer trouble yourself about it? There is a duty incumbent on your father, which unless he performs, he loses the character of a father, of natural affection, of tenderness. Do not seek to make him lose anything else by this; for every man suffers precisely where he errs. Your duty, on the other hand, is to meet the case with firmness, modesty, and mildness; otherwise you forfeit piety, modesty, and nobleness. Well, and is your judge free from danger? No; he runs an equal hazard. Why, then, are you still afraid of his decision? What have you to do with the ills of another? Meeting the case wrongly would be your own ill. Let it be your only care to avoid that; but whether sentence is passed on you or not, as it is the business of another, so the ill belongs to him. "Such a one threatens you." *Me?* No. "He censures you." Let him look to it, how he does his own duty. "He will give an unjust sentence against you." Poor wretch!

CHAPTER NINETEEN

What Is the Comparative Condition of the Philosopher, and of the Crowd?

THE first difference between one of the crowd and a philosopher is this: the one says, "I am undone on account of my child, my brother, my father"; but the other, if ever he be obliged to say, "I am undone!" reflects, and adds, "on account of myself." For the will cannot be restrained or hurt by anything to which the will does not extend, but only by itself. If, therefore, we always would incline this way, and whenever we are unsuccessful, would lay the fault on ourselves, and remember that there is no cause of perturbation and inconstancy but wrong principles, I swear to you that we have made progress. But we set out in a very different way from the very beginning. When we were children, for example, if we happened to stumble, our nurse did not chide us, but beat the stone. Why, what harm did the stone do? Was it to move out of its place for the folly of your child? Again, if we do not find something to eat when we come out of the bath, our tutor does not try to moderate our appetite, but beats the cook. Why, did we appoint you tutor of the cook, man? No; but of our child. It is he whom you are to correct and improve. By these means, even when we are grown up, we appear children. For an unmusical person is a child in music; an illiterate person, a child in learning; and an untaught one, a child in life.

CHAPTER TWENTY

That Some Advantage May Be Gained from Every Outward Circumstance

In considering intellectual impressions, almost all persons admit good and evil to lie in ourselves and not in externals. No one says that day is good, night evil, and the greatest evil that three is four; but what? That knowledge is good and error evil. Even in connection with falsehood itself there may be one good thing—the knowledge that it is falsehood. Thus, then, should it be in life also. "Health is a good; sickness an evil." No, sir. But what? A right use of health is a good; a wrong one, an evil. So that, in truth, it is possible to be a gainer even by sickness. And is it not possible by death too; by lameness?[1] Do you think Menaeceus[2] derived little good by death? "May whoever talks thus be such a gainer as he was!" Why,

---

[1] This is perhaps a reference to his own case; Epictetus was lame.

[2] The son of Creon, who killed himself, after he had been informed by an oracle that his death would bring a victory to the Thebans.

pray, sir, did not he preserve his patriotism, his magnanimity, his fidelity, his gallant spirit? And if he had lived on, would he not have lost all these? Would not cowardice, baseness, and hatred of his country, and a wretched love of life, have been his portion? Well, now; do you not think him a considerable gainer by dying? No; but I warrant you the father of Admetus was a great gainer by living on so ignobly and wretchedly as he did! For did not he die at last?

For heaven's sake, cease to be thus deluded by externals. Cease to make yourselves slaves, first of things, and then, upon their account, of the men who have the power either to bestow or to take them away. Is there any advantage, then, to be gained from these men? From all; even from a reviler. What advantage does a wrestler gain from him with whom he exercises himself before the combat? The greatest. And just in the same manner I exercise myself with this man. He exercises me in patience, in gentleness, in meekness. I am to suppose, then, that I gain an advantage from him who exercises my neck, and puts my back and shoulders in order; so that the trainer may well bid me grapple him with both hands, and the heavier he is the better for me; and yet is it not an advantage to me when I am exercised in keeping of temper? This is not knowing how to gain an advantage from men. Is my neighbor a bad one? He is so to himself, but a good one to me; he exercises my good temper, my moderation. Is my father bad? To himself; but not to me. "This is the rod of Hermes. Touch with it whatever you please, and it will become gold." No; but bring whatever you please, and I will turn it into *good*. Bring sickness, death, want, reproach, trial for life. All these, by the rod of Hermes, shall turn to advantage. "What will you make of death?" Why, what but an ornament to you; what but a means of your showing, by action, what that man is who knows and follows the will of nature? "What will you make of sickness?" I will show its nature. I will make a good figure in it; I will be composed and happy; I will not beseech my physician, nor yet will I pray to die. What need you ask further? Whatever you give me, I will make it happy, fortunate, respectable, and enviable.

No, but, "take care not to be sick—it is an evil." Just as if one should say, "Take care that the semblance of three being four does not present itself to you. It is an evil." How an evil, man? If I think as I ought about it, what hurt will it any longer do me? Will it not rather be even an advantage to me? If then I think as I ought of poverty, of sickness, of political disorder, is not that enough for me? Why then must I any longer seek good or evil in externals?

But how is it? These truths are admitted *here;*[1] but nobody carries them home, for immediately everyone is in a state of war with his servant, his neighbors, with those who sneer and ridicule him. Many thanks to Lespius[2] for proving every day that I know nothing.

CHAPTER TWENTY-ONE

Concerning Those Who Light-Heartedly Set Themselves Up as Sophists

THOSE who have merely received bare maxims are presently inclined to throw them up, as a sick stomach does its food. Digest it, and then you will not throw it up; otherwise it will be crude and impure, and unfit to eat. But show us, from what you have digested, some change in your ruling faculty; as wrestlers do in their shoulders, from their exercise and

---

[1] Namely, in the classroom.
[2] An irritating person known to the students.

their diet; as artists, in their skill, from what they have learned. A carpenter does not come and say, "Hear me discourse on the art of building"; he constructs a building, and fits it up, and shows himself master of his trade. Let it be your business likewise to do something like this; be manly in your ways of eating, drinking, dressing; marry, have children, perform the duty of a citizen; bear reproach; bear with an unreasonable brother, father, son, neighbor, companion, as becomes a man. Show us these things, that we may see that you have really learned something from the philosophers. No; but "come and hear me repeat commentaries." Go away, and seek somebody else upon whom to bestow them. "No, but I will explain the doctrines of Chrysippus to you as no one else can; I will elucidate his style in the clearest manner." If possible I will throw in some of the vehemence of Antipater and Archedemus.

And is it for this, then, that young men leave their country and their own parents, that they may come and hear you explain words? Ought they not to return patient, active, free from passion, free from perturbation; furnished with such a provision for life, that, setting out with it, they will be able to bear all events well, and derive ornament from them? But how should you impart what you have not? For have you yourself done anything else, from the beginning, but spend your time in solving syllogisms and convertible propositions and interrogatory arguments? "But such a one has a school, and why should not I have one?" Foolish man, these things are not brought about carelessly and at haphazard; but there must be a fit age, and a method of life, and a guiding God. Is it not so? No one quits the port, or sets sail, till he has sacrificed to the gods, and implored their assistance; nor do men sow without first invoking Ceres. And shall anyone who has undertaken so great a work attempt it safely without the gods? And shall they who apply to such a one, apply to him with success? What else are you doing, man, but divulging the mysteries? As if you said, "There is a temple at Eleusis,

and here is one too; there is a priest, and I will make a priest
here; there is a herald, and I will appoint a herald too; there
is a torch bearer, and I will have a torch bearer; there are
torches, and so shall there be here. The words said, the things
done, are the same. Where is the difference between one and
the other?" Most impious man! is there no difference? Are
these things of use, out of place and out of time? A man should
come with sacrifices and prayers, previously purified, and his
mind affected by the knowledge that he is approaching sacred
and ancient rites. Thus the mysteries become useful; thus we
come to have an idea that all these things were appointed by
the ancients for the instruction and correction of life. But
you divulge and publish them without regard to time and
place, without sacrifices, without purity; you have not the
garment that is necessary for a priest, nor the fitting hair nor
girdle, nor the voice, nor the age, nor have you purified yourself like him. But when you have got the words by heart, you
say, "The mere words are sacred of themselves."

These things are to be approached in another manner. It
is a great, it is a mystical affair; not given by chance, or to
everyone indifferently. Nay, mere wisdom, perhaps, is not
a sufficient qualification for the care of youth. There ought
to be likewise a certain readiness and aptitude for this, and
indeed a particular physical temperament, and, above all, a
counsel from God to undertake this office, as he counseled
Socrates to undertake the office of confuting error; Diogenes,
that of authoritative reproof; Zeno, that of dogmatical instruction. But you set up for a physician, provided with nothing but medicines, and without knowing, or having studied,
where or how they are to be applied. "Why, such a one had
medicines for the eyes, and I have the same." Have you also,
then, a faculty of making use of them? Do you know when
and how and to whom they will be of service? Why then do
you act at hazard? Why are you careless in things of the
greatest importance? Why do you attempt a matter unsuitable

to you? Leave it to those who can perform it and do it honor. Do not bring disgrace upon philosophy by your own acts; nor be one of those who cause the thing itself to be calumniated. But if mere theorems delight you, sit quietly and turn them over by yourself; but never call yourself a philosopher, nor suffer another to call you so; but say, "He is mistaken; for my desires are not different from what they were; nor my pursuits directed to other objects; nor my assents otherwise given; nor have I at all made any change from my former condition in the use of things as they appear." Think and speak thus of yourself, if you would think as you ought; if not, act at random, and do as you do; for it is appropriate to you.

CHAPTER   TWENTY-TWO

Of the Cynic Philosophy

WHEN one of his scholars, who seemed inclined to the Cynic philosophy, asked him what a Cynic must be, and what was the general plan of that sect, Let us examine it, Epictetus said, at our leisure. But this much I can tell you now, that he who attempts so great a matter without divine guidance is an object of divine wrath, and would only bring public dishonor upon himself. For in a well-regulated house no one comes and says to himself, "I ought to be the manager here." If he does, and the master returns and sees him insolently giving orders, he drags him out and has him punished. Such is the case likewise in this great city. For here, too, is a master of the family who orders everything. "*You* are the sun; you can, by making a circuit, form the year and the seasons, and increase and nourish the fruits; you can raise and calm the winds, and give an equable warmth to the bodies of men. Go; make your circuit, and thus move everything from the greatest to the least. *You* are a calf; when the lion appears, act accordingly, or you will suffer for it. *You* are a bull; come and fight; for that is expected of you and becomes you, and you can do it. *You* can lead an army to Troy; be Agamemnon. *You* can engage in single combat with Hector; be Achilles." But if Thersites had come and claimed the command, either he would not have obtained it, or, if he had, he would have disgraced himself before so many more witnesses.

So, deliberate carefully upon this undertaking; it is not what you think it. "I wear an old cloak now, and I shall have one then. I sleep upon the hard ground now, and I shall sleep so then. I will moreover take a wallet and a staff, and go about, and beg of those I meet, and begin by rebuking them; and if I see anyone using effeminate practices, or arranging his curls, or walking in purple, I will rebuke him." If you imagine this to be the whole thing, keep away; come not near it; it belongs not to you. But if you imagine it to be what it really is, and do not think yourself unworthy of it, consider how great a thing you undertake.

First, with regard to yourself; you must no longer, in any instance, appear as now. You must accuse neither God nor man. You must altogether control desire, and must transfer aversion to such things only as are controllable by moral purpose. You must have neither anger, nor resentment, nor envy, nor pity. Neither boy, nor girl, nor fame, nor dainties must have charms for you. For you must know that other men indeed fence themselves with walls and houses and darkness, when they indulge in anything of this kind, and have many concealments; a man shuts the door, places somebody before the apartment: "Say that he is out; say that he is engaged." But the Cynic, instead of all this, must defend himself with self-respect; otherwise he will be improperly exposed in the open air. This is his house, this his door, this his porter, this his darkness. He must not wish to conceal anything relating to himself; for if he does, he is gone; he has lost the Cynic character, the openness, the freedom; he has begun to fear something external; he has begun to need concealment, nor can he get it when he will. For where shall he conceal himself, or how? For if this tutor, this pedagogue[1] of the public, should happen to slip, what must he suffer? Can he, then, who dreads these things, continue wholeheartedly to supervise the conduct of other men? Impracticable, impossible.

In the first place, then, you must purify your own ruling faculty, to match this method of life. Now, the material for me to work upon is my own mind, as wood is for a carpenter, or leather for a shoemaker; and my business is a right use of things as they appear. But body is nothing to me; its parts nothing to me. Let death come when it will, either of the whole body or of part. "Go into exile." And whither? Can anyone turn me out of the universe? He cannot. But wherever I go there is the sun, the moon, the stars, dreams, auguries, communication with God. And even this preparation is by no means sufficient for a true Cynic. But it must further be known that he is a messenger sent from Zeus to men, concerning good and evil; to show them that they are mistaken, and seek the essence of good and evil where it is not, but do not observe it where it is; that he is a spy, like Diogenes, when he was brought to Philip after the battle of Chaeronea. For, in effect, a Cynic is a spy to discover what things are friendly, what hostile, to man; and he must, after making an accurate observation, come and tell them the truth; not be struck with terror, so as to point out to them enemies where there are none; nor, in any other instance, be disconcerted or confounded by appearances.

---

[1] A trusted servant who kept constant watch over the deportment of the boys of wealthy families.

He must, then, if it should so happen, be able to lift up his voice, to come upon the stage, and say, like Socrates: "O mortals, whither are you hurrying? What are you about? Why do you tumble up and down, O miserable wretches, like blind men? You are going the wrong way, and have forsaken the right. You seek prosperity and happiness in a wrong place, where they are not; nor do you give credit to another, who shows you where they are. Why do you seek this possession without? It lies not in the body; if you do not believe me, look at Myro, look at Ofellius.[1] It is not in wealth; if you do not believe me, look upon Croesus; look upon the rich of the present age, how full of lamentation their life is. It is not in public office; for otherwise, they who have been two or three times consul must be happy; but they are not. To whom shall we give heed in these things—to you who look only upon the externals of their condition, and are dazzled by appearances, or to themselves? What do they say? Hear them when they groan, when they sigh, when they pronounce themselves the more wretched and in more danger from these very consulships, this glory and splendor. It is not in empire; otherwise Nero and Sardanapalus had been happy. But not even Agamemnon was happy, though a better man than Sardanapalus or Nero. But when others sleep soundly, what is he doing?

Forth by the roots he rends his hairs.[2]

And what does he himself say?

I wander bewildered; my heart leaps forth from my bosom.

Why, which of your affairs goes ill, poor wretch—your possessions? No. Your body? No. But you have gold and brass in abundance. What then goes ill? That part of you is neglected and corrupted, whatever it be called, by which we

---

[1] Probably famous athletes or gladiators of the day.

[2] Homer, *Iliad*. See Classics Club edition, p. 144.

desire and shrink; by which we pursue and avoid. How neglected? It is ignorant of that for which it was naturally formed, of the essence of good, and of the essence of evil. It is ignorant what is its own, and what another's. And when anything belonging to others goes ill, it says, "I am undone; the Greeks are in danger!"[1] Poor ruling faculty which alone is neglected, and has no care taken of it. "They will die by the sword of the Trojans!" And if the Trojans should not kill them, will they not die? "Yes, but not all at once." Why, where is the difference? For if it be an evil to die, then whether it be all at once or singly, it is equally an evil. Will anything more happen than the separation of soul and body? "Nothing." And when the Greeks perish, is the door shut against you? Is it not in your power to die? "It is." Why then do you lament, while you are a king and hold the scepter of Zeus? A king is no more to be made unfortunate than a god. What are you, then? You are a mere shepherd, truly so called; for you weep, just as shepherds do when the wolf seizes any of their sheep; and they who are governed by you are mere sheep. But why do you come hither? Was your desire in any danger; your aversion; your pursuits; your avoidances? "No," he says, "but my brother's wife has been stolen." Is it not great good luck, then, to be rid of an adulterous wife? "But must we be held in contempt by the Trojans?" What are they— wise men, or fools? If wise, why do you go to war with them? If fools, why do you heed them?

"Where, then, does our good lie, since it does not lie in these things? Tell us, sir, you who are our messenger and spy." Where you do not expect, nor wish to seek it. For if you were willing, you would find it in yourselves; nor would you wander abroad, nor seek what belongs to others, as your own. Turn your thoughts upon yourselves. Consider the impressions which you have. What do you imagine good to be?

---

[1] Referring to Agamemnon's situation; see note on preceding page.

What is prosperous, happy, unhampered. Well, and do you not naturally imagine it great? Do you not imagine it valuable? Do you not imagine it incapable of being hurt? Where, then, must you seek prosperity and exemption from hindrance— in that which is enslaved, or free? "In the free." Is your body, then, enslaved or free? We do not know. Do you not know that it is the slave of fever, gout, defluxion, dysentery; of a tyrant; of fire, steel; of everything stronger than itself? "Yes, it is a slave."

How, then, can anything belonging to the body be un-hampered? And how can that be great or valuable, which is by nature lifeless, earth, clay? What, then; have you nothing free? "Possibly nothing." Why, who can compel you to assent to what appears false? No one. Or who, not to assent to what appears true? No one. Here, then, you see that there is some-thing in you naturally free. But which of you can desire or shun, or use his active powers of pursuit or avoidance, or pre-pare or plan anything, unless he has been impressed by an appearance of its being for his advantage or his duty? No one. You have, then, in these too something unrestrained and free. Cultivate this, unfortunates; take care of this; seek for good here.

"But how is it possible that a man destitute, naked, without house or home, squalid, unattended, an outcast, can lead a serene life?" See; God hath sent us one, to show in practice that it is possible. "Take notice of me, that I am without a country, without a house, without an estate, without a servant; I lie on the ground; have no wife, no children, no coat; but have only earth and heaven and one poor cloak. And what do I need? Am not I without sorrow, without fear? Am not I free? Did any of you ever see me disappointed of my de-sire, or incurring what I wish to avoid? Did I ever blame God or man? Did I ever accuse anyone? Have any of you seen me look discontented? How do I treat those whom you fear and stand before in awe? Is it not like poor slaves? Who that sees me does not think that he sees his own king and master?"

This is the language, this the character, this the undertaking, of a Cynic. You say no; but their mark is the wallet and the staff and a large capacity for swallowing and stowing away whatever is given them; abusing unseasonably those they meet, or showing their bare shoulder. Do you consider how you shall attempt so important an undertaking? First take a mirror. View your shoulders, examine your back, your loins. It is the Olympic games, man, for which you are to be entered; not a poor slight contest. In the Olympic games a champion is not allowed merely to be conquered and depart; but must first be disgraced in the view of the whole world —not of the Athenians alone, or Spartans, or Nicopolitans; and then he who has prematurely departed must be whipped too, and, before that, must have suffered thirst and heat, and have swallowed an abundance of dust.

Consider carefully, know yourself; consult the Divinity; attempt nothing without God; for if he counsels you, be assured that it is his will, whether you become eminent or suffer many a blow. For there is this fine circumstance connected with the character of a Cynic, that he must be beaten like an ass, and yet, when beaten, must love those who beat him as though he were the father, the brother of all.

"No, to be sure; but if anybody beats you, stand publicly and roar out, 'O Caesar! am I to suffer such things in breach of your peace? Let us go before the proconsul.'"

But what is Caesar to a Cynic, or what is the proconsul, or anyone else, but Zeus, who has given him his power, and whom he serves? Does he invoke any other but him? And is he not persuaded that, whatever he suffers of this sort, it is Zeus who does it to exercise him? Now Hercules, when he was exercised by Eurystheus, did not think himself miserable, but executed with alacrity all that was to be done. And shall he who is appointed to the combat, and exercised by Zeus, cry out and take offense at things? A worthy person, truly, to bear the scepter of Diogenes! Hear what he in a fever said to those who were passing by. "Foolish men, why do you not stay? Do you take such a journey to Olympia to see the destruction or combat of the champions; and have you no inclination to see the combat between a man and a fever?" No doubt a man of that sort would have blamed God, who had sent him into the world, for maltreating him! He took pride in his distress, demanding that those who passed by should gaze upon him. What will he blame God for? Because he is living a decent life? What charge does he bring against God? That he sets his own virtue in a clearer light? Well; and what does he say of poverty; of death; of pain? How did he compare his happiness with that of the Persian king; or rather, thought it beyond comparison! For amidst perturbations, and griefs, and fears, and disappointed desires, and incurred aversions, how can there be any entrance for happiness? And where there are corrupt principles, there must all these things necessarily be.

And when the same young man inquired whether, if a friend should desire to come to him and take care of him when he was sick, he should comply, Epictetus said, Will you find me the friend of a Cynic? For to be worthy of being numbered among his friends, a person must be a Cynic; he must share with him the scepter and the kingdom, and be a worthy minister, if he would be honored with his friendship; as Diogenes was the friend of Antisthenes; as Crates, of Diogenes. Do you think that he who only comes to him and salutes him is his friend; and that he will think him worthy of being entertained as such? If such a thought comes into your head, rather look round you for some desirable dunghill to shelter you in your fever from the north wind, that you may not perish by taking cold. But you seem to me to prefer to get into somebody's house, and to be well fed there awhile. What business have you, then, even to attempt so important an undertaking as this?

"But," said the young man, "will marriage and parentage be recognized as important duties by a Cynic?"

Grant me a community of sages, and no one there, perhaps, will readily apply himself to the Cynic philosophy. For on whose account should he there embrace that method of life? However, supposing he does, there will be nothing to restrain him from marrying and having children. For his wife will be another like himself, and so will his father-in-law, and his children will be brought up in the same manner. But as the state of things now is, like that of an army prepared for battle, it is a question whether the Cynic should be free from distraction, entirely attentive to the service of God; at liberty to walk among mankind; not tied down to common duties, nor entangled in the relations of life, which if he transgresses, he will no longer keep the character of a wise and good man; and which if he observes, there is an end of him, as the messenger and scout and herald of the gods? For consider, there are some offices due to his father-in-law, some to the other relations of his wife, some to his wife herself. Besides, after this, he is confined to the care of his family when sick, and to providing for their support. At the very least, he must have a vessel to warm water in, to bathe his child; there must be wool, oil, a bed, a cup for his wife after her delivery; and thus the furniture increases; more business, more distraction. Where, for the future, is this king whose time is devoted to the public good?—

To whom the people is trusted, and many a care?[1]

who ought to superintend others, married men, fathers of children—whether one treats his wife well or ill; who quarrels; which family is well regulated; which not—like a physician

---

[1] Homer, *Iliad*. See Classics Club edition, p. 23.

who goes about and feels the pulse of his patients: "You have a fever; you the headache; you the gout. You must abstain from food; you must eat; you must omit bathing; you must have an incision made; you be cauterized." Where shall he have leisure for this who is tied down to common duties? Must he not provide clothes for his children, and send them, with writing implements and tablets, to a schoolmaster? Must he not provide a bed for them—for they cannot be Cynics from their very birth? Otherwise, it would have been better to expose them as soon as they were born than to kill them thus. Do you see to what we bring down our Cynic; how we deprive him of his kingdom? "Well, but Crates[1] was married." The case of which you speak was a particular one, arising from love; and the woman was another Crates. But we are inquiring about ordinary and common marriages; and in this inquiry we do not find the affair much suited to the condition of a Cynic.

"How then shall he keep up society?"

For heaven's sake, do they confer a greater benefit upon the world who leave two or three brats in their stead, than those who, so far as possible, oversee all mankind—what they do, how they live; what they attend to, what they neglect, in spite of their duty? Did all those who left children to the Thebans do them more good than Epaminondas, who died childless? And did Priam, who was the father of fifty profligates, or Danaus, or Aeolus, conduce more to the advantage of society than Homer? Shall a military command, or any other post, then, exempt a man from marrying and becoming a father, so that he shall be thought to have made sufficient amends for the want of children; and shall not the kingdom of a Cynic be a proper compensation for it? Perhaps we do not

[1] Crates, a rich Theban, gave away a large fortune, and assumed the wallet and staff of a Cynic philosopher. Hipparchia, a Thracian lady, gave up wealth and friends to share his poverty, in spite of his advice to the contrary. Marriage for love was unusual in the ancient world.

understand his grandeur, nor duly represent to ourselves the character of Diogenes; but we think of Cynics as they are now, who stand like dogs watching at tables, and who have only the lowest things in common with the others; else things like these would not move us, nor should we be astonished that a Cynic will not marry nor have children. Consider, sir, that he is the father of mankind; that all men are his sons, and all women his daughters. Thus he attends to all; thus takes care of all. What! do you think it is from impertinence that he rebukes those he meets? He does it as a father, as a brother, as a minister of the common parent, Zeus.

Ask me, if you please, too, whether a Cynic will engage in the administration of the commonwealth. What commonwealth do you inquire after, foolish man, greater than what he administers? Why should he harangue among the Athenians about revenues and taxes, whose business it is to debate with all mankind—with the Athenians, Corinthians, and Romans equally—not about taxes and revenues, or peace and war, but about happiness and misery, prosperity and adversity, slavery and freedom? Do you ask me whether a man engages in the administration of the commonwealth who administers such a commonwealth as this? Ask me, too, whether he will accept any command. I will answer you again, What command, foolish one, is greater than that which he now exercises?

But he has need of a constitution duly qualified; for if he should appear consumptive, thin, and pale, his testimony has no longer the same authority. For he must not only give a proof to the layman, by the qualities of his soul, that it is possible to be a man of weight and merit without those things that strike *them* with admiration; but he must show, too, by his body, that a simple and frugal diet, under the open air, does no injury to the body. "See, I and my body bear witness to this." As Diogenes did; for he went about in hale condition, and gained the attention of the many by his mere physical aspect. But a Cynic in poor condition seems a mere beggar; all avoid him, all are offended at him; for he ought not to appear slovenly, so as to drive people from him; but even his indigence should be clean and attractive.

Much natural tact and acuteness are likewise necessary in a Cynic (otherwise he is almost worthless), that he may be able to give an answer, readily and pertinently, upon every occasion. So Diogenes, to one who asked him, "Are you that Diogenes who does not believe there are any gods?" "How so," replied he, "when I think *you* odious to them?" Again, when Alexander surprised him sleeping, and repeated,

To sleep all the night becomes not a man who gives counsel;[1]

before he was quite awake, he responded,

To whom the people is trusted, and many a care.

But, above all, the Cynic's governing principle must be clearer than the sun; otherwise he must necessarily be a common cheat and a rascal if, while himself guilty of some vice, he reproves others. For consider how the case stands. Arms and guards give a power to common kings and tyrants of reproving and of punishing delinquents, though they be wicked themselves; but to a Cynic, instead of arms and guards, conscience gives this power. When he knows that he has watched and labored for mankind; that he has slept pure, and waked still purer; and that he has regulated all his thoughts as the friend, as the minister of the gods, as a partner of the empire of Zeus; that he is ready to say, upon all occasions,

Conduct me, Zeus, and thou, O Destiny,[2]

and, "If it thus pleases the gods, thus let it be,"[3] why should he not dare to speak boldly to his own brethren, to his chil-

---

[1] Homer, *Iliad*. See Classics Club edition, p. 23.

[2] Cleanthes, in Diogenes Laertius.

[3] Plato, *Crito*. See Classics Club edition, p. 66.

dren; in a word, to his kindred? Hence he who is thus qualified is neither impertinent nor a busybody; for he is not busied about the affairs of others, but his own, when he oversees the transactions of men. Otherwise call a general a busybody, when he oversees, inspects, and watches his soldiers and punishes the disorderly. But if you reprove others at the very time that you are hiding a cake under your arm, I will ask you if you had not better go into a corner, and eat up what you have stolen. But what have you to do with the concerns of others? For what are *you?* Are you the bull in the herd, or the queen of the bees? Show me such ensigns of empire as she has from nature. But if you are a drone, and lay claim to the kingdom of the bees, don't you think that your fellow citizens will drive you out, just as the bees do the drones?

A Cynic must, besides, have so much patience as to seem insensible and like a stone to the vulgar. No one reviles, no one beats, no one affronts *him;* but he has surrendered his body to be treated at pleasure by anyone who will. For he remembers that the inferior, in whatever respect it is the inferior, must be conquered by the superior; and the body is inferior to the multitude, the weaker to the stronger. He never, therefore, enters into a combat where he can be conquered, but immediately gives up what belongs to others; he does not claim what is slavish and dependent; but in what concerns will and sense impressions you will see that he has so many eyes, you would say Argus was blind in comparison to him. Is his choice ever reckless, his pursuits ever rash, his desire ever disappointed, his aversion ever incurred, his aim ever fruitless? Is he ever querulous, ever dejected, ever envious? Here lies all his attention and application. With regard to other things, he enjoys profound quiet. All is peace. There is no robber, no tyrant for the will. But there is for the body? Yes. The estate? Yes. Offices and honors? Yes. And what cares he for these? When anyone, therefore, would frighten him with them he says: "Go look for children; masks are frightful to them; but *I* know they are only shells, and have nothing within."

Such is the affair about which you are deliberating; therefore, if you please, for heaven's sake! defer it, and first consider how you are prepared for it. Observe what Hector says to Andromache,

> *War is the sphere for all men, and for me.*[1]

Thus conscious was he of his own qualifications and of her weakness.

CHAPTER TWENTY-THREE

Concerning Such as Read and Dispute Ostentatiously

FIRST, say to yourself what you would be; and then do what you have to do. For in almost everything we see this to be the practice. Olympic champions first determine what they would be, and then act accordingly. To a racer in a longer course there must be one kind of diet, walking, anointing, and training; to one in a shorter, all these must be different; and to a Pentathlete, still more different. You will find the case the same in the manual arts. If a carpenter, you must have such and such things; if a smith, such other. For if we do not refer each of our actions to some standard, we shall act at random; if to an improper one, we shall miss our aim. Further, there is a general and a particular end. The first is, to act as

---

[1] Homer, *Iliad*. See Classics Club edition, p. 99.

a man. What is comprehended in this? To be gentle, yet not sheepish; not to be mischievous, like a wild beast. But the particular end relates to the study and choice of each individual. A harpist is to act as a harpist; a carpenter, as a carpenter; a philosopher, as a philosopher; an orator, as an orator. When, therefore, you say, "Come, and hear me discourse," observe, first, not to do this at random; and, in the next place, after you have found to what end you refer it, consider whether it be a proper one. Do you wish to be useful, or be praised? You presently hear him say, "What do I value the praise of the multitude?" And he says well; for this is nothing to a musician, or a geometrician, as such. You would be useful then. In what? Tell us, that we too may run to make part of your audience. Now, is it possible for anyone to benefit others, who has received no benefit himself? No; for neither can he who is not a carpenter, or a shoemaker, benefit anyone in respect to those arts. Would you know, then, whether you have received benefit? Produce your principles, philosopher. What is the aim and promise of desire? Not to be disappointed. What of aversion? Not to be incurred. Come, do we fulfill this promise? Tell me the truth; but, if you falsify, I will tell it to *you*. The other day, when your audience came but coldly together, and did not receive what you said with applause, you went away dejected. Again, the other day when you were praised, you went about asking everybody, "What did you think of me?" "Upon my life, sir, it was prodigious." "But how did I express myself upon that subject?" "Which?" "Where I gave a description of Pan and the Nymphs." "Most excellently." And do you tell me, after this, that you regulate your desires and aversions conformably to nature? Go away! Persuade somebody else.

Did you not, the other day, praise a man contrary to your own opinion? Did you not flatter a certain senator? Yet would you wish your own children to be like him? "Heaven forbid!"

Why then did you praise and cajole him? "He is a gifted young man, and attentive to discourses." How so? "He admires *me*." Now indeed you have produced your proof.

After all, what do you think? Don't these very people secretly despise you? When a man conscious of no good action or intention finds some philosopher saying, "You are a great genius, and of a frank and candid disposition," what do you think he says, but "This man has some need of me"? Pray tell me what mark of a great genius he has shown. You see he has long conversed with you, has heard your discourses, has attended your lectures. Has he turned his attention to himself? Has he perceived his own faults? Has he thrown off his conceit? Does he seek an instructor? "Yes, he does." An instructor how to live? No, fool, but how to talk; for it is upon this account that he admires you. Hear what he says: "This man writes with very great art, and much more finely than Dion."[1] That is quite another thing. Does he say, This is a modest, faithful, calm person? But if he said this too, I would ask him, if he is faithful, what does it mean to be a faithful man? And if he could not tell, I would add, First learn the meaning of what you say, and then speak.

While you are in this bad disposition, then, and gaping after applauders, and counting your hearers, can you be of benefit to others? "Today I had many more hearers." "Yes, many; we think there were five hundred." "You say nothing; estimate them at a thousand." "Dion never had so great an audience." "How should he?" "And they have a fine taste for discourses." "What is excellent, sir, will move even a stone." Here is the language of a philosopher! Here is the disposition of one who is to be beneficial to mankind! Here is the man, attentive to discourses, who has read the works of the Socratic philosophers, as such; not as if they were the writings of

---

[1] Probably a popular lecturer of the day.

orators, like Lysias and Isocrates! "I have often wondered by what arguments—"[1] No; "By what argument"; that is the more perfectly accurate expression. Haven't you been reading this literature as you would little odes? If you read them as you ought, you would not dwell on such trifles, but would rather consider such a passage as this: "Anytus and Melitus may kill me, but they cannot hurt me." And "I am not always disposed to defer to my friends, but to that reason which, after examination, appears to me to be the best."[2] Hence, whoever heard Socrates say, "I know something and teach it"? But he sent different people to different instructors; they came to him, desiring to be introduced to the philosophers; and he took them and introduced them. No; but, you think, as he accompanied them, he used to give them such advice as this: "Hear *me* discourse today at the house of Quadratus." Why should I hear you? Have you a mind to show me how finely you put words together, sir? And what good does that do you? "But praise me." What do you mean by praising you? "Say, Incomparable! Prodigious!" Well; I do say it. But if praise be that which the philosophers put in the category of the *good*, what have I to praise you for? If it be good to speak well, teach me, and I will praise you. "What, then; ought these things to be heard without pleasure?" By no means. I do not hear even a harpist without pleasure; but am I therefore to devote myself to playing upon the harp? Hear what Socrates says to his judges: "It would not be decent for me to appear before you, at this age, composing speeches like a boy."[3] Like a boy, he says. For it is, without doubt, a pretty accomplishment to select words and place them together, and then to read or speak them gracefully in public; and in the

---

[1] The beginning of Xenophon's Memoirs of Socrates. There was a debate among the critics, whether *argument* or *arguments* was the proper reading.

[2] Plato, *Apology*. See Classics Club edition, pp. 47-48.

[3] Plato, *Apology*. See Classics Club edition, p. 33.

midst of the discourse to observe that "he vows by all that is good, there are but few capable of these things."

But does a philosopher apply to people to hear him? Does he not attract those who are fitted to receive benefit from him, in the same manner as the sun or their necessary food does? What physician applies to anybody to be cured by him? (Though now indeed I hear that the physicians at Rome advertise for patients; but in my time they were applied to.) "I apply to you to come and hear that you are in a bad way, and that you take care of everything but what you ought; that you know not what is good or evil, and are unfortunate and unhappy." A fine advertisement! And yet, unless the discourse of a philosopher has this effect, both that and the speaker are lifeless.

Rufus used to say, "If you are at leisure to praise me, I speak to no purpose." And indeed he used to speak in such a manner, that each of us who heard him supposed that some person had gone to Rufus and accused us; he so precisely hit upon what was done by us, and placed the faults of everyone before his eyes.

The school of a philosopher is a surgery. You are not to go out of it with pleasure, but with pain; for you do not come there in health; but one of you has a dislocated shoulder; another, an abscess; a third, a fistula; a fourth, the headache. And am I, then, to sit uttering pretty, trifling thoughts and little exclamations, that, when you have praised me, you may each of you go away with the same dislocated shoulder, the same aching head, the same fistula, and the same abscess that you brought? And is it for this that young men are to travel? And do they leave their parents, their friends, their relations, and their estates, that they may praise you while you utter your clever little mottoes? Was this the practice of Socrates; of Zeno; of Cleanthes?

What then! is there not in speaking a style and manner of exhortation? Who denies it? Just as there is a manner of confutation and of instruction. But who ever, therefore, added that of *ostentation* for a fourth? For in what does the hortatory manner consist? In being able to show, to one and all, the contradictions in which they are involved; and that they care for everything rather than what they mean to care for; for they mean the things conducive to happiness, but they seek them where they are not to be found. To effect this, must a thousand seats be placed, and an audience invited; and you, in a fine robe or cloak, ascend the rostrum, and describe the death of Achilles? Forbear, for heaven's sake! to bring, so far as you are able, good works and practices into disgrace. Nothing, to be sure, gives more force to exhortation than when the speaker shows that he has need of the hearers; but tell me who, when he hears you reading or speaking, is solicitous about *himself*; or turns his attention upon himself; or says, when he is gone away, "The philosopher hit me well"? Instead of this, even though you are in high vogue, one hearer merely remarks to another, "He spoke finely about Xerxes!" "No," says the other, "I preferred what he said about the battle of Thermopylae!" Is this the audience for a philosopher?

CHAPTER TWENTY-FOUR

That We Ought Not to Yearn for Things Beyond Our Control

LET not another's disobedience to nature become an evil for you; for you were not born to be depressed and unhappy with others, but to be happy with them. And if anybody is unhappy, remember that his unhappiness is his own fault; for God made all men to enjoy felicity and peace. He has furnished all with means for this purpose; having given them some things for their own, others not for their own. Whatever is subject to restraint, compulsion, or deprivation is not their own; whatever is not subject to restraint is their own. And the essence of good and evil he has placed in things which are our own, as it became him who provides for, and protects us, with paternal care.

"But I have parted with such a one, and he is therefore in grief."

And why did he consider what belonged to another his own? Why did he not consider, while he was happy in seeing you, that you are mortal, that you are liable to change your abode? Therefore he bears the punishment of his own folly. But to what purpose, or for what cause, do you too suffer depression of spirits? Have *you* not studied these things? Like trifling, silly women, have you regarded the things you took delight in, the places, the persons, the conversations, as if they were to last forever; and do you now sit crying, because you do not see the same people, or live in the same place? Indeed, you deserve to be so overcome, and thus to become more wretched than ravens or crows, which, without groaning or

239

longing for their former state, can fly where they will, build their nests in another place, and cross the seas.

"Yes, but this happens from their want of reason."

Was reason then given to us by the gods for the purpose of unhappiness and misery, to make us live wretched and lamenting? Oh, by all means, let every one be deathless! Let nobody leave home! Let us never leave home ourselves, but remain rooted to a spot, like plants! And if any of our acquaintance should quit his abode, let us sit and cry; and when he comes back, let us dance and clap our hands like children. Shall we never wean ourselves, and remember what we have heard from the philosophers—unless we have heard them only as juggling enchanters—that the universe is one great city, and the substance one of which it is formed; that there must necessarily be a certain rotation of things; that some must give way to others, some be dissolved, and others rise in their stead; some remain in the same situation, and others be moved; but that all is full of beloved ones, first of the gods, and then of men, by nature endeared to each other; that some must be separated, others live together, rejoicing in the present, and not grieving for the absent; and that man, besides a natural greatness of mind and contempt of things independent on his own will, is likewise formed not to be rooted to the earth, but to go at different times to different places; sometimes on urgent occasions, and sometimes merely for the sake of observation. Such was the case of Odysseus, who

> *Saw the cities and watched the habits of various men;*[1]

and, even before him, of Hercules, to travel over the habitable world,

> *Observing manners, good or ill, of men;*[1]

to expel and clear away the one, and, in its stead, to introduce the other. Yet how many friends do you not think he must

---

[1] Homer, *Odyssey*. See Classics Club edition, p. 3.

have at Thebes; how many at Argos; how many at Athens; and how many did he acquire in his travels? He married, too, when he thought it a proper time, and became a father, and then quitted his children; not lamenting and longing for them, nor as if he had left them orphans; for he knew that no human creature is an orphan, but that there is a father who always, and without intermission, takes care of all. For he had not merely heard it as matter of talk, that Zeus was the father of mankind; but he esteemed and called him his own father, and performed all that he did with a view to him. Hence he was, in every place, able to live happy. But it is never possible to make happiness consistent with a longing after what is not present. For true happiness implies the possession of all which is desired, as in case of satiety with food; there must be no thirst, no hunger.

"But Odysseus longed for his wife, and sat weeping on a rock."[1]

Why do you regard Homer and his fables as authority for everything? Or, if Odysseus really did weep, what was he but a wretched man? But what wise and good man is wretched? The universe is surely ill governed, if Zeus does not take care that his subjects be happy like himself. But these are unlawful and profane thoughts; and Odysseus, if he did indeed weep and wail, was not a good man. For who can be a good man who does not know what he is? And who knows this, and yet forgets that all things made are perishable; and that it is not possible for man and man always to live together? What then? To desire impossibilities is base and foolish; it is the behavior of a stranger in the world; of one who fights against God in the only way he can, by holding false opinions.

"But my mother grieves when she does not see me."

And why has she not learned these doctrines? I do not say that care ought not to be taken that she may not lament; but

---

[1] Homer, *Odyssey*. See Classics Club edition, p. 60.

that we are not to insist absolutely upon what is not in our own power. Now, the grief of another is not in my power; but my own grief is. I will therefore absolutely suppress my own, for that is in my power; and I will endeavor to suppress another's grief so far as I am able; but I will not insist upon it absolutely, otherwise I shall fight against God; I shall resist Zeus, and oppose him in the administration of the universe; and not only my children's children will bear the punishment of this disobedience and fighting against God, but I myself too—starting, and full of perturbation, both in the daytime and in my nightly dreams; trembling at every message, and having my peace dependent on intelligence from others. "Somebody has come from Rome." "I trust no harm has happened." Why, what harm can happen to you where you are not? "From Greece." "No harm, I hope." Why, at this rate, every place may be the cause of misfortune to you. Is it not enough for you to be unfortunate where you are, but it must happen beyond sea, too, and by letters? Such is the security of your condition!

"But what if my friends there should be dead?"

What, indeed, but that those are dead who were born to die? Do you at once wish to grow old, and yet not to see the death of anyone you love? Do you not know that, in a long course of time, many and various events must necessarily happen; that a fever must get the better of one, a highwayman of another, a tyrant of a third? For such is the world we live in; such they who live in it with us. Heats and colds, improper diet, journeys, voyages, winds, and various accidents destroy some, banish others; destine one to an embassy, another to a camp. And now, pray, will you sit in consternation about all these things, lamenting, disappointed, wretched, dependent on another; and not on one or two only, but ten thousand times ten thousand?

Is this what you have heard from the philosophers; this what you have learned? Do you not know what sort of a thing warfare is? One must keep guard, another go out as a spy, another even to battle. It is neither possible, nor indeed desirable, that all should be in the same place; but you, neglecting to perform the orders of your general, complain whenever anything a little hard is commanded; and do not consider what influence you have on the army, so far as lies in your power. For, if all should imitate you, nobody will dig a trench, or throw up a rampart, or stand guard, or expose himself to danger; but everyone will appear useless to the expedition. Again, if you were a sailor in a voyage, suppose you were to fix upon one place, and there remain, and if it should be necessary to climb the mast, refuse to do it; if to run to the bow of the ship, refuse to do it! And what captain would tolerate you? Would he not throw you overboard as a useless piece of goods and mere luggage, and a bad example to the other sailors?

Thus, also, in the present case; everyone's life is a warfare, and that long and various. You must observe the duty of a soldier, and perform everything at the nod of your general, and even, if possible, divine what he would have done. For there is no comparison between the above-mentioned general and this whom you now obey, either in power or excellence of character. You are placed in an extensive command, and not in a mean post; your life is a perpetual office-holding? Do you not know that such a one must spend but little time on his affairs at home, but be much abroad, either commanding or obeying; attending on the duties either of a magistrate, a soldier, or a judge? And now, pray, would you be fixed and rooted on the same spot, like a plant?

"Why, it is pleasant."

Who denies it? And so is a soup pleasant, and a fine woman is pleasant. Is not this just what they say who make pleasure their end? Do you not perceive whose words you have uttered? That of Epicureans and debauchees. And while you follow their practices and hold their principles, do you talk to us of the doctrines of Zeno and Socrates? Why do you not throw away as far as possible those assumed traits which belong to others, and with which you have nothing to do? What else do the Epicureans desire than to sleep without hindrance, and rise without compulsion; and when they have risen, to yawn at their leisure and wash their faces; then write and read what they please; then prate about some trifle or other, and be applauded by their friends, whatever they say; then go out for a walk, and, after they have taken a turn, bathe, and then eat, and then to bed? In what manner do they spend their time there, why should I say how? For it is easily guessed.

Come now; do you also tell me what kind of life you desire to lead, who are a zealot for truth, and follower of Diogenes and Socrates? What would you do at Athens—these very same things? Why then do you call yourself a Stoic? They who falsely claim Roman citizenship are punished severely; and must those be dismissed with impunity who falsely claim so great a thing, and so venerable a title, as you? Or is this not impossible; and is there not a divine and powerful and inevitable law, which exacts the greatest punishments from those who are guilty of the greatest offenses? For what does this law say?—Let him who claims what belongs not to him be arrogant, be vainglorious, be base, be a slave; let him grieve, let him envy, let him pity; and, in a word, let him lament and be miserable.

"What then! would you have me pay my court to such a one? Would you have me frequent his door?"[1]

If reason requires it for your country, for your relations, for mankind, why should you not go? You are not ashamed to go to the door of a shoemaker when you want shoes, nor of a gardener when you want lettuce. Why, then, in regard to the rich, when you have some similar want?

---

[1] Obviously the speaker has been expected to pay court to an influential man. The transition is so abrupt as to suggest that something was lost from the manuscript here.

"Yes; but I need not be awed before a shoemaker."

Nor before a rich man.

"I need not flatter a gardener."

Nor a rich man.

"How, then, shall I get what I want?"

Why, do I bid you go in expectation of getting it? No; only that you may do your duty.

"Why, then, after all, should I go?"

That you may have gone; that you may have discharged the duties of a citizen, of a brother, of a friend. And, after all, remember that you are going as if to a shoemaker, to a gardener, who has no monopoly of anything great or respectable, though he should sell it ever so dear. You are going as if to buy lettuces worth an obolus,[1] but by no means worth a talent.[1] So here, too, if the matter is worth going to his door about, I will go; if it is worth talking with him about, I will talk with him. But if one must kiss his hand, too, and cajole him with praise, that is paying too dear. It is not expedient for myself, nor my country, nor my fellow citizens, nor my friends, to destroy what constitutes the good citizen and the friend.

"But one will appear not to have set heartily about the business, if one thus fails."

What, have you again forgotten why you went? Do you not know that a wise and good man does nothing for appearance, but everything for the sake of having acted well?

"What advantage is it, then, to him, to have acted well?"

What advantage is it to one who writes down the name of Dion without a blunder? The having written it.

"Is there no reward, then?"

Why, do you seek any greater reward for a good man than the doing what is fair and just? And yet, at Olympia, you

---

[1] The obolus was worth only a few cents; the talent, another ancient unit of weight and money, varied greatly in value with time and place, and according to whether it was of silver or gold, but it represented a substantial sum.

desire nothing else, but think it enough to be crowned victor. Does it appear to you so small and worthless a thing to be just, good, and happy? Besides, being introduced by God into this Great City [the world], and bound to discharge at this time the duties of a man, do you still want nurses and a mother; and are you conquered and made effeminate by the tears of poor weak women? Are you thus determined never to cease being an infant? Do you not know that, if one acts like a child, the older he is, so much the more he is ridiculous?

Did you never visit anyone at Athens at his own house?

"Yes; whomsoever I pleased."

Why, now you are here, be willing to visit this person, and you will still see whom you please; only let it be without meanness, without undue desire or aversion, and your affairs will go well; but their going well, or not, does not consist in going to the house and standing at the door, or the contrary; but lies within, in your own principles, when you have acquired a contempt for things uncontrollable by will, and esteem none of them your own, but hold that what belongs to you is only to judge and think, to exert rightly your aims, your desires, and aversions. What further room is there after this for flattery, for meanness? Why do you still long for the quiet you elsewhere enjoyed; for places familiar to you? Stay a little, and these will become familiar to you in their turn; and then, if you are so mean-spirited, you may weep and lament again on leaving these.

"How, then, am I to preserve an affectionate disposition?"

As becomes a noble-spirited and happy person. For reason will never tell you to be dejected and broken-hearted, or to depend on another, or to reproach either God or man. Be affectionate in such a manner as to observe all this. But if, from affection, as you call it, you are to be a slave and miserable, it is not worth your while to be affectionate. And what restrains you from loving anyone as a mortal—as a person who may be obliged to quit you? Pray did not Socrates

love his own children? But it was as became one who was
free, and mindful that his first duty was to gain the love of
the gods. Hence he violated no part of the character of a good
man, either in his defense or in fixing a penalty on himself.[1]
Nor yet before, when he was a senator or a soldier. But *we*
make use of every pretense to be mean-spirited; some on account of a child; some, of a mother; and some, of a brother.
But it is not fit to be unhappy on account of anyone, but happy
on account of all; and chiefly of God, who has constituted
us for this purpose. What! did Diogenes love nobody, who
was so gentle and benevolent as cheerfully to undergo so
many pains and miseries of body for the common good of
mankind? Yes, he did love them; but how? As became a minister of Zeus; at once caring for men, and obedient to God.
Hence the whole earth, not any particular place, was his country. And when he was taken captive he did not long for
Athens and his friends and acquaintance there, but made himself acquainted with the pirates, and endeavored to reform
them; and when he was at last sold into captivity, he lived at
Corinth just as before at Athens; and if he had gone to the
Perrhoebeans,[2] he would have been exactly the same. Thus
is freedom acquired. Hence he used to say, "Ever since Antisthenes made me free [3] I have ceased to be a slave." How
did *he* make him free? Hear what he says: "He taught me
what was my own and what not. An estate is not my own.
Kindred, domestics, friends, reputation, familiar places, manner of life, all belong to another." "What is your own, then?"

---

[1] It was the custom of Athens, in cases where no fixed punishment
was appointed by the law, to ask the criminal himself what penalty he
thought he deserved. When the judges asked Socrates this question, he
answered, "The highest honors and rewards, and to be maintained in
the Prytaneum at the public expense,"—an answer which so extremely
irritated his judges, that they immediately condemned him to death.

[2] A people towards the extremity of Greece.

[3] Diogenes was the disciple of Antisthenes.

"The right use of the phenomena of existence. He showed me that I have *this*, not subject to restraint or compulsion; no one can hinder or force me in this, otherwise than as I please.

"Who, then, after this, has any power over me—Philip, or Alexander, or Perdiccas, or the Persian king? Where can they get it? For he that is to be subdued by man must first be subdued by things. He, therefore, of whom neither pleasure, nor pain, nor fame, nor riches can get the better; and he who is able, whenever he thinks fit, to abandon his whole body with contempt and depart, whose slave can he ever be? To whom is he subject?" But if Diogenes had taken pleasure in living at Athens, and had been subdued by that manner of life, his affairs would have been at everyone's disposal; and whoever was stronger would have had the power of grieving him. How would he have flattered the pirates, think you, to make them sell him to some Athenian, that he might see again the fine Piraeus, the Long Walls, and the Acropolis? How would you see them—as a slave and a miserable wretch? And what good would that do you? "No; but as a free man." How free? See, somebody lays hold on you, takes you away from your usual manner of life, and says: "You are my slave; for it is in my power to restrain you from living as you like. It is in my power to afflict and humble you. Whenever I please, you may be cheerful once more, and set out elated for Athens."

What do you say to him who thus enslaves you? What rescuer can you find? Or dare you not so much as look up at him; but, without saying more, beg to be set free? Why, you ought to go to prison gladly, man, even speedily, outstripping your conductors. Instead of this do you regret living at Rome and long for Greece? And when you must die, will you then, too, come crying to us that you shall no more see Athens, nor walk in the Lyceum? Is it for this that you have traveled? Is it for this that you have been seeking for somebody to do you good? What good—that you may the more easily solve syllogisms and manage hypothetical arguments?

And is it for this reason you left your brother, your country, your friends, your family, that you might carry back such acquirements as these? So that you did not travel to learn constancy or tranquillity, or that, secured from harm, you might complain of no one, accuse no one; that no one might injure you; and that thus you might preserve your relations in society, without hindrance. You have made a fine traffic of it, to carry home hypothetical arguments and convertible propositions! If you please, too, sit in the market, and cry them for sale, as peddlers do their medicines.

Why will you not rather deny that you know even what you have learned, for fear of bringing a scandal upon such theorems as useless? What harm has philosophy done you—in what has Chrysippus injured you—that you should demonstrate by your actions that such studies are of no value? Had you not evils enough at home? How many causes for grief and lamentation had you there, even if you had not traveled? But you have added more; and if you ever get any new acquaintance and friends, you will find fresh causes for groaning; and, in like manner, if you attach yourself to any other country. To what purpose, therefore, do you live—to heap sorrow upon sorrow, to make you wretched? And then you tell me this is affection. What affection, man? If it be good, it cannot be the cause of any evil; if evil, I will have nothing to do with it. I was born for my own good, not evil.

"What, then, is the proper training for these cases?"

First, the highest and principal means, and as obvious as if at your very door, is this—that when you attach yourself to anything, it may not be as to a secure possession.

"How, then?"

As to something brittle as glass or earthenware; that when it happens to be broken, you may not lose your self-command. So here, too, when you embrace your child, or your brother, or your friend, never yield yourself wholly to the fair semblance, nor let the passion pass into excess; but curb it, restrain it—like those who stand behind triumphant victors, and remind them that they are men. Do you likewise remind yourself that you love what is mortal; that you love what is not your own. It is allowed you for the present, not irrevocably, nor forever; but as a fig, or a bunch of grapes, in the appointed season. If you long for these in winter, you are foolish. So, if you long for your son, or your friend, when you cannot have him, remember that you are wishing for figs in winter. For as winter is to a fig, so is every accident in the universe to those things with which it interferes. In the next place, whatever objects give you pleasure, call before yourself the opposite images. What harm is there, while you kiss your child, in saying softly, "Tomorrow you may die"; and so to your friend, "Tomorrow either you or I may go away, and we may never see each other again"?

"But these sayings are ominous."

And so are some incantations; but because they are useful, I do not mind it; only let them be useful. But do you call anything ominous except what implies some ill? Cowardice is ominous; baseness is ominous; lamentation, grief, shamelessness. These are words of bad omen; and yet we ought not to shrink from using them, as a guard against the things they mean. But do you tell me that a word is ominous which is significant of anything natural? Say, too, that it is ominous for ears of corn to be reaped; for this signifies the destruction of the corn, but not of the world. Say, too, that the fall of the leaf is ominous; and that confectionery should be produced from figs, and raisins from grapes. For all these are changes from a former state into another—not a destruction, but a certain appointed economy and administration. Such is absence, a slight change; such is death, a greater change—not from what now is nothing, but to what now is not.

"What, then; shall I be no more?"

True; but you will be something else, of which at present the world has no need; for even *you* were not produced when you pleased, but when the world had need of you. Hence a wise and good man, mindful who he is and whence he came, and by whom he was produced, is attentive only how he may fill his post regularly and dutifully before God. "Dost thou wish me still to live? Let me live free and noble, as thou desirest; for thou has made me incapable of restraint in what is my own. But hast thou no further use for me? Farewell! I have stayed thus long through thee alone, and no other; and now I depart in obedience to thee." "How do you depart?" "Still as thou wilt; as one free, as thy servant, as one sensible of thy commands and thy prohibitions. But, while I am employed in thy service, what wouldst thou have me be—a prince, or a private man; a senator, or a plebeian; a soldier, or a general; a teacher, or a master of a family? Whatever post or rank thou shalt assign me, like Socrates, I will die a thousand times rather than desert it. *Where* wouldst thou have me to be, at Rome, or at Athens; at Thebes, or at Gyaros? Only remember me there. If thou shalt send me where men cannot live in accord with nature, I will not depart unbidden, but upon a recall as it were sounded by thee. Even then I do not desert thee; Heaven forbid! but I perceive that thou hast no use for me. If a life in accord with nature be granted, I will seek no other place but that in which I am, nor any other company but those with whom I dwell."

Let these things be ready at hand, night and day. These things write; these things read; of these things talk both to yourself and others. Ask them, "Have you any help to give me in this matter?" And, again, go and ask another and another. Then, if any of those things should happen that are called disagreeable, this will surely be a relief to you, in the first place, that it was not unexpected. For it is much to be able always to say, "I knew that I begot one born to die."[1]

---

[1] This was said by Xenophon, when news was brought him that his son was killed in a battle.

Thus do you say too, "I knew that I was liable to die, to travel, to be exiled, to be imprisoned." If afterwards you turn to yourself, and seek from what quarter the event proceeds, you will presently recollect: "It is from things uncontrollable by will, not from what is my own. What then is it to me?" Then, further, which is the chief point: "Who sent this—the commander, the general, the city, the public law? Give it to me, then, for I must always obey the law in all things."

Further yet, when your imagination molests you (for this is beyond your control), strive against it, and conquer it through reason. Do not suffer it to gain strength, nor to lead you indefinitely on, beguiling you at its own will. If you are at Gyaros, don't picture to yourself the manner of living at Rome—how many pleasures you used to find there, and how many would attend your return; but dwell rather on this point: how he who must live at Gyaros may live there nobly. And if you are at Rome, don't picture to yourself the manner of living at Athens, but consider only how you ought to live where you are.

Lastly, for all other pleasures substitute the consciousness that you are obeying God, and performing not in word, but in deed, the duty of a wise and good man. How great a thing is it to be able to say to yourself: "What others are now solemnly arguing in the schools, and can state in paradoxes, I actually practice. Those qualities which are there discoursed, disputed, celebrated, I have made mine own. Zeus has been pleased to let me recognize this within myself, and himself to discern whether he has in me one fit for a soldier and a citizen, and to employ me as a witness to other men, concerning things uncontrollable by will. See that your fears were vain, your appetites vain. Seek not good from without; seek it within yourselves, or you will never find it. For this reason he now brings me hither, now sends me thither; sets me before mankind, poor, powerless, sick; banishes me to Gyaros; leads me to prison; not that he hates me—Heaven forbid! for who hates the most faithful of his servants?—nor that he neglects me, for he neglects not one of the smallest things; but to exercise me, and make use of me as a witness to others. Appointed to such a service, do I still care where I am, or with whom, or what is said of me—instead of being wholly attentive to God and to his orders and commands?"

Having these principles always at hand, and practicing them by yourself, and making them ready for use, you will never want anyone to comfort and strengthen you. For shame does not consist in having nothing to eat, but in not having wisdom enough to exempt you from fear and sorrow. But if you once acquire that exemption, will a tyrant or his guards or courtiers be anything to you? Will offices or office-seekers disturb you, who have received so great a command from Zeus? Only do not make a parade over it, nor grow insolent upon it; but show it by your actions; and though no one else should notice it, be content that you are well and blessed.

CHAPTER TWENTY-FIVE

Concerning Those Who Waver in Their Purpose

CONSIDER which of your undertakings you have fulfilled, which not, and why; which give you pleasure, which pain, in the reflection; and, if possible, recover yourself where you have failed. For the champions in this greatest of combats must not grow weary, but should even contentedly bear chastisement. For this is no combat of wrestling or boxing, where both he who succeeds and he who fails may possibly be of very great worth or of little, indeed may be very fortunate or very miserable, but this combat is for good fortune and happiness itself. What is the case, then? Here, even if we have renounced the contest, no one restrains us from renewing it, nor need we wait for another four years for the return of another Olympiad; but recollecting and recovering yourself, and returning with the same zeal, you may renew it immediately; and even if you should again yield, you may again begin; and if you once get the victory, you become like one who has never yielded. Only don't begin to do the same thing over again out of sheer habit, and end up as a bad athlete, going the whole circuit of the games, and getting beaten continuously, like quails who have run away.[1] "I am overcome in the presence of a girl. But what of it? I have been thus conquered before." "I am excited to wrath against someone. But I have been in anger before." You talk to us just as if you had come off unhurt. As if one should say to his physician, who had forbidden him to bathe, "Why, did I not bathe before?" Suppose the physician should answer him, "Well, and what was the consequence of your bathing? Were you not feverish? Didn't your head ache?" So, when you scolded somebody the other day, did you not act like an ill-natured person; like an impertinent one? Did you not feed this habit of yours by corresponding actions? When you were conquered by a pretty girl, did you come off with impunity? Why, then, do you talk of what you have done before? You ought to remember it, I think, as slaves do a whipping, so as to refrain from the same faults. "But the case is unlike; for there is pain that causes the remembrance. But what is the pain, what the punishment, of my committing these faults? For when was I ever thus trained to the avoidance of bad actions?" Yet the pains of experience, whether we will or not, have their beneficial influence.

---

[1] It would seem that a fighting quail, once defeated, submitted readily to defeat afterward.

CHAPTER TWENTY-SIX

Concerning Those Who Fear Want

ARE you not ashamed to be more fearful and mean-spirited than fugitive slaves? To what estates, to what servants, do they trust, when they run away and leave their masters? Do they not, after carrying off a little with them for the first days, travel over land and sea, contriving first one, then another, method of getting food? And what fugitive ever died of hunger? But *you* tremble, and lie awake at night, for fear you should want necessaries. Foolish man! are you so blind? Do you not see the way whither the want of necessaries leads?

"Why, where does it lead?"

Where a fever or a falling stone may lead—to death. Have you not, then, often said this to your companions? Have you not read, have you not written, many things on this point? And how often have you arrogantly boasted that you are undisturbed by fears of death!

"Yes; but my family, too, will perish with hunger."

What then? Does their hunger lead any other way than yours? Is there not the same descent, the same state below? Will you not, then, in every want and necessity, look with confidence there, where even the most rich and powerful, and kings and tyrants themselves, must descend? You indeed may descend hungry, perhaps, and they full of indigestion and drunkenness. For have you often seen a beggar who did not live to old age, nay, to extreme old age? Chilled by day and night, lying on the ground, and eating only what is barely necessary, they seem to be almost incapable of dying. But, can you not write? Can you not take care of children? Can you not be a watchman at somebody's door?

"But it is shameful to come to this necessity."

First, therefore, learn what things are shameful, and then claim to be a philosopher; but at present do not suffer even another to call you so. Is that shameful to you which is not your own act; of which you are not the cause; which has happened to you by accident, like a fever or a headache? If your parents were poor, or left others their heirs, or, though living, do not assist you, are these things shameful for you? Is this what you have learned from the philosophers? Have you never heard that what is shameful is blamable; and what is blamable must be something which deserves to be blamed? Whom do you blame for an action not his own, which he has not himself performed? Did you, then, make your father such as he is; or is it in your power to reform him? Is that permitted you? What, then; must you desire what is not permitted, and when you fail of it, be ashamed? Are you thus accustomed, even when you are studying philosophy, to depend on others, and to hope for nothing from yourself? Sigh, then, and groan, and eat in fear that you shall have no food tomorrow. Tremble, lest your servants should rob you, or run away from you, or die.

Thus live on forever, whoever you are, who have applied yourself to philosophy in name only, and as much as in you lies have disgraced its principles, by showing that they are unprofitable and useless to those who profess them. You have never made constancy, tranquillity, and serenity the object of your desires; have sought no teacher for this knowledge, but many for mere syllogisms. You have never, by yourself, confronted some delusive semblance with, "Can I bear this, or can I not bear it? What remains for me to do?" But, as if all your affairs went safe and well, you have aimed only to secure yourself in your present possessions. What are they? Cowardice, baseness, worldliness, desires unaccomplished, unavailing aversions. These are the things which you have been laboring to secure. Ought you not first to have acquired something by the use of reason, and then to have provided security for that? Whom did you ever see building a series of battlements without placing them upon a wall? And what porter is ever set where there is no door? But *you* study! Can you show me what you study?

"Not to be shaken by sophistry."

Shaken from what? Show me first what you have in your custody; what you measure, or what you weigh; and then accordingly show me your weights and measures, and to what purpose you measure that which is but dust. Ought you not to show what makes men truly happy, what makes their affairs proceed as they wish; how we may blame no one, accuse no one; how acquiesce in the administration of the universe? Show me these things. "See, I do show them," say you; "I will solve syllogisms for you." This is but the measure, O unfortunate! and not the thing measured. Hence you now pay the penalty due for neglecting philosophy. You tremble; you like awake; you take counsel with everybody, and if the result of the advice does not please everybody, you think that you have been ill-advised. Then you dread hunger, as you fancy; yet it is not hunger that you dread, but you are afraid that you will not have someone to cook for you, someone else for a butler, another to pull off your shoes, a fourth to dress you, others to rub you, others to follow you; that when you have undressed yourself in the bathing-room, and stretched yourself out, like a man crucified, you may be rubbed here and there; and the attendant may stand by, and say, "Come this way; give your side; take hold of his head; turn your shoulder"; and that when you are returned home from the bath you may cry out, "Does nobody bring anything to eat?" and then, "Clear off the tables; wipe them off."

This is your dread, that you will not be able to lead the life of a sick man. But learn the life of those in health—how slaves live, how laborers, how those who are genuine philosophers; how Socrates lived, even with a wife and children; how Diogenes; how Cleanthes, at once studying and drawing water for his livelihood. If these are the things you would have, you can possess them everywhere, and with a fearless confidence.

"In what?"

In the only thing that can be confided in; in what is sure, incapable of being restrained or taken away—your own will.

But why have you contrived to make yourself so useless and good for nothing that nobody will receive you into his house, nobody take care of you; but although, if any sound, useful vessel be thrown out of doors, whoever finds it will take it up and prize it as something gained, yet nobody will take *you* up, but everybody esteem you a loss. What, can you not so much as perform the office of a dog or a cock? Why, then, do you wish to live any longer if you are so worthless? Does any good man fear that food should fail him? It does not fail the blind; it does not fail the lame. Shall it fail a good man? A paymaster is always to be found for a soldier, or a laborer, or a shoemaker, and shall one be wanting to a good man? Is God so negligent of his own institutions, of his servants, of his witnesses, whom alone he uses for examples to the uninstructed, to show that he exists, and that he administers the universe rightly, and does not neglect human affairs, and that no evil can happen to a good man, either living or dead? What, then, is the case, when he does not bestow food? What else than that, like a good general, he has given me a signal to retreat? I obey, I follow, speaking well of my leader, praising his works. For I came when it seemed good to him; and, again, when it seems good to him, I depart; and in life it was my business to praise God within myself and to every auditor, and to the world.

Does he grant me but few things? Does he refuse me affluence? It is not his pleasure that I should live luxuriously; for he did not grant that even to Hercules, his own son; but another reigned over Argos and Mycene, while he obeyed, labored, and strove. And Eurystheus was just what he was, neither truly king of Argos, nor of Mycene; not being indeed king over himself. But Hercules was ruler and governor of the whole earth and seas; the expeller of lawlessness and injustice; the introducer of justice and sanctity. And this he effected naked and alone. Again, when Ulysses was ship-wrecked and cast away, did his helpless condition at all deject him? Did it break his spirit? No; but how did he go to Nausicaa and her attendants, to ask those necessaries which it seems most shameful to beg from another?

As some lion, bred in the mountains, confiding in strength.[1] Confiding in what? Not in glory, or in riches, or in dominion, but in his own strength; that is, in his knowledge of what is within him and without him. For this alone is what can render us free and incapable of restraint; can raise the heads of the humble, and make them look with unaverted eyes full in the face of the rich and of the tyrants; and this is what philosophy bestows. But *you* will not even set forth with confidence; but all trembling about such trifles as clothes and plate. Foolish man! have you thus wasted your time till now?

"But what if I should be ill?"

It will then be for the best that you should be ill.

"Who will take care of me?"

God and your friends.

"I shall lie in a hard bed."

But like a man.

"I shall not have a convenient room."

Then you will be ill in an inconvenient one.

"Who will provide food for me?"

They who provide for others too; you will be ill like Manes.[2]

"But what will be the end of my illness—anything but death?"

---

[1] Homer, *Odyssey*. See Classics Club edition, p. 73.
[2] In other words, you would be neglected like a slave when ill. Manes was a typical slave name.

Why, do you not know, then, that the origin of all human evils, and of baseness and cowardice, is not death, but rather the fear of death? Fortify yourself, therefore, against this. Hither let all your discourses, readings, exercises, tend. And then you will know that only in this way are men made free.

BOOK IV

CHAPTER ONE

Of Freedom

HE IS free who lives as he likes; who is not subject to compulsion, to restraint, or to violence; whose pursuits are unhindered, his desires successful, his aversions unincurred. Who, then, would wish to live in error? "No one." Who would live deceived, erring, unjust, dissolute, discontented, dejected? "No one." No wicked man, then, lives as he likes; therefore no such man is free. And who would live in sorrow, fear, envy, pity, with disappointed desires and doing that which he would avoid? "No one." Do we then find any of the wicked exempt from these evils? "Not one." Consequently, then, they are not free.

If some person who has been twice consul should hear this, he will forgive you, provided you add, "but you are wise, and this has no reference to you." But if you tell him the truth, that, in point of slavery, he does not necessarily differ from those who have been thrice sold, what but chastisement can you expect? "For how," he says, "am I a slave? My father was free, my mother free. Besides, I am a senator, too, and the friend of Caesar, and have been twice consul, and have myself many slaves." In the first place, most worthy sir, perhaps your father too was a slave of the same kind; and your mother, and your grandfather, and all your series of ancestors. But even were they ever so free, what is that to you? For what if they were of a generous, you of a mean spirit; they brave, and you a coward; they sober, and you dissolute?

"But what," he says, "has this to do with my being a slave?" Is it no part of slavery to act against your will, under compulsion, and lamenting? "Be it so. But who can compel me but the master of all, Caesar?" By your own confession, then, you have *one* master; and let not his being, as you say, master of all, give you any comfort; for then you are merely a slave in a large family. Thus the Nicopolitans, too, frequently cry out, "By the genius of Caesar we are *free!*" [1]

For the present, however, if you please, we will let Caesar alone. But tell me this. Have you never been in love with anyone, either of a servile or liberal condition? "Why, what has that to do with being slave or free?" Were you never commanded anything by your mistress that you did not choose? Have you never flattered your fair slave? Have you never kissed her feet? And yet if you were commanded to kiss Caesar's feet, you would think it an outrage and an excess of tyranny. What else is this than slavery? Have you never gone out by night where you did not desire? Have you never spent more than you chose? Have you not sometimes uttered your words with sighs and groans? Have you never borne to be reviled and shut out of doors? But if you are ashamed to confess your own follies, see what Thrasonides [2] says and does; who, after having fought more battles perhaps than you, went out by night, when Geta, his slave, would not dare to go; nay, had the slave been compelled to do it, would have gone bewailing and lamenting the bitterness of servitude. And what says he afterwards? "A contemptible girl has en-

---

[1] Nicopolis was a city where Epictetus taught.

[2] A character in one of the comedies of Menander, called *The Hated Lover.*

slaved *me*, whom no enemy ever enslaved." Wretch! to be the slave of a girl and a contemptible girl too!

Why, then, do you still call yourself free? Why do you boast your military expeditions? Then he calls for a sword, and is angry with the person who, out of kindness, denies it; and sends presents to her who hates him; and begs, and weeps, and then again is elated on every little success. But what elation? Is he raised above desire or fear?

Consider what is our idea of freedom in animals. Some keep tame lions, and feed them and even lead them about; and who will say that any such lion is free? Nay, does he not live the more slavishly the more he lives at ease? And who that had sense and reason would wish to be one of those lions? Again, how much will caged birds suffer in trying to escape? Nay, some of them starve themselves rather than undergo such a life; others are saved only with difficulty and in a pining condition; and the moment they find any opening, out they go. Such a desire have they for their natural freedom, and to be at their own disposal, and unrestrained. And what harm can this confinement do you? "What say you? I was born to fly where I please, to live in the open air, to sing when I please. You deprive me of all this, and then ask what harm I suffer?"

Hence we will allow those only to be free who will not endure captivity, but, so soon as they are taken, die and so escape. Thus Diogenes somewhere says that the only way to freedom is to die with ease. And he writes to the Persian king, "You can no more enslave the Athenians than you can enslave the fish." "How? Can I not get possession of them?" "If you do," said he, "they will leave you, and be gone like fish. For catch a fish, and it dies. And if the Athenians, too, die as soon as you have caught them, of what use are your warlike preparations?" This is the voice of a free man who had examined the matter in earnest, and, as it might be expected, found it all out. But if you seek it where it is not, what wonder if you never find it?

A slave wishes to be immediately set free. Think you it is because he is desirous to pay his fee of manumission to the officer? No, but because he fancies that, for want of acquiring his freedom, he has hitherto lived under restraint and un-prosperously. "If I am once set free," he says, "it is all prosperity; I care for no one; I can speak to all as being their equal and on a level with them. I go where I will, I come when and how I will." He is at last made free, and presently having nowhere to eat he seeks whom he may flatter, with whom he may sup. He then either submits to prostitution and endures the most infamous degradation, and if he can obtain admission to some great man's table, falls into a slavery much worse than the former; or perhaps, if the ignorant fellow should grow rich, he dotes upon some girl, laments, and is unhappy, and wishes for slavery again. "For what harm did it do me? Another clothed me, another shod me, another fed me, another took care of me when I was sick. It was only in a few things, by way of return, I could serve him.

"But now, miserable wretch! what do I suffer, in being a slave to many, instead of one! Yet, if I can be promoted to equestrian rank, I shall live in the utmost prosperity and happiness." In order to obtain this, he first deservedly suffers; and as soon as he has obtained it, it is all the same again. "But then," he says, "if I do but get a military command, I shall be delivered from all my troubles." He gets a military command. He suffers as much as the vilest rogue of a slave; and, never-theless, he asks for a second command and a third; and when he has put the finishing touch, and is made a senator, then he is a slave indeed. When he comes into the public assembly, it is then that he undergoes his finest and most splendid slavery.

It is needful not to be foolish, but to learn what Socrates taught, the nature of things; and not rashly to apply general

principles to particulars. For the cause of all human evils is the
not being able to apply general principles to special cases.
But different people have different grounds of complaint;
one, for instance, that he is sick. That is not the trouble; it is
in his principles. Another, that he is poor; another, that he
has a harsh father and mother; another, that he is not in the
good graces of Caesar. This is nothing else but not understanding how to apply our principles. For who has not an idea of
evil, that it is hurtful; that it is to be avoided; that it is by all
means to be prudently guarded against? One principle does
not contradict another, except when it comes to be applied.
What, then, is this evil that is hurtful and to be avoided?
"Not to be the friend of Caesar," says some one. He is gone;
he has failed in applying his principles; he is embarrassed; he
seeks what is not to the purpose. For if he comes to be
Caesar's friend, he is still no nearer to what he sought. For
what is it that every man seeks? To be secure, to be happy,
to do what he pleases without restraint and without compulsion. When he becomes the friend of Caesar, then does he
cease to be restrained; to be compelled? Is he secure? Is he
happy? Whom shall we ask? Whom can we better credit
than this very man who has been his friend? Come forth and
tell us whether you sleep more quietly now than before you
were the friend of Caesar. You presently hear him cry, "Leave
off, for heaven's sake! and do not insult me. You know not
the miseries I suffer; there is no sleep for me; but one comes
and says that Caesar is already awake; another, that he is just
going out. Then follow troubles and cares."

Well, and when did you use to sup the more pleasantly—
formerly, or now? Hear what he says about this too. When
he is not invited, he is distracted; and if he is, he sups like a
slave with his master, solicitous all the while not to say or do
anything foolish. And what do you think? Is he afraid of
being whipped like a slave? No such easy penalty. No, but
rather, as becomes so great a man, Caesar's friend, of losing

his head. And when did you bathe the more quietly; when did you perform your exercises in more leisure; in short, which life would you rather wish to live—your present, or the former? I could swear there is no one so stupid and insensible as not to deplore his miseries, the more he is the friend of Caesar.[1]

Since, then, neither they who are called kings nor the friends of kings live as they like, who, then, after all, is free? Seek, and you will find; for you are furnished by nature with means for discovering the truth. But if you are not able by these alone to find the consequence, hear them who have sought it. What do they say? Do you think freedom a good? "The greatest." Can anyone, then, who attains the greatest good be unhappy or unsuccessful in his affairs? "No." As many, therefore, as you see unhappy, lamenting, unprosperous —confidently pronounce them not free. "I do." Henceforth, then, we have done with buying and selling, and such like stated conditions of becoming slaves. For if these propositions hold, then, whether the unhappy man be a great or a little king—of consular or bi-consular dignity—he is not free. "Agreed."

Further, then, answer me this: do you think freedom to be something great and noble and valuable? "How should I not?" Is it possible, then, that he who acquires anything so great and valuable and noble should be of an abject spirit? "It is not." Whenever, then, you see anyone subject to another, and flattering him contrary to his own opinion, confidently say that he too is not free; and not only when he does this for a supper, but even if it be for a government, nay, a consulship. Call those indeed little slaves who act thus for the sake of little things; and call the others, as they deserve, great slaves. "Be this, too, agreed." Well, do you think freedom to be

---

[1] Compare with this section Bacon's essay, "Of Great Place." See Classics Club edition, p. 42.

something independent and self-determined? "How can it be otherwise?" When, therefore, it is in the power of another to restrain or to compel, say confidently that this man is not free. And do not pay any attention to his grandfathers or great-grandfathers, or inquire whether he has been bought or sold; but if you hear him say from his heart and with emotion, "my master," though twelve lictors should march before him,[1] call him a slave. And if you should hear him say, "Wretch that I am! What I must suffer!" call him a slave. In short, if you see him wailing, complaining, unprosperous, call him a slave, even in purple.

"Suppose, then, that he does none of these things." Do not yet say that he is free; but learn whether his principles are in any event liable to compulsion, to restraint, or disappointment; and if you find this to be the case, call him a slave, keeping holiday during the Saturnalia.[2] Say that his master is abroad; that he will come presently; and you will know what he suffers. "Who will come?" Whoever has the power either of bestowing or of taking away any of the things he desires.

"Have we so many masters, then?" We have. For, even before these, we have circumstances as our masters. Now they are many; and it is through these that the men who control the circumstances inevitably become our masters too. For no one fears Caesar himself; but death, banishment, confiscation, prison, disgrace. Nor does anyone love Caesar unless he be a person of great worth; but we love riches, the tribunate, the praetorship, the consulship. When we love or hate or fear such things, they who have the disposal of them must necessarily be our masters. Hence we even worship them as gods. For we consider that whoever has the disposal of the greatest advantages is a deity; and then further reason falsely, "But such a one has the control of the greatest advantages; there-

---

[1] Indicating a man of consular rank.
[2] Slaves enjoyed special privileges during this holiday.

fore he is a deity." For if we reason falsely, the final inference must be also false.

What is it, then, that makes a man free and independent? For neither riches, nor consulship, nor the command of provinces nor of kingdoms, can make him so; but something else must be found. What is it that keeps anyone from being hindered and restrained in penmanship, for instance? "The science of penmanship." In music? "The science of music." Therefore in life too, it must be the science of living. As you have heard it in general, then, consider it likewise in particulars. Is it possible for him to be unrestrained who desires any of those things that are within the power of others? "No." Can he avoid being hindered? "No." Therefore neither can he be free. Consider, then, whether we have nothing or everything in our own sole power—or whether some things are in our own power and some in that of others. "What do you mean?" When you would have your body perfect, is it in your own power, or is it not? "It is not." When you would be healthy? "It is not." When you would be handsome? "It is not." When you would live or die? "It is not." Body then is not our own; but is subject to everything that proves stronger than itself. "Agreed." Well, is it in your own power to have an estate when you please, and such a one as you please? "No." Slaves? "No." Clothes? "No." A house? "No." Horses? "Indeed, none of these." Well, if you desire ever so earnestly to have your children live, or your wife, or your brother, or your friends, is it in your own power? "No, it is not."

Will you then say that there is *nothing* independent, which is in your own power alone, and unalienable? See if you have anything of this sort. "I do not know." But consider it thus: can anyone make you assent to a falsehood? "No one." In the matter of assent, then, you are unrestrained and unhindered. "Agreed." Well, and can anyone compel you to exert your aims towards what you do not like? "He can; for when he threatens me with death, or fetters, he thus compels me." If, then, you were to despise dying or being fettered, would you any longer regard him? "No." Is despising death, then, an action in our power, or is it not? "It is." Is it therefore in your power also to exert your aims towards anything, or is it not? "Agreed that it is. But in whose power is my avoiding anything?" This, too, is in your own. "What then if, when I am exerting myself to walk, anyone should restrain me?" What part of you can he restrain? Can he restrain your assent? "No, but my body." Yes, as he may a stone. "Be it so. But still I cease to walk." And who claimed that walking was one of the actions that cannot be restrained? For I only said that your exerting yourself towards it could not be restrained. But wherever the body and its assistance are essential, you have already heard that nothing is in your power. "Be this, too, agreed." And can anyone compel you to desire against your will? "No one." Or to propose, or intend, or, in short, not to be beguiled by the appearances of things? "Nor this. But when I desire anything, he can restrain me from obtaining what I desire." If you desire anything that is truly within your reach, and that cannot be restrained, how can he restrain you? "By no means." And pray who claims that he who longs for what depends on another will be free from restraint?

"May I not long for health, then?" By no means; nor for anything else that depends on another; for what is not in your own power, either to procure or to preserve when you will, *that* belongs to another. Not only keep your hands from it, but even more than these, your desires. Otherwise you have given yourself up as a slave; you have put your neck under the yoke, if you admire any of the things which are not your own, but which are subject and mortal, to whichever of them you are attached. "Is not my hand my own?" It is a part of you, but it is by nature clay, liable to restraint, to compulsion; a slave to everything stronger than itself. And why do I say your hand? You ought to consider your whole body as a useful ass, with a pack-saddle on, so long as possible, so long as it is allowed. But if there should come a military conscription, and a soldier should lay hold on it, let it go. Do not resist, or murmur; otherwise you will be first beaten and lose the ass after all. And since you are thus to regard even the body itself, think what remains to do concerning things to be provided for the sake of the body. If that be an ass, the rest are but bridles, pack-saddles, shoes, oats, hay for him. Let these go too. Quit them yet more easily and expeditiously.

And when you are thus prepared and trained to distinguish what belongs to others from your own; what is liable to restraint from what is not; to esteem the one your own property, but not the other; to keep your desire, to keep your aversion, carefully regulated by this point—whom have you any longer to fear? "No one." For about what should you be afraid—about what is your own, in which consists the essence of good and evil? And who has any power over *this*? Who can take it away? Who can hinder you, any more than God can be hindered? But are you afraid for body, for possessions, for what belongs to others, for what is nothing to you? And what have you been studying all this while, but to distinguish between your own and that which is not your own; what is in your power and what is not in your power; what is liable to restraint and what is not? And for what purpose have you applied to the philosophers—that you might nevertheless be disappointed and unfortunate? No doubt you will be exempt from fear and perturbation! And what is grief to you? For whatsoever we anticipate with fear, we endure with grief. And for what will you any longer passionately wish? For you have acquired a temperate and steady desire of things dependent on will, since they are accessible and desirable; and you have no desire of things uncontrollable by will, so as to leave room for that irrational, and impetuous, and precipitate passion.

Since then you are thus affected with regard to *things*, what man can any longer be formidable to you? What has

man that he can be formidable to man, either in appearance,
or speech, or mutual intercourse? No more than horse to
horse, or dog to dog, or bee to bee. But *things* are formidable
to everyone, and whenever any person can either give these
to another, or take them away, he becomes formidable too.
"How, then, is this citadel to be destroyed?" Not by sword
or fire, but by principle. For if we should demolish the visible
citadel,[1] shall we have demolished also that of some fever,
of some fair woman—in short, the citadel [of temptation]
within ourselves; and have turned out the tyrants to whom we
are subject upon all occasions and every day, sometimes the
same tyrants, sometimes others? But here is where we must
begin; hence demolish the citadel, and turn out the tyrants
—give up body, members, riches, power, fame, magistracies,
honors, children, brothers, friends; esteem all these as belonging to others. And if the tyrants be turned out, why should I
also demolish the external citadel, at least on my own account? For what harm does it do *me* from its standing? Why
should I turn out the guards? For in what point do they affect
me? It is against others that they direct their fasces, their
staves, and their swords. Have I ever been restrained from
what I willed, or compelled against my will? Indeed, how is
this possible? I have placed my pursuits under the direction
of God. Is it his will that I should have a fever? It is my will
too. Is it his will that I should pursue anything? It is my
will too. Is it his will that I should desire? It is my will too. Is
it his will that I should obtain anything? It is mine too. Is
it not his will? It is not mine. Is it his will that I should be
tortured? Then it is my will to be tortured. Is it his will that
I should die? Then it is my will to die. Who can any longer

---

[1] The metaphor of the citadel in the passage which follows seems
somewhat confused. The tyrant is represented as a false judgment about
wealth; the citadel or Acropolis, as the wealth itself, and this is dangerous only so long as the tyrant (false judgment) prevails. Once that
is overthrown, wealth itself need not be destroyed.

restrain or compel me, contrary to my own opinion? No more than Zeus.

It is thus that cautious travelers act. Does someone hear that the road is beset by robbers? He does not set out alone, but waits for the retinue of an ambassador or quaestor or pro-consul, and when he has joined himself to their company, goes along in safety. Thus does the prudent man act in the world. There are many robberies, tyrants, storms, distresses, losses of things most dear. Where is there any refuge? How can he go alone unattacked? What retinue can he wait for, to go safely through his journey? To what company shall he join himself—to some rich man; to some consular senator? And what good will that do me? He may be robbed himself, groaning and lamenting. And what if my fellow-traveler him-self should turn against me and rob me? What shall I do? I say I will be the friend of Caesar. While I am his companion, no one will injure me. Yet before I can become illustrious enough for this, what must I bear and suffer! How often, and by how many, must I be robbed! And then, if I do become the friend of Caesar, he too is mortal; and if, by any accident, he should become my enemy, where can I best retreat—to a desert? Well, and may not a fever come there? What can be done, then? Is it not possible to find a fellow-traveler safe, faithful, brave, incapable of being surprised? A person who reasons thus, understands and considers that if he joins himself to God, he shall go safely through his journey.

"How do you mean, join himself?" That whatever is the will of God may be *his* will too; that whatever is not the will of God may not be his. "How, then, can this be done?" Why, how otherwise than by considering the workings of God's power and his administration? What has he given me to be my own, and independent? What has he reserved to himself? He has given me whatever depends on will. The things within my power he has made incapable of hindrance or restraint. But how could he make a body of clay incapable of hindrance?

Therefore he has subjected possessions, furniture, house, children, wife, to the revolutions of the universe. Why, then, do I fight against God? Why do I will to retain that which depends not on will; that which is not granted absolutely, but how—in such a manner and for such a time as was thought proper? But he who gave takes away. Why, then, do I resist? Besides being a fool, in contending with a stronger than myself, I shall be unjust, which is a more important consideration. For from where did I get these things when I came into the world? My father gave them to me. And who gave them to him? And who made the sun; who the fruits; who the seasons; who their connection and relations with each other?

And after you have received all, and even your very self, from God, are you angry with the giver, and do you complain, if he takes anything away from you? Who are you; and for what purpose did you come? Was it not he who brought you here? Was it not he who showed you the light? Has not he given you companions? Has not he given you senses? Has not he given you reason? And as whom did he bring you here—was it not as a mortal? Was it not as one to live with a little portion of flesh upon earth, and to see his administration; to behold the spectacle with him, and partake of the festival for a short time? After having beheld the spectacle and the solemnity, then, as long as it is permitted you, will you not depart when he leads you out, adoring and thankful for what you have heard and seen? "No; but I would enjoy the feast still longer." So would the initiated in the mysteries, too, be longer in their initiation; so, perhaps, would the spectators at Olympia see more athletes. But the solemnity is over. Go away. Depart like a grateful and modest person; make room for others. Others, too, must be born as you were; and when they are born must have a place, and habitations, and necessaries. But if the first do not give way, what room is there left? Why are you insatiable, never satisfied? Why do you crowd the world?

"But I would have my wife and children with me too." Why, are they *yours*? Are they not the Giver's? Are they not his who made *you* also? Will you not then give up what belongs to another? Will you not yield to your Superior? "Why, then, did he bring me into the world upon these conditions?" Well, if it is not worth your while, depart. He has no need of a discontented spectator. He wants such as will share the festival; make part of the chorus; who will extol, applaud, celebrate the solemnity. He will not be displeased to see the wretched and fearful dismissed from it. For when they were present they did not behave as at a festival, nor fill a proper place, but lamented, found fault with the Deity, with their fortune, with their companions. They were insensible both of their advantages and of the powers which they received for far different purposes—the powers of magnanimity, nobleness of spirit, fortitude, and that which now concerns us, freedom. "For what purpose, then, have I received these things?" To use them. "How long?" As long as he who lent them pleases. If, then, they are not necessary, do not make an idol of them, and they will not be so; do not tell yourself that they are necessary, when they are not.

This should be our study from morning till night beginning with the least and frailest things, as with earthernware, with glassware. Afterwards proceed to a suit of clothes, a dog, a horse, an estate; thence to yourself, body, members, children, wife, brothers. Look everywhere around you, and be able to detach yourself from these things. Correct your principles. Permit nothing to cleave to you that is not your own; nothing to grow to you that may give you agony when it is torn away. And say, when you are daily training yourself as you do here, not that you act the philosopher, which may be a presumptuous claim, but that you are asserting your freedom.

For this is true freedom. This is the freedom that Diogenes gained from Antisthenes, and declared it was impossible that he should ever after be a slave to anyone. Hence, when he was taken prisoner, how did he treat the pirates? Did he call any of them master? I do not mean the name, for I am not afraid of a word, but of the disposition from whence the word proceeds. How did he reprove them for feeding their prisoners ill? How was he sold? Did he seek a master? No, but a slave. And when he was sold, how did he converse with his lord? He immediately disputed with him whether he ought to be dressed or shaved in the manner he was; and how he ought to bring up his children. And where is the wonder? For if the same master had bought someone to instruct his children in gymnastic exercises, would he in those exercises have treated him as a servant or as a master? And so if he had bought a physician or an architect. In every department the skillful must necessarily be superior to the unskillful.

What else, then, can he be but master, who possesses the universal knowledge of life? For who is master in a ship? The pilot. Why? Because whoever disobeys him is a loser. "But a master can put me in chains." Can he do it, then, without being a loser? "I think not, indeed." But because he must be a loser, he evidently must not do it; for no one acts unjustly without being a loser. "And how does he suffer, who puts his own slave in chains?" What think you? From the very fact of chaining him. This you yourself must grant, if you would hold to the doctrine that man is not naturally a wild, but a gentle, animal. For when is it that a vine is in a bad condition? "When it is in a condition contrary to its nature." How is it with a cock? "The same." It is therefore the same with a man also. What is his nature—to bite and kick and throw into prison and cut off heads? No, but to do good, to assist, to indulge the wishes of others. Whether you will or not, then, he is in a bad condition whenever he acts unreasonably. "And so was not Socrates in a bad condition?" No, but his judges and accusers were. "Nor Helvidius,[1] at Rome?" No, but his

---

[1] A prominent Stoic senator.

murderer. "How do you mean?" Why, the same as you do when you say that a cock is not in a bad condition which is victorious, and yet badly wounded; but rather that one which is conquered and comes off unhurt. Nor do you call a dog happy which neither hunts nor toils, but when you see him perspiring, and distressed, and panting with the chase. Is that a paradox? If we say that the evil of everything consists in what is contrary to its nature, is this a paradox? Do you not say it with regard to other things? Why, therefore, in the case of man alone, do you take a different view? But further, it is no paradox to say that by nature man is gentle and social and faithful. "No, it is not." How then is it a paradox to say that, when he is whipped, or imprisoned, or beheaded, he is not hurt? If he suffers nobly, does he not come off even the better and a gainer? But is he not hurt who suffers the most miserable and shameful evils, who, instead of a man, becomes a wolf, a viper, or a hornet?

Come, then; let us recapitulate what has been agreed on. The man who is unrestrained, who has all things in his power as he wills, is free; but he who may be restrained or compelled or hindered, or thrown into any condition against his will, is a slave. "And who is unrestrained?" He who desires none of those things that belong to others. "And what are those things which belong to others?" Those which are not in our power, either to have or not to have; or to have them thus or so. Body, therefore, belongs to another; its parts to another; property to another. If, then, you attach yourself to any of these as your own, you will be punished as he deserves who desires what belongs to others. This is the way that leads to freedom, this the only deliverance from slavery, to be able at length to say, from the bottom of one's soul,

> *Conduct me, Zeus, and thou, O Destiny,*
> *Wherever your decrees have fixed my lot.*[1]

---

[1] A Fragment from the *Hymn* of Cleanthes.

But what say you, philosopher? A tyrant calls upon you to speak something unbecoming you. Will you say it, or will you not? "Stay, let me consider." Would you consider *now?* And what did you think about when you were in the schools? Did you not study what things were good and evil, and what indifferent? "I did." Well, and what were the opinions which pleased us? "That just and fair actions were good; unjust and base ones, evil." Is living a good? "No." Dying, an evil? "No." A prison? "No." And what did a mean and dishonest speech, the betraying a friend, or the flattering a tyrant, appear to us? "Evils." Why, then, are you still considering, and have not already considered and come to a resolution? For what sort of a consideration is this: "Whether I ought, when it is in my power, to procure myself the greatest good, instead of procuring myself the greatest evil." A fine and necessary consideration, truly, and deserving mighty deliberation!

Why do you trifle with us, man? No one ever needed to consider any such point; nor, if you really imagined things fair and honest to be good, things base and dishonest to be evil, and all others things indifferent, would you ever be in such a perplexity as this, or near it; but you would presently be able to distinguish by your understanding as you do by your sight. For do you ever have to consider whether black is white, or whether light is heavy? Do you not follow the plain evidence of your senses? Why, then, do you say that you are now considering whether things indifferent are to be avoided, rather than evils? The truth is, you have no principles; for things indifferent do not impress you as such, but as the greatest evils; and these last, on the other hand, as things of no importance.

For thus has been your practice from the first. "Where am I? If I am in the school and there is an audience, I talk as the philosophers do; but if I am out of the school, then away

THE DISCOURSES OF EPICTETUS

with this stuff that belongs only to scholars and fools." This man is accused by the testimony of a philosopher, his friend; this philosopher turns parasite; another hires himself out for money; a third does that in the very senate. When one is not governed by appearances, then his principles speak for themselves. You are a poor cold lump of prejudice, consisting of mere phrases, on which you hang as by a hair. You should preserve yourself firm and practical, remembering that you are to deal with real things. In what manner do you hear— I will not say that your child is dead, for how could you possibly bear that?—but that your oil is spilled, your wine consumed? If only someone, while you are bawling, would say this: "Philosopher, you talk quite otherwise when in the schools. Why do you deceive us? Why, when you are a worm, do you call yourself a man?" I should be glad to be near one of these philosophers while he is reveling in debauchery, that I might see how he demeans himself, and what sayings he utters; whether he remembers the title he bears and the discourses which he hears, or speaks, or reads.

"And what is all this to freedom?" It lies in nothing else than this—whether you rich people approve or not. "And who affords evidence of this?" Who but yourselves? You who have a powerful master, and live by his motion and nod, and faint away if he does but look sternly upon you, who pay your court to old men and old women, and say, "I cannot do this or that, it is not in my power." Why is it not in your power? Did you not just now contradict me, and say you were free? "But Aprylla [1] has forbidden me." Speak the truth, then, slave, and do not run away from your masters nor deny them, nor dare to assert your freedom, when you have so many proofs of your slavery. One might indeed find some excuse for a person compelled by love to do something contrary to his opinion, even when at the same time he sees what is best with-

---

[1] Probably some rich old woman.

out having resolution enough to follow it, since he is in the grip of something overpowering, and in some measure divine.

But who can endure you, who are in love with old men and old women, and perform menial offices for them, and bribe them with presents, and wait upon them like a slave when they are sick; at the same time wishing they may die, and inquiring of the physician whether their disease is yet mortal? And again, when for these great and venerable magistracies and honors you kiss the hands of the slaves of others; so that you are the slave of those who are not free themselves! And then you walk about in state, a praetor or a consul. Do I not know how you came to be praetor; how you received the consulship; who gave it to you? For my own part, I would not even live, if I must live by Felicio's [1] means, and bear his pride and slavish insolence. For I know what a slave is, blinded by what he thinks good fortune.[2]

"Are you free yourself, then?" you may ask. By heaven, I wish and pray for it. But I own I cannot yet face my masters. I still pay a regard to my body, and set a great value on keeping it whole; though, for that matter, it is not whole. But I can show you one who was free, that you may no longer seek an example. Diogenes was free. "How so?" Not because he was of free parents, for he was not; but because he was so in himself; because he had cast away all which gives a handle to slavery; nor was there any way of getting at him, nor anywhere to lay hold on him, to enslave him. Everything sat loose upon him; everything was merely tied on. If you laid hold on his possessions, he would rather let them go than follow you for them; if on his leg, he let go his leg; if his body, he let go his body; acquaintance, friends, country, just the same. For he knew the source from which he had received them, and from whom, and upon what conditions he received

---

[1] One of Nero's freedmen.

[2] Undoubtedly a reference to his master, Epaphroditus, who had been a slave of Nero.

them. But he would never have forsaken his true parents, the gods, and his real country [the universe]; nor have suffered anyone to be more dutiful and obedient to them than he; nor would anyone have died more readily for his country than he. He never had to inquire whether he should act for the good of the whole universe; for he remembered that everything that exists has its source in its administration, and is commanded by its ruler.

Accordingly, see what he himself says and writes. "Upon this account," said he, "O Diogenes, it is in your power to converse as you will with the Persian monarch and with Archidamus, king of the Lacedemonians." Was it because *he* was born of free parents? Or was it because *they* were descended from slaves, that all the Athenians, and all the Lacedemonians, and Corinthians, could not converse with them as they pleased; but feared and paid court to them? Why then is it in your power, Diogenes? "Because I do not esteem this poor body as my own. Because I want nothing. Because this and nothing else is a law to me." These were the things that enabled him to be free.

And that you may not think I am showing you the example of a man clear of incumbrances, without a wife or children or country or friends or relations, to bend and draw him aside, take Socrates, and consider him, who had a wife and children, but held them not as his own; had a country, friends, relations, but held them only so long as it was proper, and in the manner that was proper; submitting all these to the law and to the obedience due to it. Hence, when it was proper to fight, he was the first to go out, and exposed himself to danger without the least reserve. But when he was sent by the thirty tyrants to apprehend Leon,[1] because he esteemed it a base

---

[1] Socrates, with four other persons, was commanded by the Thirty Tyrants of Athens to fetch Leon, a leader of the opposition, from the isle of Salamis, in order to be put to death. His companions executed their commission; but Socrates remained at home, and chose rather to

action, he did not even deliberate about it; though he knew that, perhaps, he might die for it. But what did that signify to him? For it was something else that he wanted to preserve, not his mere flesh; but his fidelity, his honor, free from attack or subjection. And afterwards, when he was to make a defense for his life, does he behave like one having children, or a wife? No, but like a man alone in the world. And how does he behave, when required to drink the poison? When he might escape, and Crito would have him escape from prison for the sake of his children, what did he say? Does he think it a fortunate opportunity? How should he? But he considers what is becoming, and neither sees nor regards anything else. "For I am not desirous," he says, "to preserve this pitiful body; but that part which is improved and preserved by justice, and impaired and destroyed by injustice." Socrates is not to be basely preserved. He who refused to vote for what the Athenians commanded; he who despised the thirty tyrants; he who held such discourses on virtue and mortal beauty—such a man is not to be preserved by a base action, but is preserved by dying, instead of running away. For a good actor is saved when he stops when he should stop, rather than acting beyond his time.

"What then will become of your children?" "If I had gone away into Thessaly, you would have taken care of them; and will there be no one to take care of them when I am departed to Hades?"[1] You see how he ridicules and plays with death. But if it had been you or I, we should presently have proved by philosophical arguments that those who act unjustly are to be repaid in their own way; and should have added, "If I escape I shall be of use to many; if I die, to none." Nay, if it had been necessary, we should have crept through a mouse-

---

expose his life to the fury of the tyrants, than be accessory to the death of an innocent person. He would most probably have fallen a sacrifice to their vengeance, if the Oligarchy had not shortly after been dissolved. See Classics Club edition of Plato's *Apology*, p. 51.

[1] Plato, *Crito*. See Classics Club edition, p. 78.

hole to get away. But how should *we* have been of use to any-body? Where could we be of use? If we were useful alive, should we not be of still more use to mankind by dying when we ought and as we ought? And now the remembrance of the death of Socrates is not less, but even more useful to the world than that of the things which he did and said when alive.

Study these points, these principles, these discourses; con-template these examples if you would be free, if you desire the thing in proportion to its value. And where is the wonder that you should purchase so good a thing at the price of other things, be they never so many and so great? Some hang them-selves, others break their necks, and sometimes even whole cities have been destroyed for that which is reputed freedom; and will not you for the sake of the true and secure and in-violable freedom, repay God what he has given when he de-mands it? Will you study not only, as Plato says, how to die, but how to be tortured and banished and scourged; and, in short, how to give up all that belongs to others?

If not, you will be a slave among slaves, though you were ten thousand times a consul; and even though you should rise to the palace, you will be a slave none the less. And you will feel that, though philosophers (as Cleanthes says) do, perhaps, talk contrary to common opinion, yet it is not contrary to reason. For you will find it true, in fact, that the things that are eagerly followed and admired are of no use to those who have gained them; while they who have not yet gained them imagine that, if they are acquired, every good will come along with them; and then, when they are acquired, there is the same feverishness, the same agitation, the same nausea, and the same desire for what is absent. For freedom is not procured by a full enjoyment of what is desired, but by controlling the desire. And in order to know that this is true, take the same pains about these which you have taken about other things. Hold vigils to acquire a set of principles that will make you free. Instead of a rich old man, pay your court to a philosopher. Be

seen about his doors. You will not be disgraced by being seen
there. You will not return empty or without profit if you
approach him as you ought. However, try at least. The trial
is not dishonorable.

Of Social Intercourse

To this point you must devote yourself before all others: not
to be so attached to any one of your former acquaintances
or friends as to descend to behavior like his; otherwise you
will ruin yourself. But if it comes into your head, "I shall
appear odd to him, and he will not treat me as before," remember that there is nothing to be had for nothing; nor is it
possible that he who acts in the same manner as before should
not remain the same person.

Choose, then, whether you will be loved by those who
formerly loved you, and be like your former self; or be better,
and not meet with the same treatment. For if this last is preferable, immediately incline altogether this way, and let no
other kind of reasoning draw you aside; for no one can improve while he is wavering. If, then, you prefer this to everything, if you would be fixed only on this, and employ all your
pains about it, give up everything else. Otherwise this wavering will affect you in both directions; you will neither make a
due improvement, nor preserve the advantages you had before. For before, by setting your heart entirely on things of
no value, you were agreeable to your companions. But you
cannot excel in both styles; you must necessarily lose as much
of the one as you partake of the other.

If you do not drink with those with whom you used to drink, you cannot appear equally agreeable to them. Choose, then, whether you would be a drunkard, and agreeable to them, or sober, and disagreeable to them. If you do not sing with those with whom you used to sing, you cannot be equally dear to them. Here too, then, choose which you will. For if it is better to be modest and decent than to have it said of you "what an agreeable fellow," give up the rest; renounce it; withdraw yourself; have nothing to do with it. But if this does not please you, turn your whole force to the opposite way. Be one of the debauchees; one of the adulterers. Act accordingly, and you will obtain what you wish. Jump up in the theater, too, and roar out in praise of the dancer. But characters so different are not to be confounded. You cannot act both Thersites and Agamemnon. If you would be Thersites, you must be hump-backed and bald; if Agamemnon, tall and handsome and faithful to those who are under your care.

CHAPTER THREE

What Things Are to Be Exchanged for Other Things

WHEN you have lost anything external, always consider what you acquire in place of it; and if this is of more value, never call yourself a loser—whether it be a horse for an ass; an ox for a sheep; a good action for a piece of money; a due composure of mind for a dull jest; or modesty for indecent talk. By continually remembering this, you will preserve your character such as it ought to be. Otherwise, consider that you are spending your time in vain; and all that to which you are now applying your mind, you are about to spill and overturn. And little is needed, merely a small deviation from reason, to destroy and upset all.

A pilot does not need so much apparatus to overturn a ship as to save it; but if he heads too much into the wind, it is lost; even if he should not do it purposely, but only because he is thinking of something else for a moment, it is lost. Such is the case in life, too. If you do but nod a little, all that you have hitherto accomplished is gone. Take heed, then, to the appearances of things. Watch over them. It is no small matter that you are guarding; but modesty, fidelity, constancy, docility, innocence, fearlessness, serenity—in short, freedom.

For what will you sell these? Consider what the purchase is worth. "But shall I not get such a thing in return?" Consider, if you do not get it, what it is that you have instead. Suppose I have decency, and another the office of tribune; I have modesty, and he the praetorship? But I do not applaud where it is unbecoming; I will pay no undeserved honor; for I am free, and the friend of God, so as to obey him willingly; and I must not value anything else, neither body, nor possessions, nor fame—in short, nothing. For it is not his will that I should value them. If this had been his pleasure, he would have placed in them my good, which now he has not done; therefore I cannot transgress his commands.

Seek in all things your own highest good; and for the rest, be content to take simply what has been given you, in so far as you can make a rational use of it, contented with this alone. Otherwise you will be unfortunate, disappointed, restrained, hindered. These are the established laws, these the statutes. Of these laws one ought to be an expositor, and to these obedient, rather than to those of Masurius and Cassius.[1]

---

[1] Two famous lawyers of the day.

CHAPTER FOUR

Concerning Those Who Earnestly Desire a Tranquil Life

REMEMBER that it is not only the desire of riches and power that debases us and subjects us to others, but even the desire of quiet, leisure, learning, or traveling. For, in general, reverence for any external thing whatever makes us subject to others. What is the difference, then, whether you desire to be a senator or not to be a senator? What is the difference, whether you desire power or to be out of power? What is the difference, whether you say, "I am in a bad way, I have nothing to do; but am tied down to books, as inactive as if I were dead"; or "I am in a bad way, I have no leisure to read"? For as levees and power are among things external and uncontrollable by will, so likewise is a book. For what purpose would you read? Tell me. For if you rest merely in being amused and learning something, you are insignificant and miserable. But if you refer it to the proper end, what is that end but a life truly prosperous? And if reading does not procure you a prosperous life, of what use is it? "But it does procure a prosperous life (say you); and therefore I am uneasy at being deprived of it." And what sort of prosperity is that which everything can hinder—I do not say Caesar alone, or Caesar's friend, but a crow, a man practicing the flute, a fever, or ten thousand other things? Nothing is so essential to prosperity as that it should be permanent and unhindered.

Suppose I am now called to do something. I go, therefore, and will be attentive to the bounds and measures which ought to be observed; that I may act modestly, steadily, and without desire or aversion as to externals. In the next place, I observe other men, what they say, and how they move; and not in any mean spirit, nor to have something to censure or ridicule; but I turn to myself. "Am I also guilty of the same faults; and how then shall I shake them off?" or, "I once thus erred, but, God be thanked, not now." Well, when you have done thus, and been employed on such things, have you not done as good a work as if you had read a thousand lines or written as many? For are you uneasy at not reading while you are eating? When you eat, or bathe, or exercise, are you not satisfied with doing it in a manner corresponding to what you have read? Why, then, do you not reason in like manner about everything? When you approach Caesar or any other person, if you preserve yourself dispassionate, fearless, sedate; if you are rather an observer of what is done than the subject of observation; if you do not envy those who are preferred to you; if you are not overcome by the occasion, what do you lack? Books? How, or to what end? For these are not the real preparation for living, but living is made up of things very different. Just as if a champion, when he enters the lists, should begin crying because he is not still exercising outside. It was for this that you were exercised. For this were the dumb-bells, the dust, and your young antagonists. And do you now seek for these when it is the time for actual business? This is just as if, in forming our opinions, when perplexed between true and false semblances, we should, instead of practically distinguishing between them, merely peruse dissertations on evidence.

What, then, is the trouble? That we have neither learned by reading, nor by writing, how to deal practically with the semblances of things according to the laws of nature. But we stop at learning what is said, and, being able to explain it to others, at solving syllogisms and arranging hypothetical arguments. Hence where the study is, there, too, is the hindrance. Do you desire absolutely what is out of your power? Be restrained then, be hindered, be disappointed. But if we were to read dissertations about the exertion of our efforts, not merely to see what might be said about our efforts, but to exert them well; on desire and aversion, that we might not be disappointed of our desires, nor incur our aversions; on the duties of life, that mindful of our relations, we might do nothing irrational nor inconsistent with them; then we should not be provoked at being hindered in our reading; but should be contented with the performance of actions suitable to us, and should learn a new standard of computation. Not, "Today I have perused so many lines; I have written so many"; but, "Today I have used my efforts as the philosophers direct. I have restrained my desires absolutely; I have applied my aversion only to things controllable by will. I have not been terrified by such a one, nor put out of countenance by such another. I have exercised my patience, my abstinence, my beneficence." And thus we should thank God for what we ought to thank him.

But now we resemble the crowd in another way also, and do not know it. One is afraid that he shall not be in power; you, that you shall. By no means be afraid of it, man; but as you laugh at him, laugh at yourself. For there is no difference, whether you thirst like one in a fever, or dread water like him who is bit by a mad dog. Else how can you say, like Socrates, "If it so pleases God, so let it be"? Do you think that Socrates, if he had fixed his desires on the leisure of the Lyceum or the Academy, or the conversation of the youth there, day after day, would have made so many campaigns as he did, so readily? Would not he have lamented and groaned: "How wretched am I! now must I be miserable here, when I might be sunning myself in the Lyceum"? Was that your business in life, then, to sun yourself? Was it not to be truly successful; to be unrestrained and free? And how could he have been Socrates, if he had lamented thus? How could he after that have written hymns in a prison?

In short, then, remember this, that so far as you prize anything external to your own will, you impair that will. And not only power is external to it, but the being out of power too; not only business, but leisure too. "Then must I live in this tumult now?" What do you call a tumult? "A multitude of people." And where is the hardship? Suppose it to be the Olympic games. Think it a public assembly. There, too, some bawl out one thing, some another; some push the rest. The baths are crowded. Yet who of us is not pleased with these assemblies, and does not grieve to leave them? Do not be hard to please, and squeamish at what happens. "Vinegar is disagreeable, for it is sour. Honey is disagreeable, for it upsets my digestion. I do not like vegetables." "So I do not like retirement, it is a desert; I do not like a crowd, it is a tumult." Why, if things are so disposed that you are to live alone or with few, call this condition repose, and make use of it as you ought. Talk with yourself, judge of the appearances presented to your mind; train your mental habits to accuracy. But if you happen on a crowd, call it one of the public games, a grand assembly, a festival. Endeavor to share in the festival with the rest of the world. For what sight is more pleasant to a lover of mankind than a great number of men? We see companies of oxen or horses with pleasure. We are highly delighted to see a great many ships. Who is sorry to see a great many men? "But they stun me with their noise." Then your hearing is hindered; and what is that to you? Is your faculty of making a right use of the appearances of things hindered too? Or who can restrain you from using your desire and aversion, your powers of pursuit and avoidance, in accord with nature? What tumult is sufficient for this?

Do but remember the general rules. What is mine; what not mine? What is allotted me? What does God will that I do now? What does he not will? A little while ago it was his will that you should be at leisure, should talk with yourself, write about these things, read, hear, prepare yourself. You have had sufficient time for this. At present he says to you,

"Come now to the combat. Show us what you have learned; how you have wrestled." How long would you exercise by yourself? It is now the time to show whether you are one of those champions who merit victory, or of those who go about the world conquered in all the circle of games. Why, then, are you out of humor? There is no combat without a tumult. There must be many preparatory exercises, many shouts of applause, many masters, many spectators. "But I would live in quiet." Why, then, lament and groan as you deserve. For what greater punishment is there to those who are uninstructed and disobedient to the orders of God, than to grieve, to mourn, to envy; in short, to be disappointed and unhappy?

Are you not willing to deliver yourself from all this? "And how shall I deliver myself?" Have you not heard that you must absolutely control desire, and apply aversion to such things only as are controllable by will; that you must consent to resign all—body, possessions, fame, books, tumults, power, exemption from power? For if you once swerve from this course, you are a slave; you are under subjection; you are made liable to restraint, to compulsion; you are altogether the property of others. But have that maxim of Cleanthes always ready,

Conduct me, Zeus; and thou, O Destiny.[1]

Is it your will that I should go to Rome? Conduct me to Rome. To Gyaros? To Gyaros. To Athens? To Athens. To prison? To prison. If you once say, "When may I go to Athens?" you are undone. This desire, if it be unaccomplished, must necessarily render you disappointed; and if fulfilled, vain respecting what ought not to elate you; if, on the contrary, you are hindered, then you are wretched through incurring what you do not like. Therefore give up all these things.

"Athens is a fine place." But it is a much finer thing to be happy, serene, tranquil, not to have your affairs dependent

---

[1] See footnote on p. 276.

on others. "Rome is full of tumults and visits." But prosperity is worth all difficulties. If, then, it be a proper time for these, why not get rid of your aversion? Why must you be burdened like an ass, and cudgeled like one? Otherwise, consider that you must always be a slave to him who has the power to procure your discharge—to everyone who has the power of hindering you—and must worship him like your evil genius.

The only way to real prosperity (let this rule be at hand morning, noon, and night) is a resignation of things uncontrollable by will; to esteem nothing as property; to deliver up all things to the Deity and to fortune; to leave the control of them to those whom Zeus has made such; to be ourselves devoted to that only which is really ours—to that which is incapable of restraint—and whatever we read or write or hear, to refer all to this.

Therefore I cannot call anyone industrious, if I hear only that he reads or writes; nor do I call him so even if he adds the whole night to the day, unless I know to what end he applies it. For not even you would call him industrious who sits up for the sake of a girl; nor do I. But if he does it for fame, I call him ambitious; if for money, avaricious; if from the desire of learning, bookish; but not industrious. But if he applies his labor to his ruling faculty, in order to treat and regulate it in accord with nature, then only I call him industrious. Never praise or blame any person on account of outward actions that are common to all; but only on account of principles. These are the peculiar property of each individual, and the things which make actions good or bad.

Mindful of this, enjoy the present and accept all things in their season. If you meet in action any of those things which you have made a subject of study, rejoice in them. If you have laid aside ill-nature and reviling; if you have lessened your harshness, indecent language, recklessness, effeminacy; if you are not moved by the same things as formerly, or in the same manner as formerly—you may keep a perpetual festival, today for success in one affair, tomorrow for another. How much better a reason for sacrifice is this than obtaining a consulship or a government! These things you have from yourself and from the gods. Remember this—who it is that gave them, and to whom and for what purpose. Accustomed to these reasonings, can you still think that it makes any difference what place God allots you? Are not the gods everywhere at the same distance? Do they not everywhere have the same view of what is going on?

CHAPTER FIVE

Concerning the Quarrelsome and Brutal

A WISE and good person neither quarrels with anyone himself, nor, as far as possible, suffers another to do so. The life of Socrates affords us an example of this too, as well as of other things; since he not only everywhere avoided quarreling himself, but tried to prevent others from quarreling. See in Xenophon's *Symposium* how many quarrels he ended; how, again, he bore with Thrasymachus, with Polus, with Callicles; how with his wife, how with his son, who attempted to confute him, and caviled at him. For he well remembered that no one is master of the ruling faculty of another; and therefore he desired nothing but what was his own. "And what is that?" Not that any particular person should be dealt with in accord with nature, for that belongs to others; but that while they act in their own way, as they please, he should nevertheless live in accord with nature, only doing what belongs to himself, in order to make them also live in harmony with nature. For this is the point that a wise and good person has in view. To have the command of an army? No; but if it be allotted him, to properly apply his own powers in that sphere. To marry? No; but if marriage be allotted him, to act in this sphere also in harmony with the laws of nature. But if he expects perfection in his wife or his child, then he asks to have that for his own which really belongs to others. And wisdom consists in this very point, to learn what things are our own and what belong to others.

What room is there then for quarreling, to a person thus disposed? For does he wonder at anything that happens? Does it appear strange to him? Does he not prepare for worse and more grievous injuries from bad people than actually happen to him? Does he not reckon it so much gained if they come short of the last extremities? Such a one has reviled you. You are much obliged to him that he has not struck you. But he has struck you too. You are much obliged to him that he has not wounded you too. But he has wounded you too. You are much obliged to him that he has not killed you. For when did he ever learn, or from whom, that he is a gentle, that he is a social, animal; that the very injury itself is a great mischief to him who inflicts it?

As, then, he has not learned these things, nor believes them, why should he not follow what appears to be for his interest? Your neighbor has thrown stones. What then; is it any fault of yours? But your goods are broken. What then; are you a piece of furniture? No, but your essence consists in the faculty of will. What behavior then is assigned you in return? If you consider yourself as a wolf, you can bite back, throw more stones. But if you ask the question as a man, then examine your treasure; see what faculties you have brought into the world with you. Are they fitted for ferocity, for revenge? When is a horse miserable? When he is deprived of his natural faculties; not when he cannot crow, but when he cannot run. And a dog? Not when he cannot fly, but when he cannot hunt. Is not a man, then, also unhappy in the same manner;

not he who cannot strangle lions or perform great athletic feats (for he has received no faculties for this purpose from nature); but he who has lost his rectitude of mind, his fidelity? This is he who ought to receive public condolence for the misfortunes into which he is fallen; not, by heaven! either he who has the misfortune to be born or to die, but he whose misfortune it is while he still lives to lose what is his own; not his paternal possessions, his paltry estate or his house, his lodging or his slaves, for none of these are a man's own, but all these belong to others, are servile, dependent, and given [by the Gods] now to one person, now to another; but his personal qualifications as a man, the impressions which he brought into the world stamped upon his mind; such as we look for in money, accepting or rejecting it accordingly. "What impression has this piece of money?" "Trajan's." "Give it to me." "Nero's."[1] Throw it away. It is false; it is good for nothing. So in the other case. "What stamp have his principles?" "Gentleness, social affection, patience, good-nature." Bring him hither. I receive him. I make such a man a citizen; I receive him for a neighbor, a fellow traveler. Only see that he does not have the stamp of Nero. Is he passionate? Is he resentful? Is he querulous? Would he, if he took the fancy, break the heads of those who fell in his way? Why then do you call him a man? For is everything determined by a mere outward form? Then say, just as well, that a piece of wax is an apple, or that it has the smell and taste too. The external figure is not enough; nor, consequently, is it sufficient to constitute a man that he has a nose and eyes, if he have not the proper principles of a man. Such a one does not understand reason, or apprehend when he is confuted. He is like an ass. Another is dead to the sense of shame. He is a worthless creature; anything rather than a man. Another seeks whom he

---

[1] Nero being declared an enemy by the Senate, his coin was, in consequence of this, prohibited and destroyed.

may kick or bite; so that he is neither sheep nor ass. But what then? He is a wild beast.

"Well, but would you have me despised, then?" By whom —by those who know you? And how can they despise you who know you to be gentle and modest? But perhaps by those who do not know you? And what is that to you? For no other artist troubles himself about those ignorant of art. "But people will be much readier to attack me." Why do you say *me?* Can anyone hurt your will, or restrain you from treating, in harmony with nature, the phenomena of existence? Why, then, are you disturbed and desirous to make yourself appear formidable? Why do you not make public proclamation that you are at peace with all mankind, however they may act; and that you chiefly laugh at those who suppose they can hurt you? "These wretches neither know who I am, nor in what consist my good and evil; nor how little they can touch what is really mine." Thus the inhabitants of a fortified city laugh at the besiegers. "What trouble, now, are these people giving themselves for nothing! Our wall is secure; we have provisions for a very long time, and every other preparation." These are what make a city fortified and impregnable; and nothing but its principles make the human soul secure. For what wall is so strong, what body so impenetrable, what possession so un-alienable, what dignity so secured against stratagems? All things else, everywhere else, are mortal, easily captured; and whoever in any degree fixes his mind upon them must neces-sarily be subject to perturbation, despair, terrors, lamenta-tions, disappointed desires, and the incurring of what he would avoid.

And will we not fortify, then, the only citadel that is granted us; and withdrawing ourselves from what is mortal and servile, diligently improve what is immortal and by nature free? Do we not remember that no one either hurts or benefits another; but only the views which we hold concerning every-thing? It is this that hurts us; this that overturns us. Here is the fight, the sedition, the war. It was nothing else that made Eteocles and Polynices enemies,[1] but their views concerning empire, and their principles concerning exile, namely, that the one seemed the extreme of evil, the other the greatest good. Now, the very nature of everyone is to pursue good, to avoid evil; to consider him an enemy and betrayer who deprives us of the one and involves us in the other, though he be a brother, or a son, or father. For nothing is more nearly related to us than good. So that if good and evil consist in externals, there is no affection between father and son, brother and brother; but on sides there are enemies, betrayers, sycophants. But if a right choice be the only good, and a wrong one the only evil, what further room is there for quarreling, for reviling? About what? About what means nothing to us. And against whom? Against the ignorant, against the unhappy, against those who are deceived in the most important respects.

Mindful of this, Socrates lived in his own house, patiently bearing a furious wife, a senseless son. For what were the effects of her fury? The throwing as much water as she pleased on his head, the trampling a cake under her feet.[2] "And what is this to me, if I think such things nothing to me? This very point is my business; and neither a tyrant, nor a master, shall restrain my will; nor multitudes, though I am a single person; nor one ever so strong, though I am ever so weak. For this is given by God to everyone, free from restraint."

These principles make friendship in families, concord in cities, peace in nations. They make a person grateful to God, everywhere courageous, as dealing with things merely foreign

---

1 Eteocles and Polynices were the sons of Oedipus who in a quarrel over the kingdom of Thebes killed each other.

2 Alcibiades sent a fine cake as a present to Socrates. This so provoked the jealousy of his wife Xantippe, that she threw it down and stamped upon it. Socrates only laughed, and said, "Now you will have no share in it yourself."

and of minor importance. But we, alas! are able indeed to write and read these things, and to praise them when they are read; but very far from being convinced by them. In that case, what is said of the Lacedemonians,

Lions at home, foxes at Ephesus,[1]

may be applied to us, too; lions in the school, but foxes outside.

CHAPTER SIX

To Those Who Are Annoyed at Being Pitied

IT vexes me, say you, to be pitied. Is this your affair, then, or theirs who pity you? And further, how is it in your power to prevent it? "It is, if I show them that I do not need pity." But are you now in such a condition as not to need pity, or are you not? "I think I am. But these people do not pity me for what, if anything, would deserve pity, my faults; but for poverty, and want of power, and sicknesses, and deaths, and other things of that kind." Are you, then, prepared to convince the world that none of these things is in reality an evil; but that it is possible for a person to be happy, even when he is poor, and without honors and power? Or are you prepared to put on the appearance of being rich and powerful? The last of these is the part of an arrogant, silly, worthless fellow. Observe, too, by what means this fiction must be carried on. You must hire some poor slaves, and get possessed of a few

[1] The campaigns of the Lacedemonians were less successful in Asia Minor; they became wary and foxlike.

little pieces of plate, and often show them in public; and though they are the same, endeavor to conceal that they are the same; you must have gay clothes and other finery, and make a show of being honored by the great; and endeavor to sup with them, or be thought to sup with them; and use some vile arts with your person, to make it appear handsomer and genteeler than it really is. All this you must contrive, if you would take the second way not to be pitied.

And the first is impracticable as well as tedious, to undertake the very thing that Zeus himself could not do—to convince all mankind what things are really good and evil. Is this granted you? The only thing granted you is to convince yourself; and you have not yet done that; and yet do you undertake to convince others? Why, who has lived so long with you as you have with yourself? Who is so likely to have faith in you, in order to be convinced by you, as yourself? Who is more truly a well-wisher or a friend to you than yourself? How is it, then, that you have not yet convinced yourself? Are things not now upside down? What you were studying was this: to learn to be exempt from grief, perturbation, and meanness, and to be free. Have you not heard, then, that the only way that leads to this is to give up what is beyond the control of will; to withdraw from it, and confess that it belongs to others? To what order of things belongs another's opinion about you? "Things uncontrollable by will." Is it nothing then to you? "Nothing." While you are still piqued and disturbed about it, then, do you consider that you are convinced concerning good and evil?

Letting others alone, then, why will you not be your own scholar and teacher? Let others look to it, whether it be for their advantage to think and act contrary to nature; but no one is nearer to me than myself. What means this? I have heard the reasonings of philosophers, and assented to them; yet, in fact, I am not the more relieved. Am I so stupid? And yet, in other things to which I had an inclination, I was not found very stupid; but I quickly learned grammar, and how to wrestle, and geometry, and the solution of syllogisms. Has not reason, then, convinced me? And yet there is no one of the other things that I so much approved or liked from the very first. And now I read concerning these subjects, I hear discourses upon them, I write about them, and I have not yet found any principle more sure than this. What, then, do I need? Is not this the difficulty, that the contrary principles are not removed out of my mind? Is it not that I have not strengthened these opinions by exercise, nor practiced them in action; but, like arms thrown aside, they are grown rusty, and do not suit me? Yet neither in wrestling, nor writing, nor reading, nor solving syllogisms, am I contented with merely learning; but I apply in every way the forms of arguments which are presented to me, and I invent others; and the same of convertible propositions. But the necessary principles by which I might become exempted from fear, grief, and passion, and be unrestrained and free, I do not exercise, nor bestow on them the proper care. And then I trouble myself what others will say of me; whether I shall appear to them worthy of regard; whether I shall appear happy.

Will you not see, foolish man, what you can say of *yourself;* what sort of person you appear to *yourself* in your opinions, in your desires, in your aversions, in your pursuits, in your preparation, in your intention, in the other proper works of a man? But instead of that, do you trouble yourself whether others pity you? "Very true. But I am pitied without reason." Then are you not pained by this? And is not he who is in pain to be pitied? "Yes." How, then, are you pitied without reason? For you render yourself worthy of pity by what you suffer upon being pitied.

What says Antisthenes, then? Have you never heard?—"It is kingly, O Cyrus, to do well and to be ill spoken of." My head is well, and all around me think it aches. What is that to me? I am free from a fever; and they sympathize with me as if I had one. "Poor soul, what a long while have you had this fever!" I say, too, with a dismal countenance, Yes, indeed, it is now a long time that I have been ill. "What can be the consequence, then?" What pleases God. And at the same time I secretly laugh at those who pity me.

What prevents me, then, from doing the same in my moral life? I am poor, but I have right principles concerning poverty. What is it to me, then, if people pity me for my poverty? I am not in power and others are; but I have such opinions as I ought to have concerning power and the want of power. Let them consider well who pity me. I am neither hungry, nor thirsty, nor cold. But because they are hungry and thirsty, they suppose me to be so too. What can I do for them? Am I to go about making proclamation, and saying, Do not deceive yourselves, good people, I am very well; I care for neither poverty, nor want of power, nor anything else but right principles? These I possess unrestrained, and care for nothing further.

But what trifling is this! How have I right principles when I am not contented to be what I am; but am in agony as to how I shall appear? "But others will get more, and be preferred to me." Well, what is more reasonable than that they who take pains for anything should get most in that particular direction in which they take pains? They have taken pains for power; you, for right principles. They, for riches; you, for a proper use of the phenomena of existence. See whether they have the advantage of you in that for which you have taken pains, and which they neglect; if they judge better concerning the natural bounds and limits of things; if their desires are less often disappointed than yours, if they are less likely to fall into what they would avoid; if they aim better in their intentions, in their purposes, in their pursuits; if they preserve a becoming behavior as men, as sons, as parents, and so on with the other relations of life. But if they are in power, and you not, why will you not speak the truth to yourself; that you do nothing for the sake of power, but that they do everything? It were very reasonable that he who carefully seeks anything should be less successful than he who neglects it! "No; but since I take care to have right principles, it is more reasonable that I should excel." Yes, in respect to what you take pains about, your principles. But give up to others the things in which they have taken more pains than you. Else it is just as if, because you have right principles, you should expect to aim an arrow better than an archer, or to forge better than a smith.

In that case cease to take pains about principles, and apply yourself to those things which you wish to possess, and then begin crying, if you do not succeed; for you deserve to cry. But now you claim that you are engaged and absorbed in other things; and they say well that no man can be of two trades. One man, as soon as he rises and goes out, seeks to whom he may pay his compliments, whom he may flatter, to whom he may send a present, how he may please the favorite; how, by doing mischief to one, he may oblige another. Whenever he prays, he prays for things like these; whenever he sacrifices, he sacrifices for things like these. To these he transfers the Pythagorean percept,

Let not the stealing god of Sleep surprise.

[1] *Where have I failed* in point of flattery? *What have I done* —anything like a free, brave-spirited man? If he should find anything of this sort, he rebukes and accuses himself. "What business had you to say that? For could you not have lied? Even the philosophers say there is no objection against telling a lie."

But, on the other hand, if you have in reality been careful about nothing else but to make a right use of the phenomena of existence; then, as soon as you are up in the morning, consider

---

[1] The portions of the questions in italics are from the *Golden Verses* of Pythagoras. Epictetus represents the self-seeker as applying them to his own wretched aims.

what you need in order to be free from passion; what, to enjoy tranquillity? "In what do I consist—merely in body, in estate, in reputation? None of these. What, then? I am a reasonable creature. What, then, is required of me?" Meditate upon your actions. Where have I failed in any requisite for prosperity? What have I done, either unfriendly or unsocial? What have I omitted that was necessary in these points?

Since there is so much difference, then, in your desires, your actions, your wishes, would you yet have an equal share with others in those things about which you have not taken pains, and they have? And do you wonder, after all, and are you out of humor, if they pity you? But they are not out of humor, if you pity them. Why? Because they are convinced that they are in possession of their proper good; but you are not convinced that you are. Hence you are not contented with your own condition, but desire theirs; whereas they are contented with theirs, and do not desire yours. For if you were really convinced that it is you who are in possession of what is good, and that they are mistaken, you would not so much as think what they say about you.

CHAPTER   SEVEN

On Freedom from Fear

WHAT makes a tyrant formidable? His guards, say you, and their swords; they who protect his bedchamber, and they who keep out intruders. Why, then, if you bring a child to him amidst these guards, is it not afraid? Is it because the child does not know what they mean? Suppose, then, that anyone knows what is meant by guards, and that they are armed with swords; and for that very reason comes in the tyrant's way, since, on account of some misfortune, he wishes to die, and seeks to die easily by the hand of another. Does such a man fear the guards? No; for he desires the very thing that makes them formidable. Well, then; if anyone, being without an absolute desire to live or die, but indifferent to it, comes in the way of a tyrant, what prevents his approaching him without fear? Nothing. If, then, another should think concerning his estate, or wife, or children, as this man thinks concerning his body; and, in short, from some madness or folly should be of such a disposition as not to care whether he has them or not; but just as children, playing with shells, are busied with the play, but not with the shells, so he should pay no regard to these affairs, except to carry on the play with them, what tyrant, what guards, or swords are any longer formidable to such a man?

And is it possible that anyone should be thus disposed towards these things from madness, and the Galileans [1] from mere habit; yet that no one should be able to learn, from reason and demonstration, that God made all things in the world, and made the whole world itself unrestrained and perfect, and all its parts for the use of the whole? All other creatures are indeed denied the capacity of understanding the governance of the world; but a reasonable being has abilities for the consideration of all these things—both that itself is a part, and what part; and that it is fit the parts should submit to the whole. Besides, being by nature constituted noble, magnanimous, and free, the rational animal, man, sees that some of the things around him are unrestrained and in his power, and others are restrained and in the power of others—the unrestrained, such as depend on will; the restrained, such as do not depend on it.

---

[1] Unquestionably Epictetus meant the Christians. Although he was a contemporary of St. Paul, he knew little of the struggling new sect; obviously he knew of the obstinacy with which they clung to their faith under persecution.

And for this reason, if he regards his own good and interest to consist in things unrestrained and in his own power, he will be free, prosperous, happy, safe, magnanimous, pious, thankful to God for everything, never finding fault with anything, never censuring anything that is brought about by him. But if he esteems his good and his interest to consist in externals, and things uncontrollable by will, he must necessarily be restrained, be hindered, be enslaved to those who have the power over those things which he admires and fears; he must necessarily be irreverent, as supposing himself injured by God, and unjust, as claiming more than his share; he must necessarily, too, be abject and base.

Why may not he who discerns these things live with an easy and light heart, quietly awaiting whatever may happen, and bearing contentedly what has happened? Shall it be poverty? Bring it; and you shall see what poverty is when it is met well. Would you have power? Bring troubles too along with it. Banishment? Wherever I go, it will be well with me there; for it was well with me here—not on account of the place, but of the principles which I shall carry away with me; for no one can deprive me of these; on the contrary, they alone are my property, and cannot be taken away; and their possession suffices me wherever I am, or whatever I do.

"But it is now time to die." Why do you say die? Do not talk of the thing in a tragic strain; but state the thing as it is, that it is time for your material part to revert whence it came. And where is the terror of this? What part of the world is going to be lost? What is going to happen that is new or prodigious? Is it for this that a tyrant is formidable? Is it on this account that the swords of his guards seem so large and sharp? Try these things upon others. For my part I have examined the whole. No one has authority over me. God has made me free; I know his commands; after this no one can enslave me. I have a proper vindicator of my freedom; proper judges. Are you the master of my body? But what is that to me? Of my little estate? But what is that to me? Of banishment and chains? Why, all these again, and my whole body, I give up to you; make a trial of your power whenever you please, and you will find how far it extends.

Whom, then, can I any longer fear—those who guard the chamber? Lest they should do—what?—shut me out? If they find me wanting to come in, let them. "Why do you come to the door, then?" Because it is fitting for me that, while the play lasts, I should play too. "How then are you incapable of being shut out?" Because, if I am not admitted, I would not wish to go in; but would much rather that things should be as they are, for I esteem what God wills to be better than what I will. To him I yield myself, as a servant and a follower. My pursuits, my desires, my very will, must coincide with his. Being shut out does not affect me; but those who push to get in. Why, then, do not I push too? Because I know that there is no really good thing distributed to those who get in. But when I hear anyone congratulated on the favor of Caesar, I ask what he has got. "A province." Has he the needed wisdom also? "A public office." Has he also knowledge enough to administer it? If not, why should I push my way in?

Someone scatters nuts and figs. Children scramble and quarrel for them; but not men, for they think them trifles. But if anyone should scatter broken pottery, not even children would scramble for the fragments. Provinces are being distributed; let children look to it. Money; let children look to it. Military command, a consulship; let children scramble for them. Let them be shut out, be beaten, kiss the hands of the giver or of his slaves. But to me they are mere figs and nuts. "What then is to be done?" If you miss them, while he is throwing them, do not trouble yourself about it; but if a fig should fall into your lap, take it, and eat it; for one may pay so much regard even to a fig. But if I am to stoop and throw down a rival, or be thrown down by another, and flatter those who succeed, a fig is not worth this, nor is any other of those things which are not really good, and which the philosophers have persuaded me not to esteem as good.

Show me the swords of the guards. "See how large and how sharp they are." What, then, can these great and sharp swords do? "They kill." And what can a fever do? "Nothing else." And a falling tile? "Nothing else." Do you then wish me to be bewildered by all these things, and to worship them, and to go about as a slave to them all? Heaven forbid! But having once learned that everything that is born must likewise die, that the world may not be at a standstill, nor the course of it hindered, I no longer see any difference, whether this be effected by a fever, or a tile, or a soldier; but if any comparison is to be made, I know that the soldier will effect it with less pain and more speedily. Since then I neither fear any of those things which he can inflict upon me, nor covet anything which he can bestow, why do I stand any longer in awe of a tyrant? Why am I amazed at him? Why do I fear his guards? Why do I rejoice, if he speaks kindly to me, and receives me graciously; and why boast to others of my reception? For is he Socrates or Diogenes, that his praise should show what I am? Or have I set my heart on imitating his manners? But to keep up the play I go to him and serve him, so long as he commands nothing unreasonable or improper. But if he should say to me, "Go to Salamis, and bring Leon," [1] I bid him seek another, for I play no longer. "Lead him away." I follow as a part of the play. "But your head will be taken off." And will his own remain on forever; or yours, who obey him? "But you will be thrown out unburied." [2] If I am identical with my corpse, I shall be thrown out; but if I am something else than the corpse, speak more handsomely, as the thing is, and do not think to frighten me. These things are frightful to children and fools. But if anyone who has once entered into the school of a

[1] See note, pp. 280-281.

[2] As a final insult to the dead. Diogenes asked that his corpse be thrown out unburied.

philosopher knows not what he himself is, then he deserves to be frightened, and to flatter the last object of flattery; if he has not yet learned that he is neither flesh, nor bones, nor nerves, but is that which makes use of these, and regulates and comprehends the phenomena of existence.

"Well; but these reasonings make men despise the laws." And what reasonings, then, make those who use them more obedient to the laws? But the law of fools is no law. And yet, see how these reasonings make us properly disposed, even towards such persons, since they teach us not to assert against them any claim wherein they can surpass us. They teach us to give up body, to give up estate, children, parents, brothers, to yield everything, to let go everything, excepting only principles; which even Zeus has excepted and decreed to be everyone's own property. What unreasonableness, what breach of the laws, is there in this? Where you are superior and stronger, there I give way to you. Where, on the contrary, I am superior, you submit to me; for this has been my study, and not yours. Your study has been to walk upon a marble floor, to be attended by your servants and clients, to wear fine clothes, to have a great number of hunters, fiddlers, and players. Do I lay any claim to these?

On the other hand, have you made a study of principles, or even of your own reason? Do you know of what parts it consists; how they are combined and joined, and with what powers? Why, then, do you take it amiss, if another, who has studied them, has the advantage of you in these things? "But they are of all things the greatest." Well; and who restrains you from being conversant with them, and attending to them ever so carefully? Or who is better provided with books, with leisure, with assistants? Only turn your thoughts now and then to these matters; bestow but a little time upon your own ruling faculty. Consider what is the power you have, and where it came from, this power that uses all other things, that examines them all, that chooses, that rejects. But while you employ yourself merely about externals, you will possess them in a way that no one else can match; but everything else will be, just as you choose to have it, sordid and neglected.

CHAPTER EIGHT

To Those Who Hastily Assume the Philosophic Dress

NEVER commend or censure anyone for common actions, nor attribute to them either skillfulness or unskillfulness; and thus you will at once be free both from rashness and ill-nature. Such a one bathes hastily. Does he therefore do it badly? Not at all. But what is he doing? He bathes hastily. "Is everything well done, then?" By no means. But what is done from good principles is well done; what from bad ones, ill. Till you know from what principle anyone acts, neither commend nor censure the action. But the principle is not easily discerned from the external appearance. This man is a carpenter. Why? He uses an ax. What proof is that? This man is a musician, for he sings. What proof is that? Another is a philosopher. Why? Because he wears a cloak and long hair. What then do mountebanks wear? And so, when people see any of these acting indecently, they presently say, "See what the philosopher does." But they ought rather, from his acting indecently, to say that he is no philosopher. For if indeed the essence of philosophic pursuits is to wear a cloak and long hair, they say right; but if it be rather to keep himself free from faults, since he does not fulfill his profession, why do they not deprive him of his title?

For this is the way with regard to other arts. When we see anyone handle an ax awkwardly, we do not say, "What is the use of this art? See how poorly carpenters work," but we say the very contrary, "This man is no carpenter; for he handles an ax awkwardly." So, if we hear anyone sing badly, we do not say, "Observe how musicians sing," but rather, "This fellow is no musician." It is with regard to philosophy alone that people behave like this. When they see anyone acting inconsistently with the profession of a philosopher, they do not take away his title; but assuming that he is a philosopher, and then reasoning from his improper behavior, they infer that philosophy is of no use.

"What then is the reason for this?" Because we pay some regard to the idea which we have of a carpenter and a musician, and so of other artists, but not of a philosopher; which idea being thus vague and confused, we judge of it only from external appearances. And of what other art do we form our opinion from the dress or the hair? Has it not principles too, and materials, and an aim? What, then, are the materials of a philosopher—a cloak? No, but reason. What his aim—to wear a cloak? No, but to have his reason in good order. What are his principles? Are they how to get a great beard, or long hair? No, but rather, as Zeno expresses it, to know the elements of reason, what is each separately and how linked together, and what their consequences.

Why, then, will you not first see, whether when misbehaving he fulfills his profession, before you proceed to blame his way of acting? Whereas now, when acting soberly yourself, you say, in regard to whatever he appears to do amiss, "Observe the philosopher!" as if it were proper to call a person who does such things a philosopher. And again, "This is philosophical!" But you do not say, "Observe the carpenter, or observe the musician," when you know one of them to be an adulterer, or see him to be a glutton. So, in some small degree, you realize what the profession of a philosopher is, but are misled and confounded by your own carelessness. And, indeed, even those called philosophers enter upon their profession by means which are sometimes good and sometimes bad. As soon as they have put on the cloak and let their beards grow, they cry, "I am a philosopher." Yet no one says, "I am a musician," merely because he has bought a fiddle and fiddlestick; nor, "I am a smith," because he is dressed in the cap and apron. But they take their name from their art, not from their garb.

For this reason, Euphrates [1] was in the right in saying, "I long endeavored to conceal my embracing the philosophic life; and it was of use to me. For, in the first place, I knew that whatever I did right I did not for spectators, but for myself. I ate in a seemly manner, for my own approbation. I preserved composure of look and manner, all for God and myself. Then, as I struggled alone, I alone was in danger. Philosophy was in no danger, on my doing anything shameful or unbecoming; nor did I hurt the rest of the world, which, by doing wrong as a philosopher, I might have done. For this reason, they who were ignorant of my intention, used to wonder that while I conversed and lived entirely with philosophers, I never took up the character. And where was the harm, that I should be discovered to be a philosopher by my actions, rather than by the usual badges? See how I eat, how I drink, how I sleep, how I endure, how I forbear; how I assist others; how I direct my desires and aversions; how I preserve the natural and acquired relations, without confusion and without obstruction. Judge me on the basis of this, if you can. But if you are so deaf and blind that you would not suppose Hephaestus himself to be a good smith, unless you saw the cap upon his head, where is the harm of not being recognized by so foolish a judge?"

It was thus, too, that Socrates concealed himself from the multitude; and some even came and desired him to introduce

[1] See note, p. 194.

them to philosophers. Was he accustomed to be displeased, then, like us; and to say, What! do you not take *me* for a philosopher? No, he took them and introduced them; contented with merely being a philosopher, and rejoicing in feeling no annoyance that he was not thought one. For he remembered his business; and what is the business of a wise and good man—to have many pupils? By no means. Let those who have made that their aim see to that. Well, then; is it to be a perfect master of difficult theorems? Let others see to that too. What, then, was his position, and what did he desire to be? What constituted his hurt or advantage? "If," said he, "anyone can still hurt me, I am accomplishing nothing. If I depend for my advantage upon another, I am nothing. Have I any wish unaccomplished? Then I am unhappy." To such a combat he invited everyone, and, in my opinion, yielded to no one. But do you think it was by making proclamation, and saying, "I am such a man"? Far from it; but by being such a man. For it is folly and insolence to say, "I am passive and undisturbed. Be it known to you, mortals, that while you are disturbed and vexed about things of no value, I alone am free from all perturbation." Are you, then, so little satisfied with your exemption from pain, that you must needs make proclamation: "Come hither, all you who have the gout, or the headache, or a fever, or are lame, or blind; and see *me*, free from every sickness"? This is vain and shocking, unless you can show, like Aesculapius, by what method of cure they may presently become as free from sickness as yourself, and can bring your own health as a proof of it.

Such is the Cynic who is honored with the scepter and diadem of Zeus; who says, "That you may see, O mankind, that you do not seek happiness and tranquillity where it is, but where it is not, behold, I am sent as an example to you from God—I who have neither estate, nor house, nor wife, nor children, nor even a bed, coat, or furniture. And yet see how healthy I am. Try me; and if you see me free from worry, hear the remedies, and how I was cured." This now is an attitude both benevolent and noble. But consider whose business it is. That of Zeus, or of him whom he judges worthy of this office; that he may never show to the world anything to impeach his own testimony for virtue and against externals.

Neither pallid of hue, nor wiping tears from his cheek.[1]

And not only this, but he does not desire or seek for company or place or amusement, as boys do the vintage time, or holidays; being always fortified by virtuous shame, as others are by walls and gates and sentinels.

But now, they who have only such an inclination to philosophy as weak stomachs have to some kinds of food, of which they will presently grow sick, expect to hasten to the scepter, to the kingdom. They let their hair grow, assume the cloak, bare the shoulder, wrangle with all they meet; and if they see anyone in a thick, warm coat, must needs wrangle with him. First harden yourself against all weather, man. Consider your inclination; whether it be not that of a man with a weak stomach, or of a woman with the cravings of pregnancy. Try first to conceal what you are; philosophize a little while by yourself. Fruit is produced thus: the seed must first be buried in the ground, lie hid there some time, and grow up by degrees, that it may come to perfection. But if it produces the ear before the stalk has its proper joints, it is imperfect, and of the garden of Adonis.[2] Now *you* are a poor plant of this kind. You have blossomed too soon; the winter will kill you. See what farmers say about seeds of any sort, when the warm weather comes too early. They are in great anxiety for fear the seeds should shoot out too luxuriantly; and then one frost

---

[1] Homer, *Odyssey.* See Classics Club edition, p. 143.

[2] At the feast of Adonis there were carried about little earthen pots filled with mold, in which grew herbs. These were called gardens of Adonis, an expression which came to be proverbially applied to things unfruitful or immature.

may blight them and expose their weakness. Beware you, too, O man. You have shot out luxuriantly; you have sprung forth towards a trifling fame, before the proper season. You think you are somebody, as a fool may among fools. You will be taken by the frost; or rather, you are already frozen downward at the root; you still blossom, indeed, a little at the top, and therefore you think you are still alive and flourishing.

Let us, at least, ripen naturally. Why do you lay us open? Why do you force us? We cannot yet bear the air. Suffer the root to grow; then the first, then the second, then the third joint of the stalk to spring from it; and thus nature will force out the fruit, whether I will or not. For who that is charged with such principles, but must perceive, too, his own powers, and strive to put them in practice. Not even a bull is ignorant of his own powers, when any wild beast approaches the herd, nor does he wait for anyone to encourage him; nor does a dog when he spies some wild animal. And if I have the powers of a good man, shall I wait for you to encourage me for my own proper actions? But believe me, I do not yet have the equipment. Why, then, would you wish me to be withered before my time, as you are?

CHAPTER NINE

To a Man Who Had Grown Shameless

WHEN you see another in power, set this against it, that you have the advantage of not needing power. When you see another rich, see what you have instead of riches; for if you have nothing in their stead, you are miserable. But if you have the advantage of not needing riches, know that you have something more than he has, and of far greater value. Another has a handsome wife; you the satisfaction of not desiring a handsome wife. Do you think these are small matters? And what would not those very persons give, who are rich and powerful, and possess handsome wives, if they were only able to despise riches and power, and those very women whom they love and whom they possess! Do you not know what the thirst of a man in fever is? It has no resemblance to that of a person in health. The latter drinks and is satisfied. But the other, after being delighted a very little while, is nauseated, the water becomes bile, he is sick at his stomach, and becomes more thirsty than ever. It is the same with avarice, ambition, lust. Presently comes jealousy, fear of loss, unbecoming words, designs, and actions.

"And what," say you, "do I lose?" You were modest, man, and are so no longer. Have you lost nothing? Instead of Chrysippus and Zeno, you read Aristides [1] and Evenus.[2] Have you lost nothing, then? Instead of Socrates and Diogenes, you admire the man who can corrupt and seduce most women. You would be handsome, by decking your person, when you

---

[1] An indecent poet of Miletus.
[2] A writer of amorous verses.

are not really so. You love to appear in fine clothes, to attract female eyes; and if you anywhere meet with a good perfumer, you think yourself lucky. But formerly you did not so much as think of any of these things; but only where you might find a decent discourse, a worthy person, a noble design. For this reason, you used to appear like a man both at home and abroad; to wear a manly dress; to hold discourses worthy of a man. And after this, do you still say you have lost nothing? What, then; do men lose nothing but money? Is not modesty lost? Is not decency lost? Or can he who loses these suffer no injury? You indeed perhaps no longer think anything of this sort to be an injury. But there was once a time when you accounted this to be the only injury and hurt; when you were anxiously afraid lest anyone should shake your regard from such discourses and actions.

See, it is not shaken by another, but by yourself. Fight against yourself, recover yourself to decency, to modesty, to freedom. If you had formerly been told any of these things of me, that one prevailed on me to commit adultery, to wear such a dress as yours, or to be perfumed, would you not have gone and laid violent hands on the man who thus abused me? And will you not now help yourself? For how much easier is that sort of assistance? You need not kill, or fetter, or affront, or go to law with anyone; but merely talk with yourself, the person who will most readily be persuaded by you, and with whom no one has greater weight than you. And, in the first place, condemn your actions; but when you have condemned them, do not despair of yourself, nor be like those spiritless people who, when they have once given way, abandon themselves entirely, and are carried along as by a torrent. Take example from the wrestling masters. Has the boy fallen down? Get up again, they say; wrestle again, till you have acquired strength. React in the same manner yourself. For be assured that there is nothing more easily prevailed upon than the human soul. You need but will, and it is done, it is set right;

as, on the contrary, you need but nod over the work, and it is ruined. For both ruin and recovery are from within.

"And, after all, what good will this do me?" What greater good do you seek? From being impudent, you will become modest; from indecent, decent; from dissolute, sober. But if you seek any greater things than these, do as you are doing. It is no longer in the power of any God to save you.

CHAPTER   TEN

What Ought We to Despise
and What Value

THE doubts and perplexities of all men are concerning externals—what they shall do; how it will be; what will be the event; whether this thing will happen, or that. All this is the talk of persons engaged in things uncontrollable by will. For who says, How shall I avoid giving assent to the false; how, turn away from the true? If anyone is of such a good disposition as to be anxious about these things, I will remind him: "Why are you anxious? It is in your own power. Be assured. Do not hastily give your assent before you have applied those tests prescribed by nature." Again, if he is anxious, for fear lest he should fail of what he seeks or incur what he shuns, I will first embrace him, because, slighting what others are fluttered and terrified about, he takes care of what is his own, where his very being is; then I will say to him: "If you would not fail of what you seek, or incur what you shun, desire nothing that belongs to others; shun nothing that lies beyond your own control; otherwise you must necessarily be disappointed in what you seek, and incur what you shun." Where is the difficulty here? Where the room for, How is it to take place? How is it to turn out? And, Will this happen, or that?

Is not the future uncontrollable by will? "Yes." And does not the essence of good and evil consist in what is within the control of will? It is in your power, then, to treat every event in harmony with nature? Can anyone restrain you? "No one." Then do not say to me any more, How is it to take place? For, however it be, you will set it right, and the outcome will be fortunate for you.

Pray what would Hercules have been, if he had said, "What can be done to prevent a great lion, or a large boar, or savage men, from coming in my way?" Why, what is that to you? If a large boar should come in your way, you will fight the greater combat; if wicked men, you will deliver the world from wicked men. "But then if I should die by this means?" You will die as a good man, in the performance of a gallant action. For since, at all events, one must die, one must necessarily be found doing something, either tilling, or digging, or trading, or serving a consulship, or sick with indigestion or dysentery. At what employment, then, would you have death find you? For my part, I would have it to be some humane, beneficent, public-spirited, noble action. But if I cannot be found doing any such great things, yet, at least, I would be doing what I cannot be prevented from doing, what is given me to do—that is, correcting myself, improving that faculty which makes use of the phenomena of existence to procure tranquillity, and give to each of the human relations of life its due; and if I am so fortunate, advancing still further to the security of judging right.

If death overtakes me in such a situation, it is enough for me if I can stretch out my hands to God, and say, "The opportunities which I have received from thee of comprehending and obeying thy administration, I have not neglected. As far as in me lay, I have not dishonored thee. See how I have used my perceptions; how my convictions. Have I at any time found fault with thee? Have I been discontented at thy dispensations, or wished them otherwise? Have I transgressed the relations of life? I thank thee that thou hast brought me into being. I am satisfied with the time that I have enjoyed the things which thou hast given me. Receive them back again, and distribute them as thou wilt; for they were all thine, and thou gavest them to me."

Is it not enough to depart from the world in this state of mind? And what life is better and more becoming than that of such a man; or what ending happier? But in order to attain these advantages, there are no inconsiderable risks to be encountered. You cannot seek a consulship and these things too, nor toil for an estate and these things too, nor take charge of your slaves and yourself too. But if you insist on anything of what belongs to others, then what is your own is lost. This is the nature of the affair. Nothing is to be had for nothing. And where is the wonder? If you would be consul, you must watch, run about, kiss hands, rot away at the doors of other men, say and do many slavish things, send gifts to many, daily presents to some. And for what result? Twelve bundles of rods;[1] to sit three or four times on the tribunal; to provide the games of the circus, and suppers in baskets to all the world; or let anyone show me what there is in it beyond this. Will you, then, employ no expense and no pains to acquire peace and tranquillity, to sleep sound while you do sleep, to be thoroughly awake while you are awake, to fear nothing, to be anxious for nothing? But if anything belonging to you be lost or idly wasted, while you are thus engaged, or another gets what you ought to have had, will you immediately begin fretting at what has happened? Will you not compare the exchange you have made—how much for how much? But you

---

[1] The fasces, sign of the consular office.

would have such great things for nothing, I suppose. And how can you?

Two trades cannot be combined; you cannot bestow your care both upon externals and your own ruling faculty. But if you would have the former, let the latter alone; or you will succeed in neither, while you are drawn in different ways by the two. On the other hand, if you would have the latter, let the former alone. "The oil will be spilled, the furniture will be spoiled"; but still I shall be free from passion. "There will be a fire when I am out of the way, and the books will be destroyed"; but still I shall make a right use of the phenomena of existence. "But I shall have nothing to eat." If I am so unlucky, dying is a safe harbor. That is the harbor for all—death; that is the refuge; and for that reason there is nothing difficult in life. You may go out of doors when you please, and be troubled with smoke no longer.[1]

Why, then, are you anxious? Why break your rest? Why do you not calculate where your good and evil lie, and say, "They are both in my own power; nor can any deprive me of the one, nor involve me against my will in the other." Why, then, do not I lay myself down and snore? What is my own is safe. Let what belongs to others look to itself, who carries it off, how it is distributed by him who has the disposal of it. Who am I, to will that it should be so and so? For is the option given to me? Has anyone made me the dispenser of it? What I have in my own disposal is enough for me. I must make the best I can of this. Other things must be as their master pleases.

Does anyone who has these things before his eyes lie sleepless, and shift from side to side? What would he have, or what does he need—Patroclus,[2] or Antilochus, or Menelaus? Why, did he ever think any one of his friends immortal? When was it not obvious that on the morrow, or the next day, he

---

[1] This reference is to suicide.

[2] This whole paragraph refers to the lament of Achilles over Patroclus. *Iliad,* xix, 315, etc. See Classics Club edition, p. 305.

himself or that friend might die? "Yes, very true," he says; "but I reckoned that he would survive me, and bring up my son." Because you were a fool, and reckoned upon uncertainties. Why, then, do you not blame yourself, instead of sitting in tears, like a girl? "But he used to set my dinner before me." Because he was alive, foolish man; but now he cannot. But Automedon will set it before you; and if he should die, you will find somebody else. What if the vessel in which your meat used to be cooked should happen to be broken; must you die of hunger because you have not your old vessel? Do you not send and buy a new one?

> *What greater evil could afflict my breast?*[1]

Is *this* your evil, then? And, instead of removing it, do you accuse your mother, that she did not foretell it to you, that you might have spent your whole life in grieving from that time forward?

Do you not think now that Homer composed all this on purpose to show us that the noblest, the strongest, the richest, the handsomest of men may nevertheless be the most unfortunate and wretched, if they have not the principles they need?

---

[1] Homer, *Iliad,* Classics Club edition, p. 305.

CHAPTER ELEVEN

Of Cleanliness

SOME persons doubt whether the love of society be comprehended in the nature of man; and yet these very persons, it
seems to me, do not doubt that cleanliness is included in it;
and that by this, if by anything, man is distinguished from
brute animals. When, therefore, we see any animal cleaning
itself, we are apt to cry, with wonder, that it is like a human
being. On the contrary, if an animal is censured, we are presently apt to say, by way of excuse, that it is not a human
being. Such excellence do we suppose to be in man, which
we first received from the gods. For as they are by nature
pure and uncorrupt, in proportion as men approach to them
by reason, they are tenacious of purity and cleanliness. But
since it is impracticable that their essence, composed of such
materials, should be absolutely pure, it is the office of reason
to endeavor to render it as pure as possible.

The first and highest purity or impurity, then, is that which
is formed in the soul. But you will not find the impurity of
the soul and body to be alike. For what stain can you find in
the soul, unless it be something which renders it impure in its
operations? Now, the operations of the soul are its pursuits
and avoidances, its desires, aversions, preparations, intentions,
assents. What, then, is that which renders it unclean and dirty
in these operations? Nothing else than its wrong judgments.
So that the impurity of the soul consists in wicked principles,
and its purification in forming right principles; and that is pure
which has right principles, for that alone is unmixed and un-
defiled in its operations.

Now we should, as far as possible, endeavor after something like this in the body, too. It is unavoidable that when

man has such mixtures in his body there must be a discharge of superfluous mucus from the nose. For this reason nature has made hands, and the nostrils themselves as channels to let out the moisture; nor can this be neglected with propriety. It is unavoidable that the feet should get muddy and soiled from what they pass through. Therefore nature has prepared water and hands. It is unavoidable that some uncleanness must remain on the teeth after eating. Therefore, she says, rinse your teeth. Why? That you may be a man, and not a wild beast, or a swine. It was impossible but that, from perspiration and the pressure of the clothes, something dirty and necessary to be cleaned should remain upon the body. For this there is water, oil, hands, towels, scrapers, niter, and other necessary apparatus for its purification. But not you; a smith indeed will get the rust off his iron, and have proper instruments for that purpose; and you yourself will have your plates washed before you eat, unless you are quite dirty and slovenly; but you will not wash or purify your body. "Why should I?" say you. I tell you again, in the first place, that you may be like a man; and, in the next, that you may not offend those with whom you converse. Do you think it fitting to smell offensively? Be it so. But is it fitting as regards those who sit near you; who are placed at the table with you; who salute you? Either go into a desert, as you deserve, or live solitary at home, and be the only sufferer. But to what sort of character does it belong to live in a city, and behave so carelessly and inconsiderably? If nature had trusted even a horse to your care, would you have overlooked and neglected him? Yet now, without being aware of it, you do something like this. Consider your body as committed to you, instead of a horse. Wash it, rub it, take care that no one will turn away from you in disgust. Who is not more disgusted at a foul, unwhole-some-looking sloven, than at a person who has been acci-dentally spattered with dung? The stench of the one is external and acquired; but that which arises from want of care is a kind of inward putrefaction.

"But Socrates bathed but seldom." [1] Yet his person looked clean, and was so agreeable and pleasing, that the most beautiful and noble youths were fond of him, and desired rather to sit by him than by those who had the finest persons. He might have omitted both bathing and washing, if he had pleased; and yet his amount of bathing had its effect. Cold water may supply the place of the warm bath. "But Aristophanes calls him one of the pallid, barefooted philosophers." Oh, yes, and he says, too, that he walked in the air, and stole clothes from the palaestra. Yet all who have written of Socrates affirm quite the contrary; that he was not only agreeable in his conversation, but in his person too. And, again, they write the same of Diogenes. For we ought not to frighten the world from philosophy by the appearance of our persons; but to show our serenity of mind, as in all other ways, in the care of our persons. "See, all of you, that I have nothing; that I want nothing. Without house, without city, and an exile (if that happens to be the case), and without a home, I live more easily and prosperously than the noble and rich. Look upon my person, too, that it is not injured by coarse fare." But if anyone should tell me this, bearing the habit and the visage of a condemned criminal, what god should persuade me to come near philosophy, when it makes people like that? Heaven forbid! I would not do it, even if I was sure to become a wise man for my pains.

I declare, for my own part, I would rather that a young man, on his first inclination to philosophy, should come to me finically dressed, than with his hair neglected and dirty. For there appears in him some idea of beauty and desire of decency; and where he imagines it to be, there he applies his endeavors. One has nothing more to do but to point it out to

---

[1] What is probably meant here is that Socrates bathed at home in cold water rather than at the public baths.

him, and say, "You seek beauty, young man, and you do well. Be assured, then, that it springs from the rational part of you. Seek it there, where the pursuits and avoidances, the desires and aversions, are concerned. Herein consists your excellence; but the paltry body is by nature clay. Why do you trouble yourself, to no purpose, about it? You will be convinced by time, if not otherwise, that it is nothing." But if he should come to me grimy and dirty, with mustaches drooping to his knees, what can I say to him; by what comparison allure him? For what has he studied which has any resemblance to beauty, that I may transfer his attention, and say that beauty is not there, but here? Would you have me tell him that beauty consists not in filth, but in reason? For has he any desire of beauty? Has he any appearance of it? Go, and argue with a hog not to wallow in the mud.

It was because he was a young man who loved beauty, that Polemo was touched by the discourses of Xenocrates. For he began with some zeal the study of beauty, though he sought in the wrong place. And, indeed, nature has not made the brutes which live with man dirty. Does a horse wallow in the mud; or a good dog? But swine do, and dirty geese, and worms, and spiders, which are banished to the greatest distance from human society. Will you, then, who are a man, choose not to be even one of the animals that are conversant with man; but rather a worm or a spider? Will you not bathe sometimes, be it in whatever manner you please? Will you not wash yourself? If you don't care for hot water, use cold. Will you not come clean, that they who converse with you may have some pleasure in you? But will you accompany us, in your uncleanness, even to the temples, where all unclean ways are forbidden?

What, then; would anybody have you adorn yourself to the utmost? By no means, except in those things where our nature requires it—in reason, principles, actions; but in our persons only so far as neatness requires; so far as not to give offense. But if you hear that it is not right to wear purple, you must go, I suppose, and roll your cloak in the mud, or tear it.[1] "But how can I have a fine cloak?" You have water, man; wash it. What an amiable youth is here! How worthy this old man to love and be loved! A fit person to be trusted with the instruction of our sons and daughters, and attended by young people as occasion may require—to read them lectures from a dunghill! Every deterioration takes its origin from something human; but this almost dehumanizes a man.

CHAPTER TWELVE

Of Taking Pains

WHEN you cease to take pains for a little while, do not fancy that you may begin again whenever you please; but remember this, that by means of the fault of today, your affairs must necessarily be in a worse condition for the future. The first and worst evil is that there arises a habit of neglect; and then a habit of postponing effort, and constantly procrastinating as to one's successes and good behavior and orderly thought and action. Now, if procrastination as to anything is advantageous, it must be still more advantageous to omit it altogether; but if it be not advantageous, why do you not take pains all the time? "I wish to play today." What then? Ought you not to take proper pains about it? "I wish to sing." But why not take proper pains about it? For there is no part of life exempted, about which pains are not needed. For will you

---

[1] That is, carry the precept to extremes.

do anything the worse by taking pains, and the better by neglect? What else in life is best performed by heedless people? Does a smith forge the better by heedlessness? Does a pilot steer more safely by heedlessness? Or is any other, even of the minutest operations, best performed heedlessly? Do you not perceive that, when you have let your mind loose, it is no longer in your power to call it back, either to propriety, or modesty, or moderation? But you do everything at haphazard; you merely follow your inclinations.

"To what, then, am I to direct my attention?"

Why, in the first place, to those universal maxims which you must always have at hand; and not sleep, or arise, or drink, or eat, or converse without them: that no one is the master of another's will; and that it is in the will alone that good and evil lie. No one, therefore, is my master, either to procure me any good, or to involve me in any evil; but I alone have the disposal of myself with regard to these things. Since these, then, are secured to me, what need have I to be troubled about externals? What tyrant inspires fear? What disease? What poverty? What offense? "I have not pleased such a one." Is he my concern then? Is he my conscience? "No." Why, then, do I trouble myself any further about him? "But he is thought to be of some consequence." Let him look to that; and they who think him so. But I have one whom I must please, to whom I must submit, whom I must obey—God, and those who surround him. He has intrusted me with myself, and made my will subject to myself alone, having given me rules for the right use of it. If I follow the proper rules in syllogisms, in convertible propositions, I do not heed or regard anyone who says anything contrary to them. Why, then, am I vexed at being censured in matters of greater consequence? What is the reason of this perturbation? Nothing else, but that in this instance I want practice. For every science despises ignorance and the ignorant; and not only the sciences, but even the arts. Take any shoemaker, take any smith you will, and he may laugh at the rest of the world, so far as his own business is concerned.

In the first place, then, these are the maxims we must have ready, and do nothing without them, but direct the soul to this mark; to pursue nothing external, nothing that belongs to others, but as he who has the power has appointed. Things controllable by will are to be pursued always; and the rest as may be permitted. Besides this, we must remember who we are, and what name we bear, endeavoring to use all the circumstances of life in their proper relations: what is the proper time for singing, what for play, and in what company; what will be the consequence of our performance; whether our companions will despise us, or we ourselves; when to employ raillery, and whom to ridicule; upon what occasions to comply, and with whom; and then, in complying, how to preserve our own character.

Wherever you deviate from any of these rules, the damage is immediate; not from anything external, but from the very action itself. "Well, then, is it possible by these means to be faultless?" Impracticable; but this is possible, to use a constant endeavor to be faultless. For we shall have cause to be satisfied, if, by never remitting our pains, we shall be exempt at least from a few faults. But now, when you say you will begin to take pains tomorrow, be assured that it is the same thing as if you said, "Today I will be shameless, impertinent, base, it shall be in the power of others to grieve me; I will be passionate, I will be envious today." See to how many evils you give yourself up. "But all will be well tomorrow." How much better today! If it be for your interest tomorrow, how much more today, that it may be in your power tomorrow too, and that you may not again defer it until the third day.

CHAPTER THIRTEEN

To Those Who Talk Too Much
About Their Own Affairs

WHEN anyone appears to us to discourse frankly of his own affairs, we too are somehow tempted to disclose our secrets to him; and we consider this to be acting with frankness—first, because it seems unfair that when we have heard the affairs of our neighbor, we should not in return communicate ours to him; and besides, we think that we shall not appear of a frank character, in concealing what belongs to ourselves. Indeed it is often said, "I have told you all my affairs; and will you tell me none of yours? How happens this?" Lastly, it is supposed that we may safely trust him who has already trusted us; for we imagine that he will never discover our affairs, for fear we should in turn discover his. It is thus that the thoughtless are caught by the soldiers at Rome. A soldier sits by you in a civilian's dress, and begins to speak ill of Caesar. Then you, as if you had received a pledge of his fidelity, by his first beginning the abuse, say likewise what you think; and so you are led away in chains to execution.

Something like this is the case with us in general. But when one has safely intrusted his secrets to me, shall I, in imitation of him, trust mine to anyone who comes in my way? The case is different. I indeed hold my tongue because I am of such a disposition; but he goes and tells everybody what he has heard; and then, when I come to find it out, if I happen to be like him, from a desire of revenge, I tell what he has told me, and we are both discredited. But if I remember that one man does not hurt another, but that everyone is hurt or profited by his own actions, I may indeed keep to this, not to do anything like him; yet, by my own foolish talking, I suffer what I do suffer.

"Yes; but it is unfair, when you have heard the secrets of your neighbor, not to tell him your own secrets." Did I ask you for your secrets, sir? Did you tell me your affairs upon condition that I should tell you mine in return? If you are a gossip, and take all you meet for friends, would you have me too become like you? But what if the case is this; that you did right in trusting your affairs to me, but it is not right that I should trust you? Would you have me run headlong, and fall? This is just as if I had a sound barrel, and you a leaky one; and you should come and deposit your wine with me, to be put into my barrel; and then should take it ill that, in my turn, I did not trust you with my wine. No. You have a leaky barrel. How, then, are we any longer upon equal terms? You have intrusted your affairs to an honest man, and a man of honor; one who finds his help or harm in his own actions alone, and in nothing external. Would you have me intrust mine to you, who have dishonored your own will, and who would get a paltry sum, or a post of power or preferment at court, even if it required you to kill your own children, like Medea? Where is the fairness in this? But show me that you are faithful, honorable, steady; show me that you have principles conducive to friendship; show me that your vessel is not leaky, and you shall see that I will not wait for you to intrust your affairs to me, but I will come and entreat you to hear mine. For who would not make use of a good vessel? Who despises a benevolent and friendly adviser? Who will not gladly receive one to share the burden, as it were, of his difficulties; and by sharing, to make it lighter?

"Well, but I trust you, and you do not trust me." In the first place, you do not really trust me; but you are a gossip, and therefore can keep nothing in. For if the former be the case, trust only me. But now, whenever you see a man at leisure, you sit down by him and say: "My dear friend, there is not a man in the world who wishes me better, or has more

kindness for me, than you; I entreat you to hear my affairs."
And you act this way with people with whom you have not
the least acquaintance. But if you do trust me, it is plainly as
a man of fidelity and honor, and not because I have told you
my affairs. Let me alone, then, till I reciprocate this opinion.
Convince me that if a person has told his affairs to anyone,
it is a proof of his being a man of fidelity and honor. For if
this were the case, I would go about and tell my affairs to the
whole world, if I could thus become a man of fidelity and
honor; but for this a man needs principles of no ordinary sort.

If, then, you see anyone taking pains for things that belong
to others, and subjecting his will to them, be assured that this
man has a thousand things to compel and restrain him. He has
no need of burning pitch, or the torturing wheel, to make him
tell what he knows; but the nod of a girl, for instance, will
shake his purpose; the good will of a courtier; the desire of
an office, of an inheritance; ten thousand other things of that
sort. It must therefore be remembered, in general, that con-
fidences require faithfulness and faithful principles. And
where, at this time, are these easily to be found? Pray let anyone show me a person of such a disposition as to say, I concern
myself only for those things which are my own, incapable
of restraint, and by nature free. This I esteem the essence of
good. Let the rest be as God grants; it makes no difference to
me.

I

THERE are things which are within our power, and there are things which are beyond our power. Within our power are opinion, aim, desire, aversion, and, in one word, whatever affairs are our own. Beyond our power are body, property, reputation, office, and, in one word, whatever are not properly our own affairs.

Now, the things within our power are by nature free, unrestricted, unhindered; but those beyond our power are weak, dependent, restricted, alien. Remember, then, that if you attribute freedom to things by nature dependent, and take what belongs to others for your own, you will be hindered, you will lament, you will be disturbed, you will find fault both with gods and men. But if you take for your own only that which is your own, and view what belongs to others just as it really is, then no one will ever compel you, no one will restrict you, you will find fault with no one, you will accuse no one, you will do nothing against your will; no one will hurt you, you will not have an enemy, nor will you suffer any harm.

Aiming therefore at such great things, remember that you must not allow yourself any inclination, however slight, towards the attainment of the others; but that you must entirely quit some of them, and for the present postpone the rest. But if you would have these, and possess power and wealth likewise, you may miss the latter in seeking the former; and you will certainly fail of that by which alone happiness and freedom are procured.

Seek at once, therefore, to be able to say to every unpleasing semblance, "You are but a semblance and by no means the real thing." And then examine it by those rules which you have; and first and chiefly, by this: whether it concerns the things which are within our own power, or those which are not; and if it concerns anything beyond our power, be prepared to say that it is nothing to you.

2

Remember that desire demands the attainment of that of which you are desirous; and aversion demands the avoidance of that to which you are averse; that he who fails of the object of his desires is disappointed; and he who incurs the object of his aversion is wretched. If, then, you avoid only those undesirable things which you can control, you will never incur anything which you avoid; but if you avoid sickness, or death, or poverty, you will run the risk of wretchedness. Withdraw aversion, then, from all things that are not within our power, and apply it to things undesirable, which are within our power. But for the present altogether restrain desire; for if you desire any of the things not within our own power, you must necessarily be disappointed; and you are not yet secure of those which are within our power, and so are legitimate objects of desire. Where it is practically necessary for you to pursue or avoid anything, do even this with discretion, and gentleness, and moderation.

3

With regard to whatever objects either delight the mind, or contribute to use, or are tenderly beloved, remind yourself of what nature they are, beginning with the merest trifles: if you have a favorite cup, that it is but a cup of which you are fond—for thus, if it is broken, you can bear it; if you embrace your child, or your wife, that you embrace a mortal—and thus, if either of them dies, you can bear it.

4

When you set about any action, remind yourself of what nature the action is. If you are going to bathe, represent to yourself the incidents usual in the bath—some persons splashing, others jostling, others scolding, others stealing. And thus you will more safely go about this action, if you say to yourself, "I will now go to bathe, and keep my own will in harmony with nature." And so with regard to every other action. For thus, if any impediment arises in bathing, you will be able to say, "It was not only to bathe that I desired, but to keep my will in harmony with nature; and I shall not keep it thus, if I am out of humor at things that happen."

5

Men are disturbed not by things, but by the views which they take of things. Thus death is nothing terrible, else it would have appeared so to Socrates. But the terror consists in our notion of death, that it is terrible. When, therefore, we are hindered, or disturbed, or grieved, let us never blame anyone but ourselves; that is, our own judgments. It is the action of an uninstructed person to reproach others for his own misfortunes; of one entering upon instruction, to reproach himself; and of one perfectly instructed, to reproach neither others nor himself.

6

Be not elated at any excellence not your own. If a horse should be elated, and say, "I am handsome," it might be endurable. But when you are elated, and say, "I have a handsome horse," know that you are elated only on the merit of the horse. What then is your own? The use of the phenomena of existence. So that when you are in harmony with nature in this respect, you will be elated with some reason; for you will be elated at some good of your own.

7

As in a voyage, when the ship is at anchor, if you go on shore to get water, you may amuse yourself with picking up a shellfish or a mushroom in your path, but your thoughts ought to be bent towards the ship, and perpetually attentive, lest the captain should call, and then you must leave all these things, that you may not have to be carried on board the vessel, tied up like a sheep; thus likewise in life, if, instead of a mushroom or shellfish, such a thing as a wife or a child be granted you, there is no objection; but if the captain calls, run to the ship, leave all these things, and never look behind. But if you are old, never go far from the ship, lest you should be missing when called for.

8

Demand not that events should happen as you wish; but wish them to happen as they do happen, and your life will be serene.

9

Sickness is an impediment to the body, but not to the will, unless itself pleases. Lameness is an impediment to the leg, but not to the will; and say this to yourself with regard to everything that happens. For you will find it to be an impediment to something else, but not truly to yourself.

10

Upon every accident, remember to turn towards yourself and inquire what faculty you have to deal with it. If you encounter a handsome person, you will find continence the faculty needed; if pain, then fortitude; if reviling, then patience. And when thus habituated, the phenomena of existence will not overwhelm you.

11

Never say of anything, "I have lost it"; but, "I have restored it." Has your child died? It is restored. Has your wife died? She is restored. Has your estate been taken away? That likewise is restored. "But it was a bad man who took it." What is it to you by whose hands he who gave it has demanded it again? While he permits you to possess it, consider it as something not your own, as travelers do an inn.

12

If you would improve, lay aside such reasonings as these: "If I neglect my affairs, I shall have no income; if I do not punish my servant, he will be good for nothing." For it were better to die of hunger, exempt from grief and fear, than to live in affluence, but troubled; and it is better that your servant should be bad than you unhappy.

Begin therefore with little things. Is a little oil spilt or a little wine stolen? Say to yourself, "This is the price paid for peace and tranquillity; and nothing is to be had for nothing." And when you call your servant, consider that it is possible he may not come at your call; or, if he does, that he may not do what you wish. But it is not at all desirable for him, and very undesirable for you, that it should be in his power to cause you any disturbance.

13

If you would improve, be content to be thought foolish and dull with regard to externals. Do not desire to be thought to know anything; and though you should appear to others to be somebody, distrust yourself. For be assured, it is not easy at once to keep your will in harmony with nature, and to secure externals; but while you are absorbed in the one, you must of necessity neglect the other.

14

If you wish your children and your wife and your friends to live forever, you are foolish; for you wish things to be in your power which are not so; and what belongs to others to be your own. So likewise, if you wish your servant to be without fault, you are foolish; for you wish vice not to be vice, but something else. But if you wish not to be disappointed in your desires, that is in your own power. Exercise, therefore, what is in your power. A man's master is he who is able to confer or remove whatever that man seeks or shuns. Whoever then would be free, let him wish nothing, let him avoid nothing, which depends on others; else he must necessarily be a slave.

15

Remember that you must behave as at a banquet. Is anything brought round to you? Put out your hand, and take a moderate share. Does it pass by you? Do not stop it. Is it not yet come? Do not yearn in desire towards it, but wait till it reaches you. So with regard to children, wife, office, riches; and you will some time or other be worthy to feast with the gods. And if you do not so much as take the things which are set before you, but are able even to forego them, then you will not only be worthy to feast with the gods, but to rule with them also. For, by thus doing, Diogenes and Heraclitus, and others like them, deservedly became divine, and were so recognized.

16

When you see anyone weeping in sorrow, either that his son has gone abroad, or that he has suffered in his affairs, take care not to be overcome by the apparent evil; but discriminate, and be ready to say, "What hurts this man is not this occurrence itself—for another man might not be hurt by it—but the view he chooses to take of it." As far as conversation goes, however, do not hesitate to sympathize with him, and if need be, to groan with him. Take heed, however, not to groan inwardly too.

17

Remember that you are an actor in a play the character of which is determined by the author—if short, then in a short one; if long, then in a long one. If it be his pleasure that you should enact a poor man, see that you act it well; or a cripple, or a ruler, or a private citizen. For this is your business, to act well the given part; but to choose it, belongs to God.

18

When a raven happens to croak unluckily, be not overcome by appearances, but discriminate, and say, "None of these portents are for *me;* but either to my paltry body, or property, or reputation, or children, or wife. But to *me* all portents are lucky, if I will. For whatsoever happens, it belongs to me to derive advantage therefrom."

19

You can be unconquerable, if you enter into no combat in which it is not in your own power to conquer. When, therefore, you see anyone eminent in honors or power, or in high esteem on any other account, take heed not to be bewildered by appearances and to pronounce him happy; for if the essence of good consists in things within our own power, there will be no room for envy or jealousy. But, for your part, do not desire to be a general, or a senator, or a consul, but to be free; and the only way to this is a disregard of things which lie not within our own power.

20

Remember that it is not he who gives abuse or blows who insults; but the view we take of these things as insulting. When, therefore, anyone provokes you, be assured that it is your own opinion which provokes you. Try, therefore, in the first place, not to be bewildered by appearances. For if you once gain time and respite, you will more easily command yourself.

21

Let death and exile, and all other things which appear terrible, be daily before your eyes, but death chiefly; and you will never entertain any abject thought, nor too eagerly covet anything.

22

If you have an earnest desire towards philosophy, prepare yourself from the very first to have the multitude laugh and sneer, and say, "He is returned to us a philosopher all at once"; and "Whence this supercilious look?" Now, for your part, do not have a supercilious look; but keep steadily to those things which appear best to you, as one appointed by God to this particular station. For remember that, if you are persistent, those very persons who at first ridiculed will afterwards admire you. But if you are conquered by them, you will incur a double ridicule.

23

If you ever happen to turn your attention to externals, for the pleasure of anyone, be assured that you have ruined your scheme of life. Be contented, then, in everything, with being a philosopher; and if you wish to be taken for one, appear so to yourself, and you will succeed.

24

Let not such considerations as these distress you: "I shall live in discredit, and be nobody anywhere." For if discredit be an evil, you can no more be involved in evil through another, than in baseness. Is it any business of yours, then, to get power, or to be admitted to an entertainment? By no means. How then, after all, is this discredit? And how is it true that you will be nobody anywhere; when you ought to be somebody in those things only which are within your own power, in which you may be of the greatest consequence? "But my friends will be unassisted." What do you mean by unassisted? They will not have money from you; nor will you make them Roman citizens. Who told you, then, that these are among the things within our own power, and not rather the affairs of others? And who can give to another the things which he himself has not? "Well, but get money, then, that we too may have a share." If I can get money with the preservation of my own honor and fidelity and self-respect, show me the way, and I will get it; but if you require me to lose my own proper good, that you may gain what is no good, consider how unreasonable and foolish you are. Besides, which would you rather have, a sum of money, or a faithful and honorable friend?

Rather assist me, then, to gain this character, than require me to do those things by which I may lose it. Well, but my country, say you, as far as depends upon me, will be unassisted. Here, again, what assistance is this you mean? It will not have porticos or baths of your providing? And what signifies that? Why, neither does a smith provide it with shoes, nor a shoemaker with arms. It is enough if everyone fully performs his own proper business. And were you to supply it with another faithful and honorable citizen, would he not be of use to it? Yes. Therefore neither are you yourself useless to it. "What place, then," say you, "shall I hold in the state?" Whatever you can hold with the preservation of your fidelity and honor. But if, by desiring to be useful to that, you lose these, how can you serve your country, when you have become faithless and shameless?

25

Is anyone preferred before you at an entertainment, or in courtesies, or in being called on for advice? If these things are good, you ought to rejoice that he has them; and if they are evil, do not be grieved that you do not have them. And remember that you cannot be permitted to rival others in externals, without using the same means to obtain them. For how can he who will not haunt the door of any man, will not attend him, will not praise him, have an equal share with him who does these things? You are unjust, then, and unreasonable, if you are unwilling to pay the price for which these things are sold, and would have them for nothing. For how much are lettuces sold? An obolus,[1] for instance. If another, then, paying an obolus, takes the lettuces, and you, not paying it, go without them, do not imagine that he has gained any advantage over you. For as he has the lettuces, so you have the obolus which you did not give. So, in the present case, you have not been invited to such a person's entertainment, because you have not paid him the price for which a supper is sold. It is sold for praise; it is sold for personal attention. Give him, then, the value, if it be for your advantage. But if you would at the same time not pay the one, and yet receive the other, you are unreasonable and foolish. Have you nothing, then, in place of the supper? Yes, indeed you have: not to praise him whom you do not like to praise; not to bear the insolence of his lackeys.

---

[1] See note, p. 245.

26

The will of nature may be learned from things upon which we are all agreed. As, when our neighbor's boy has broken a cup, or the like, we are ready at once to say, "These are casualties that will happen"; be assured, then, that when your own cup is likewise broken, you ought to be affected just as when another's cup was broken. Now apply this to greater things. Is the child or wife of another dead? There is no one who would not say, "Such is the fate of man." But if anyone's own child happens to die, it is immediately, "Alas! how wretched am I!" It should be always remembered how we are affected on hearing the same thing concerning others.

27

As a mark is not set up for the sake of missing the aim, so neither does the nature of evil exist in the world.[1]

28

If a person had delivered up your body to some passer-by, you would certainly be angry. And do you feel no shame in delivering up your own mind to any reviler, to be disconcerted and troubled?

29 [2]

30

Duties are universally measured by relations. Is a certain man your father? In this are implied, taking care of him; submitting to him in all things; patiently receiving his reproaches,

---

1 Virtue is the mark which God has set up for us to aim at; missing it is our fault, not his. Likewise, our failures do not indicate that there is anything wrong in the universe, in nature, but only in us.

2 This chapter, except some minor differences, is the same as the fifteenth of the third book of the Discourses.

his correction. But he is a bad father. Is your natural tie, then, to a *good* father? No, but to a father. Is a brother unjust? Well, preserve your own just relation towards him. Consider not what *he* does, but what *you* are to do, to keep your own will in a state of harmony with nature. For another cannot hurt you, without your consent. You will then be hurt when you consent to be hurt. In this manner, therefore, if you acquire the habit of regarding your relations with your neighbor, citizen, commander, you will discover in this way what duties to expect from them.

31

Be assured that the essence of piety towards the gods lies in this, to form right opinions concerning them, as existing, and as governing the universe justly and well. And fix yourself in this resolution, to obey them, and yield to them, and willingly follow them amidst all events, as being ruled by the most perfect wisdom. For thus you will never find fault with the gods, nor accuse them of neglecting you. This result cannot be secured in any other way than by withdrawing yourself from things which are not within our own power, and by making good or evil to consist only in those which are. For if you suppose any other things to be either good or evil, it is inevitable that, when you are disappointed of what you wish, or incur what you would avoid, you should reproach and blame their authors. For every creature is naturally formed to flee and abhor things that appear hurtful, and that which causes them; and to pursue and admire those which appear beneficial, and that which causes them. It is impracticable, then, that one who supposes himself to be hurt should rejoice in the person who, as he thinks, hurts him; just as it is impossible to rejoice in the hurt itself.

Hence, also, a father is reviled by his son, when he does not impart the things which seem to be good; and this made

Polynices and Eteocles[1] mutually enemies, that empire seemed good to both. On this account the farmer reviles the gods; the sailor, the merchant, or those who have lost wife or child. For where our interest is, there too is piety directed. So that whoever is careful to regulate his desires and aversions as he ought is thus made careful of piety likewise. But it also becomes incumbent on everyone to offer libations and sacrifices and first-fruits, according to the customs of his country, purely, and not heedlessly nor negligently; not in a niggardly way, nor yet extravagantly.

32

When you have recourse to divination, remember that you know not what the event will be, and you come to learn it of the diviner; but of what nature it is you knew before coming; at least, if you are of philosophic mind. For if it is among the things not within our own power, it can by no means be either good or evil. Do not, therefore, bring with you to the diviner either desire or aversion—else you will approach him trembling—but first clearly understand that every event is indifferent, and nothing to *you*, of whatever sort it may be; for it will be in your power to make a right use of it, and this no one can hinder. Then come with confidence to the gods as your counselors; and afterwards, when any counsel is given you, remember what counselors you have assumed, and whose advice you will neglect, if you disobey. Come to divination, as Socrates prescribed, in cases of which the whole consideration relates to the event, and in which no opportunities are afforded by reason, or any other art, to discover the matter in view. When, therefore, it is our duty to share the danger of a friend or of our country, we ought not to consult the oracle as to whether we shall share it with them or not. For though the diviner should forewarn you that the auspices are unfavorable, this means no more than that either death or mutila-

---

[1] See note, p. 296.

tion or exile is portended. But we have reason within us; and
it directs us, even with these hazards, to stand by our friend
and our country. Attend, therefore, to the greater diviner,
the Pythian God, who once cast out of the temple him who
neglected to save his friend.[1]

33

Begin by prescribing to yourself some character and demeanor, such as you may preserve both alone and in company.

Be silent for the most part; or speak merely what is needful,
and in few words. We may, however, enter sparingly into
discourse sometimes, when occasion calls for it; but let it not
run on any of the common subjects, as gladiators, or horse-
races, or athletic champions, or food, or drink—the vulgar
topics of conversation; and especially do not talk about people, so as either to blame, or praise, or make comparisons. If
you are able, then, by your own conversation, bring over
that of your company to proper subjects; but if you happen
to find yourself among strangers, be silent.

Let not your laughter be loud, frequent, or abundant.

Avoid taking oaths, if possible, altogether; at any rate, so
far as you are able.

Avoid entertainments given by strangers and those ignorant
of philosophy; but if ever an occasion calls you to them, keep
your attention upon the stretch, that you may not imper-
ceptibly slide into vulgarity. For be assured that if a person
be ever so pure himself, yet, if his companion be corrupted, he
who converses with him will be corrupted likewise.

Provide things relating to the body no farther than absolute
need requires; as meat, drink, clothing, house, retinue. But
cut off everything that looks towards show and luxury.

---

[1] This refers to an anecdote given in full by Simplicius, in his com-
mentary on this passage, of a man assaulted and killed, on his way to
consult the oracle, while his companion, deserting him, took refuge
in the temple, till cast out by the Deity.

Before marriage, guard yourself with all your ability from unlawful intercourse with women; yet be not uncharitable or severe to those who are led into this, nor frequently boast that you yourself do otherwise.

If anyone tells you that such a person speaks ill of you, do not make excuses about what is said of you, but answer: "He was ignorant of my other faults, else he would not have mentioned these alone."

It is not necessary for you to appear often at public spectacles; but if ever there is a proper occasion for you to be there, do not appear more solicitous for any other than for yourself; that is, wish things to be only just as they are, and only the best man to win; for thus nothing will go against you. But abstain entirely from acclamations and derision and violent emotions. And when you come away, do not talk a great deal on what has passed, except in so far as it contributes to your own improvement. For it would appear by such discourse that you were dazzled by the show.

Be not prompt or ready to attend public readings,[1] but if you do attend, preserve your gravity and dignity, and yet avoid making yourself disagreeable.

When you are going to confer with anyone, and especially with one who seems your superior, represent to yourself how Socrates or Zeno would behave in such a case, and you will not be at a loss to meet properly whatever may occur.

When you are going before anyone in power, fancy to yourself that you may not find him at home, that you may be shut out, that the doors may not be opened to you, that he may not notice you. If, with all this, it be your duty to go, bear what happens, and never say to yourself, "It was not worth so much." For this is vulgar, and like a man bewildered by externals.

In society, avoid a frequent and excessive mention of your

---

1 This was the customary way of introducing any new literary work to the public.

own actions and dangers. For however agreeable it may be to yourself to allude to the risks you have run, it is not equally agreeable to others to hear your adventures. Avoid likewise an endeavor to excite laughter. For this may slip easily into vulgarity, and, besides, may be apt to lower you in the esteem of your acquaintance. Lapsing into obscene language is likewise dangerous. Therefore when anything of this sort happens, use the first fit opportunity to rebuke him who makes advances that way; or, at least, by silence and blushing and a serious look, show yourself to be displeased by such talk.

34

If you are dazzled by the semblance of any promised pleasure, guard yourself against being bewildered by it; but let the affair wait your leisure, and procure yourself some delay. Then bring to your mind both points of time—that in which you shall enjoy the pleasure, and that in which you will repent and reproach yourself, after you have enjoyed it—and sat before you, in opposition to these, how you will rejoice and applaud yourself, if you abstain. And even though it should appear to you a seasonable gratification, take heed that its enticements and allurements and seductions may not overcome you; but set in opposition to this, how much better it is to be conscious of having gained so great a victory.

35

When you do something which you have decided ought to be done, never avoid being seen doing it, even though the world should misunderstand it; for if you are not acting rightly, shun the action itself; if you are, why fear those who wrongly censure you?

36

As the proposition, Either it is day, or it is night, has meaning when separated, but none at all when combined; so, at a feast, to choose the largest share is very suitable to the bodily appetite, but utterly inconsistent with social feeling. Remember, then, when you eat with another, not only the value to the body of those things which are set before you, but also the value of proper courtesy towards your host.

37

If you have assumed any character beyond your strength, you have both demeaned yourself ill in that, and neglected one which you might have filled with success.

38

As in walking you take care not to tread upon a nail, or turn your foot, so likewise take care not to hurt the ruling faculty of your mind. And if we were to guard against this in every action, we should enter upon action more safely.

39

The body is to everyone the proper measure of its possessions, as the foot is of the shoe. If, therefore, you stop at this, you will keep the measure; but if you move beyond it, you must necessarily be carried forward, as down a precipice; as in the case of a shoe, if you go beyond its fitness to the foot, it comes first to be gilded, then purple, and then studded with jewels. For to that which once exceeds the fit measure there is no limit.

40

Women from fourteen years old are flattered by men with the title of ladies. Therefore, perceiving that they are regarded only as qualified to give men pleasure, they begin to adorn themselves, and in that to place all their hopes. It is worth while, therefore, to try that they may perceive themselves honored only so far as they appear beautiful in their demeanor, and modestly virtuous.

41

It is a mark of small intellect, to spend much time in things relating to the body; as to be immoderate in exercises, in eating and drinking, and in the discharge of other animal functions. These things should be done incidentally and our main strength be applied to our reason.

42

When any person treats you badly, or speaks ill of you, remember that he acts or speaks from an impression that it is right for him to do so. Now, it is not possible that he should follow what appears right to you, but only what appears so to himself. Therefore, if he judges from false appearances, he is the person hurt; since he too is the person deceived. For if anyone takes a true proposition to be false, the proposition is not hurt, but only the man is deceived. Setting out, then, from these principles, you will meekly bear with a person who reviles you; for you will say upon every occasion, "It seemed so to him."

43

Everything has two handles: one by which it may be borne, another by which it cannot. If your brother acts unjustly, do not lay hold on the affair by the handle of his injustice, for by that it cannot be borne; but rather by the opposite, that he is your brother, that he was brought up with you; and thus you will lay hold on it as it ought to be borne.

44

These reasonings have no logical connection: "I am richer than you; therefore I am your superior." "I am more eloquent than you; therefore I am your superior." The true logical connection is rather this: "I am richer than you; therefore my possessions must exceed yours." "I am more eloquent than you; therefore my style must surpass yours." But you, after all, consist neither in property nor in style.

45

Does anyone bathe hastily? Do not say that he does it badly, but hastily. Does anyone drink much wine? Do not say that he does ill, but that he drinks a great deal. For unless you perfectly understand his motives, how should you know if he acts ill? Thus you will not risk yielding to any appearances but such as you fully comprehend.

46

Never proclaim yourself a philosopher; nor make much talk among the ignorant about your principles, but show them by actions. Thus, at an entertainment, do not say how people ought to eat; but eat as you ought. For remember that thus Socrates also universally avoided all ostentation. And when persons came to him, and desired to be introduced by him to philosophers, he took them and introduced them; so well did he bear being overlooked. So if talk of philosophical principles should arise among the ignorant, be for the most part silent. For there is great danger in hastily throwing up what is undigested. And if anyone tells you that you know nothing, and you are not hurt, then you may be sure that you have really entered on your work. For sheep do not hastily throw up the grass, to show the shepherds how much they have eaten; but, inwardly digesting their food, they produce it outwardly in wool and milk. Thus, therefore, do not make an exhibition of your principles before the ignorant; but of the results which come from these principles when digested.

47

When you have learned to nourish your body frugally, do not compliment yourself upon it; nor, if you drink water, be saying on every occasion, "I drink water." But first consider how much more frugal are the poor than we, and how much more patient of hardship. If at any time you would inure yourself by exercise to labor and privation, for your own sake and not for the public, do not attempt great feats; but when you are violently thirsty, just rinse your mouth with water, and tell nobody.

48

The condition and characteristic of an ordinary person is that he never looks for either help or harm from himself, but only from externals. The condition and characteristic of a philosopher is that he looks to himself for all help or harm. The marks of one who is making progress are that he censures no one, praises no one, blames no one, accuses no one; says nothing concerning himself as being anybody, or knowing anything. When he is in any instance hindered or restrained, he accuses himself; and if he is praised, he smiles to himself at the person who praises him; and if he is censured, he makes no defense. But he goes about with the caution of a convalescent, careful not to harm anything that is doing well, but not yet quite secure. He restrains desire; he transfers his aversion to those things only which thwart the proper use of our own will; he employs his energies moderately in all directions; if he appears stupid or ignorant, he does not care; and, in a word, he keeps watch over himself as over an enemy lying in ambush.

49

When anyone shows himself vain, on being able to understand and interpret the works of Chrysippus, say to yourself: "Unless Chrysippus had written obscurely, this person would have had nothing to be vain of."

But what do I desire? To understand nature, and follow her. I ask, then, who interprets her; and hearing that Chrysippus does, I have recourse to him. I do not understand his writings. I seek, therefore, one to interpret them. So far there is nothing to value myself upon. And when I find an interpreter, what remains is to make use of his instructions. This alone is the valuable thing. But if I admire merely the interpretation, what do I become more than a grammarian, instead of a philosopher, except, indeed, that instead of Homer I interpret Chrysippus? When anyone, therefore, desires me to read Chrysippus to him, I rather blush, when I cannot exhibit actions that are harmonious and consonant with his discourse.

50

Whatever rules you have adopted, abide by them as laws, and as if you would be impious to transgress them; and pay no attention to what anyone says of you, for this, after all, is no concern of yours. How long, then, will you delay to demand of yourself the noblest improvements, and in no instance to transgress the judgments of reason? You have received the philosophic principles with which you ought to be conversant: and you have been conversant with them. For what other master, then, do you wait as an excuse for this delay in self-reformation? You are no longer a boy, but a grown man. If, therefore, you will be negligent and slothful, and always add procrastination to procrastination, purpose to purpose, and fix day after day in which you will attend to yourself, you will without realizing it continue to accomplish nothing, and, living and dying, remain of ordinary mind. This instant, then, think yourself worthy of living as a mature man who is making progress.

Let whatever appears to be the best, be to you an inviolable law. And if any instance of pain or pleasure, glory or disgrace, be set before you, remember that now is the combat, now the Olympiad comes on, nor can it be put off; and that by one failure and defeat honor may be lost—or won. Thus Socrates became perfect, improving himself by everything, following reason alone. And though you are not yet a Socrates, you ought, however, to live as one seeking to be a Socrates.

51

The first and most necessary topic in philosophy is the practical application of principles, as, We ought not to lie; the second is that of demonstrations, as, Why it is that we ought not to lie; the third, that which gives strength and logical connection to the other two, as, Why this is a demonstration. For what is demonstration? What is a consequence; what a contradition; what truth; what falsehood? The third point is then necessary on account of the second; and the second on account of the first. But the most necessary, and that whereon we ought to rest, is the first. But we do just the contrary. For we spend all our time on the third point, and employ all our diligence about that, and entirely neglect the first. Therefore, at the same time that we lie, we are very ready to show how it is demonstrated that lying is wrong.

52

Upon all occasions we ought to have these maxims ready at hand:

> *Conduct me, Zeus, and thou, O Destiny,*
> *Wherever your decrees have fixed my lot.*
> *I follow cheerfully; and, did I not,*
> *Wicked and wretched, I must follow still.*[1]

> *Whoe'er yields properly to Fate is deemed*
> *Wise among men, and knows the laws of Heaven.*[2]

And this third:

"O Crito, if it thus pleases the gods, thus let it be." "Anytus and Melitus may kill me indeed; but hurt me they cannot." [3]

---

[1] Cleanthes, in Diogenes Laertius, quoted also by Seneca, Epistle 107.
[2] Euripides, Fragments.
[3] Plato, *Crito*. See Classics Club edition, p. 66.